RECONCILING MEMORIES

To the Memory of

Theodore W. Moody
Professor of History and Fellow of
The University of Dublin, Trinity College,
Member of the Academic Council
and Executive Board of
The Irish School of Ecumenics
(1971-1984)

and

Frank Wright
Lecturer in Political Science, Queens University Belfast,
member of the Corrymeela Community,
vital participant in the Reconciliation of Memories project,
who died before he could take up his appointment as
Professor of Peace Studies at the University of Limerick

Both men dedicated their lives to the work of
reconciling memories in Ireland

Edited by Alan D. Falconer and Joseph Liechty

Reconciling Memories

the columba press

This new enlarged edition published in 1998 by

the columba press

55A Spruce Avenue, Stillorgan Industrial Park, Blackrock, Co Dublin

Cover by Bill Bolger
Origination by The Columba Press
Printed in Ireland by Colour Books Ltd, Dublin

ISBN 1 85607 232 0

Acknowledgements (Second Edition)
We are grateful to Fr Noel Barber, editor of *Studies,* for allowing us to use four articles first published in the summer 1989 edition of that journal. They are the chapters by Donald Shriver, Geiko Müller-Fahrenholz, Carol Birkland, and Frank Wright ('Northern Ireland and the British-Irish Relationship'). We are also grateful to Fr Bernard Treacy, editor of *Doctrine and Life,* for permission to use Joseph Liechty's 'Repentance and Peace in Ireland', which first appeared in the February 1994 edition. And as with the first edition, we are indebted to the patience and skill of Seán O Boyle and his staff at the Columba Press.

Our primary debt, however, is to the Women's World Day of Prayer (UK Committee). Without their generous funding, this second edition would not have have been possible.

Contents

Preface to the Second Edition
    Alan D. Falconer and Joseph Liechty   7
Preface to the First Edition   *Alan D. Falconer*   9

MEMORY

Remembering   *Alan D. Falconer*   11
Re-membering the Future
    Lionel Chircop   20
The Reconciliation of Memories   *Mark Santer*   30

THEORY

Myth and the Critique of Tradition   *Richard Kearney*   37
Reconciliation of Cultures: Apocalypse Now   *Séamus Deane*   57
Reconciliation as Remembrance: 'It takes two to know one'
    Joe Harris   63
Reconciliation: An Ecumenical Paradigm   *Maurice Bond*   83

HISTORY

Reconciliation of Histories   *Margaret Mac Curtain*   99
Testing the depth of Catholic/Protestant enmity:
    The case of Thomas Leland's *History of Ireland,* 1773
    Joseph Liechty   108
Reconciling the Histories of Protestant and Catholic
    in Northern Ireland   *Frank Wright*   128
History and Reconciliation: Frank Wright, Whitley Stokes
    and the Vortex of Antagonism   *Joseph Liechty*   149

DYNAMICS OF RECONCILIATION AND POLITICAL APPLICATIONS

The Reconciling Power of Forgiveness   *Alan D. Falconer*   177

Forgiveness and Community   *Gabriel Daly*   195

A Struggle for Justice and Reconciliation:
    Forgiveness in the Politics of the American
    Black Civil Rights Movement, 1955-68
    Donald W. Shriver, Jr   216

On Shame and Hurt in the Life of Nations:
    A German Perspective *Geiko Müller-Fahrenholz*   232

Silence that Leads to Peace   *Carol J. Birkland*   242

Northern Ireland and the British-Irish Relationship
    Frank Wright   248

Repentance and Peace: A Challenge to the Churches
    Joseph Liechty   261

The Contributors   270

Preface to the Second Edition

Alan D. Falconer and Joseph Liechty

A decade has passed since *Reconciling Memories* first appeared, a decade which has demonstrated even more trenchantly the need for such reconciliation and for the processes which can lead to it. The end of the Cold War, for example, marked by the collapse of the Berlin Wall; the re-emergence of ethnic conflict in the former Yugoslavia; violent conflict in Rwanda; and the end of apartheid in South Africa – all show the need for reconciling memories if there is to be any hope for resolving conflict and creating a society in which differing communities are valued.

When the Irish School of Ecumenics embarked on its project – Towards the Reconciliation of Memories – over a decade ago, the purpose was to analyze the relationship of communities in Ireland to each other and to identify the role and the responsibility of the churches in working to reconcile communities. In the first phase of the study, scholars from the disciplines of philosophy, history, education, the social sciences, literary criticism, and theology were brought together to analyze the experiences and perceptions of the different communities in Ireland. This analysis made it clear that the most significant reconciling contribution the churches could make, to inter-church relations and to broader social reconciliation, was the recovery of a theology of forgiveness, which must be grounded in the acceptance by all parties that each has shared responsibility for creating a situation in which religious, social, and political identities have been formed and sustained as communities-in-opposition. It was and remains a timely contribution.

The Reconciliation of Memories project was originally conducted in and directed towards Ireland (and to a lesser extent towards relationships between Ireland and Britain). A second phase of the project, however, was to solicit articles on processes of reconciliation in other situations of conflict. Those essays were published in 1989 in a special issue of *Studies,* the Irish Jesuit quarterly journal. Subsequently the method of analysis, the theology of forgiveness, and the understanding of forgiveness as a continuing process have found resonance in many other parts of the world, e.g. the Maori-Pakeha relations in New Zealand, and the reconciliation of Afro-American and white communities in Tulsa, Oklahoma, to name but two. This resonance suggests that now is a kairos for forgiveness – the decisive moment to engage in such risky undertakings as forgiveness requires.

Of course, such a process also pertains to issues within and between churches. The language of the reconciliation of memories has now entered the vocabulary and agenda of the ecumenical movement, as is evident in the reports of bilateral dialogues and the literature of the World Council of Churches and the Roman Catholic Church.

This second edition of *Reconciling Memories* includes all the papers from the original edition. Alan Falconer's original 'Introduction' now appears as 'Remembering' and incorporates additional material, principally from his contribution to the 1989 *Studies* edition on reconciling memories. Although some other authors have chosen to update aspects of their papers, the changes have been few and minor; most of the papers spoke to a particular time and place, and they continue to make their best contribution when so situated. They have worn well. They offer a method of analysis and a style of interdisciplinary engagement which provide stimulation for those in other places as they seek to critically analyze their situations.

This edition also offers seven new papers. Four of them – by Donald Shriver, Geiko Müller-Fahrenholz, Carol Birkland, and Frank Wright ('Northern Ireland and the British-Irish Relationship') – were first published in *Studies* in 1989. Of the three remaining new papers, the first version of Joseph Liechty's 'History and Reconciliation' was presented to a Reconciling Memories conference in Derry in 1989, while both Lionel Chircop's paper and Joseph Liechty's 'Repentance and Peace in Ireland' were inspired by engagement with the themes of reconciliation and memory.

Preface to the First Edition

Alan D. Falconer

In his Nobel Lecture in 1980, Czeslaw Milosz observed that 'the new obsession is the refusal to remember.' During my first year as a teacher in the Irish School of Ecumenics, an incident occurred which would seem to run counter to that suggestion.

At that time, one of the courses of lectures given to the students concerned 'the Irish situation', in which an analysis of the history, politics, socio-economic and religious dimensions of Irish societies was undertaken by an English sociologist. Invariably, the Irish born students found this course problematic. One such student eventually became so angry that he articulated his frustrations and as a final seal to his statement produced from his wallet a certificate. 'This certificate,' he said, 'was given to my family at the time of the Famine. It is a certificate of disjunction from their land. I carry it in my wallet with me all the time.'

That memory had imprisoned the student. Undoubtedly the Famine was a tale of human disaster on an immense scale. Unquestionably, the Famine had political repercussions in Ireland. Yet that event of one and a quarter centuries ago seemed to determine the way that Irish student acted today. He was not in a position to enter any positive relations with people from England.

To a Scotsman, there seemed to be an inability to interpret history. During the same period as the Famine, after all, an equally incredible tale of human misery and exploitation had occurred. Whole families and clans were removed from their lands in Scotland, in what has been called 'The Highland Clearances', so that sheep could be reared. Sheep were a more economically sound investment in the Highlands than people, so the people were shipped to Canada or the United States or they made their way to the Lowlands of Scotland seeking shelter and work. The Highland Clearances were no less inhuman in their effect than the Famine in

Ireland, yet memory of the clearances does not seem to have the same imprisoning effect. For many in Ireland, as Oliver MacDonagh notes in his *States of Mind*, the past is contemporary. A first impression then, might be that the observation of Milosz that 'the new obsession is the refusal to remember' would not be true in Ireland.

In years subsequent to that incident, opportunity to explore the question of the understanding of history informally with Professor Theo Moody presented itself on many occasions. From these conversations emerged the idea of exploring this further in a series of consultations. During this period the Field Day group were exploring the way in which the identity of the Anglo-Irish, Ulster Scot and Catholic Nationalist traditions in Ireland could be described and re-interpreted. Yet various questions still required exploration. How does a member of any of these traditions appropriate the history, literature and memories of that tradition, and have these traditions given any space to the fact that they had been responsible for the identity of the other traditions also? The history of the different traditions on these islands was and is interdependent. A third question might be the fact that each tradition was identified with a particular expression of Christianity, yet the churches seemed to be unable to break through the captivity of the memories of the different traditions, despite the fact that 'to remember' in the Bible is to participate in a liberating event.

These questions set the agenda for the various papers in this volume. The contributions were presented at different consultations held in Dublin in April 1986 and Edinburgh and London in March 1987. In the light of comments made in discussion at the various consultations, some of the contributions have undergone development. The complexity of recording those discussions, however, since different papers were presented on different occasions, other than those of Frank Wright and myself which were delivered on the three occasions, has made it impossible to offer a digest of the proceedings. The papers are therefore offered as a contribution to the exploration of an idea. It is not that in Ireland 'the new obsession is the refusal to remember' as Czeslaw Milosz observed, but that the pervasive memories need to be reconciled, so that the different communities might be liberated.

Remembering

Alan D. Falconer

Introduction: Memory and Identity

John Hewitt, the Northern Irish poet, in 'Postscript 1984' writes:

> The years deceived: our unforgiving hearts,
> by myths and old antipathies betrayed,
> flared into sudden acts of violence
> in daily shocking bulletins relayed,
> and through our dark dream-clotted consciousness
> hosted like banners in some black parade.
>
> Now with compulsive resonance they toll;
> Banbridge, Ballykelly, Darkley, Crossmaglen,
> summoning pity, anger and despair,
> by grief of kin, by hate of murderous men
> till the whole tarnished map is stained and torn,
> not to be read as pastoral again.[1]

Hewitt well conveys the cyclical sense of history so evident in the memory of the different traditions in Ireland.

Among the Protestant community there is a 'siege mentality'. Protestants tend to remember those occasions in their history when they had been under siege from Roman Catholic forces. Thus the history lessons emphasise 1641 when the Earls rose against the Protestants to try to reclaim the land given to the incomers; and subsequent dates highlight those occasions when a similar situation arose and when a state of siege ensued, e.g. the Siege of Derry (1690). The siege mentality arises from the sense of the repetitiveness of history. It informs the rhetoric and the politics of Northern Ireland. This memory imprisons the community, and makes it difficult to pursue a more open attitude to other communities. As Hewitt puts it:

11

Now with compulsive resonance they toll;
Banbridge, Ballykelly, Darkley, Crossmaglen,
summoning pity, anger and despair

These are contemporary instances which seem to repeat an old story.

While there exists a 'siege mentality' among Protestants in Northern Ireland, there is a 'coercion mentality' among Roman Catholics – a sense of being colonised and of having freedom limited by another community. Within this coercion mentality is a memory that independence and freedom have had to be sought through force of arms. The Proclamation of the Republic on Easter Monday 1916 refers to six previous occasions when this pattern of history had occurred – 1916 being the seventh such occasion. Whether it is 1778, 1782, 1793, 1825, or 1916, the same forces operate in the same fashion. As the historian Oliver MacDonagh notes, 'There is a constant relationship between the oscillation of coercion and conciliation on the part of the overlord and the oscillation of negotiations and the threat of violence upon the part of the subjected.'[2] Here also is evident a cyclical attitude to history – a sense that the same forces are at work constantly in the story, and thus in the memory of the community.[3]

Once again, history holds a community captive. The culture, traditions, songs, religious commitment, political ideals, embodied above all in the literature and poetry of the community, are important vehicles communicating and challenging the identity of the society. The awareness of the history of the community highlights the struggles, ideals and mistakes made by and in relation to the community. The cohesiveness and sense of direction of the community is nourished by its memories. The importance of 'memories' for the nourishing of 'identity' is particularly evident in Ireland. Events in the seventeenth and early twentieth centuries are celebrated in song, poem, 'history lessons' and the gathering of the community.[4] The hurt, dislocation, and deaths of the famine and clearances condition peoples' response to others, and are the subject of a considerable literature.[5] The achievements and the struggles of individuals and groups, the sense of awakening and the oppressive weight of despair, evident in the literature, songs and postures of communities in Ireland, have shaped the very identity of the communities.

These memories, however, can not only shape the identities of the various communities, but also imprison them. The awareness of the cyclical nature of history is seen to match the intricate patterns of Irish Celtic art. Each community, as it phrases its identity, assumes it does so independently of other communities. However, Iain Crichton Smith, the Scots poet, has trenchantly observed:

The anthology of memories of the other is a book I hadn't reckoned on ...[6]

The identity of each community has been shaped by the actions, attitudes and declarations of other communities. Both siege and coercion mentalities are reactions to the actions of others. The definition has been crafted over and against 'the other'.

This identity-in-opposition was true not only for political attitudes. It is also evident in the theological stances of the communities. The different Christian traditions sought to provide a framework for interpreting the experience of their communities. The Protestants understood that God had placed them on Irish soil for a purpose. Therefore they had a relationship with God like the Covenant. They were the Covenant people and they had to remain faithful to God. No matter what trials and tribulations they experienced, no matter how many times they were violently under attack, they would remain faithful – even if they became a remnant. They therefore interpreted their experience of constantly being under seige in terms of the theology of the covenant and of the remnant. Throughout nineteenth- and twentieth-century politics in Ireland, the Protestant community has been invited to sign solemn leagues and covenants. This theology has provided a basic framework for the discourse of the politicians.

The Roman Catholic community, because of their experience of oppression, identified their situation with the suffering of Christ. They developed a victim theology identifying themselves with the crucified Christ – always in the hope of resurrection. It is not without significance that the Irish 1916 rising is an Easter rising. After this failed attempt, there appeared posters throughout Dublin of the Pietà. The suffering martyrs lie in the arms of Mother Erin. A theology and politics of blood sacrifice and martyrdom emerged. This interpretation appears in the political rhetoric of the community and is brought to consciousness in the annual orations of politicians at the gravesides of these early fighters for independence.

These theological interpretations of the experiences of the communities expressed their pain and suffering, gave a framework which was used to explain every new atrocity, and provided a prism for interpreting Irish society. The memory of the events and the interpretation provided an identity for the communities which was an identity-in-opposition. This was reinforced by a confessional theology which was often conducted in a way which asserted the difference between one community and another in Ireland. As one example of this – from the tradition of the Church of Ireland – one might cite T. C. Hammond's book *The One Hundred Texts,* which highlights what is deemed to be the one hundred basic texts in the Bible. The author proceeds briefly to show how Anglicans have understood these texts correctly, and then at great length shows how the Roman Catholic Church has misunderstood them. That such a theological method is not yet dead may be seen in the well written and irenic booklet by Victor Griffin, Dean of St Patrick's Cathedral, Dublin, entitled *Anglican and Irish: What we Believe.* Despite its title, which implies that it is a basic primer of contemporary Irish Anglican thought, the booklet is an attempt to overcome some of the traditional difficulties which Anglicans have had with some Roman Catholic theological positions, e.g. scripture and tradition, Mary, the saints, the papacy. The impression might still be received, however, that Anglican Irish identity is an identity phrased in opposition to Roman Catholicism.

That this is not simply an Anglican tendency has been emphasized by Prof Patrick Corish of St Patrick's College, Maynooth, in his study of *The Irish Catholic Experience.* He notes that post-Reformation Roman Catholic theological education (particularly from 1604) emphasized the importance of learning the theological treatises rather than the Bible. Through the appropriation of these treatises it was felt that Roman Catholic identity would be affirmed as an identity-in-opposition to Protestants. 'Now to be a Catholic, was not to be a Protestant.'[7] Presbyterians also found ways to emphasize difference and identity-in-opposition, through the mechanism of public disputations with Roman Catholic thinkers.

This identity-in-opposition has led to an emphasis on the independence of each tradition in Ireland. The communities have found it difficult to listen to each other. The 'other' has not been part of their world view. Yet it is quite clear that identity is interdependent.

Through this analysis of one situation, we have seen the way in which community identities are nourished by memories – particularly memories of past atrocities visited by one community or group on another. These memories, it is clear, provide a framework for interpreting or understanding the world. Every new atrocity, every new action by the other community evokes the memory of the past. In our analysis, we have also seen the way in which churches have been important actors in phrasing the identity of communities as communities-in-opposition. They have in this instance – as in many other conflict situations – provided a theology which provides an interpretative framework for the communities. The churches also are locked into this identity-in-opposition. The churches are also intrinsic to the conflict.

Ireland is not of course the only context in which 'memories' play a role. The novels, poetry and autobiographical works of Elie Wiesel and Primo Levi[8] respond in terms of the Holocaust to what Wiesel has called 'the Jewish obsession with memory'.[9] The novels of Franz Kafka and Milan Kundera explore in their contexts the way in which attempts have been made to form a completely new identity by controlling or changing or erasing the memory of a people; they reflect on the importance of memory as the root from which the self understanding of their identities by individuals and groups emerges.[10]

The divisive impact of memory is everywhere evident in our world. Writing of Africa, Cesaire cries out:

In my memory are the lagoons.
They are covered by skulls of the dead.
My memory is wrapped in blood.
My memory has its girdle of corpses.[11]

The memories of poverty, oppression and violence associated with the slave trade and colonialism in Africa determine present attitudes and relationships, as is evident in the relationship of African countries to the former colonial powers. For Pakeha and Maori peoples in New Zealand, for white and native American communities in the United States of America, and for conflicting parties in

situations around the world (some of which are discussed by contributors to this volume), memories of past atrocities and destructive
relationships determine relationships and make the resolution of
conflict difficult and traumatic. Memory is an important element
in the shaping of contemporary identities and contemporary conflicts.

Memory and Liberation

Since memory plays such an important role in the phrasing of
identity, the over-riding question which needs to be addressed in
the context of our contemporary world is how might the activity of
remembering become a liberating process rather than a statement of
a situation of captivity? Are we condemned to perpetuate our ident-
ities-in-opposition, to view each other as a threat?

Throughout the Hebrew scriptures and the New Testament, the
people of God are continually being enjoined to 'remember' or to
'do this in memory of'. The context for this activity of remembering is that of worship. At the great autumn festival of the people of
Israel, when thanks are being given for the sustenance of the community through the harvest, the community is invited to remember
God's gracious activity in all aspects of life. The formula which the
community recited (e.g. Deut 26:5-10) recounted God's liberating
presence with the people through the events of their history, and
above all the celebrations focused on the Exodus. This memorial of
the Exodus liberation experience was particularly evident in the annual Passover celebration. Here the people were enabled to engage
in a concrete re-living of their deliverance as the People of God.
Their identity as a community was once again re-affirmed as they
remembered their slavery and journey to freedom. Such a re-living
was also an act of thanksgiving to God, for entering into a
Covenant relationship with the community, and for sealing that
Covenant with the community meal (Ex 12:1-14), which was re-
enacted annually.

In participating in this Passover meal, as an expression of 'remembering', the community through its burnt offering gave
thanks to God for being united with the community. They made a
peace offering signifying the community of life between God and
the community, and ate a meal together accompanying it with a

supplication for liberation, salvation and unity as the people of God. Finally, they made a sin offering and a guilt offering as an act of reparation for sin committed by individuals and by the community.[12]

In their activity of remembering, therefore, as they ate together, the people of Israel were enabled to re-live, mystically and sacramentally, the events of the deliverance and exodus from Egypt. The past became contemporaneous. They experienced again that deliverance in the context of their own time. However, part of the appropriating of that memory was the taking of responsibility for their sins, both as individuals and as a community, whereby they had failed to live as a sign of liberation, but had themselves participated in the abuse of the humanity of other people.

As a movement which emerged within the people of Israel, these same perspectives are evident in the self-understanding of the early Christians. The link between the sacrament of the Lord's supper and the Passover is evident, even though dispute still centres on the question of whether the Last Supper was in fact a celebration of the Passover meal itself.[13] The early Christians, however, through this meal celebration experienced liberation as they obeyed the injunction to 'do this in memory of me'. The words used by the early church, e.g. *anamnesis,* are an attempt to translate into Greek the Hebrew vocabulary evident in the Passover celebration. This word 'anamnesis' is central to the two accounts of the Lord's supper, from which all celebrations of the Lord's supper or eucharist have emerged. Through this remembering, once again the past is contemporary, and the liberating activity of God is experienced. Both in the accounts of the Lord's supper and in the extended meditation on the memorial and sacrifice of Christ in the Letter to the Hebrews, the word 'memorial' is paralleled with 'remission of sins'. The new Covenant with God, reconciliation and union, is the fruit of the remission of sins through the incarnation, ministry, dying and rising of Jesus Christ, with which events we become contemporary in the celebration of 'do this in memory of me'.

The Hebrew and New Testament understanding of 'remembering', then, makes of memory-memorial a dynamic process where the past is contemporary. The identity and self-understanding of the community is celebrated, responsibility is accepted, and forgiveness of sin sought.

The reconciliation that results from this way of remembering will be honest and vital, never cheap. Such reconciliation entails recognising the interdependence of our histories, even appropriating each other's histories, through which each will empower the other to be free. Through the reconciliation of memories a new identity is born. The Scots poet Edwin Muir phrases this vision thus:

Now in this iron reign
I sing the liberty
Where each asks from each
what each most wants to give
And each awakes in each
What else would never be,
Summoning so the rare
Spirit to breathe and live.[14]

Remembering in Ireland

In 1936 or 1937, John Hewitt wrote a one-act dramatisation centred on the confrontation of folk who had been caught up in the massacre at the Gobbins, Islandmagee, in 1641. Of this drama, entitled *The Bloody Brae,* he wrote:

The story which I invented turned into a plea for forgiveness for the wrongs of our past and tolerance between the communities.[15]

Hewitt has grasped well the parameters of 'remembering' in the Irish situation, and the costliness of the process. Only through the celebration of memories in this way will liberation from the captivity to the past be possible. Otherwise, the celebration of our memories will condemn us to captivity by the past.

Notes:

1. John Hewitt, *Freehold and other Poems* (Belfast: Blackstaff Press, 1986), 26f.
2. Oliver MacDonagh, *States of Mind: A Study of Anglo-Irish Conflict 1780-1980* (London: George Allen & Unwin, 1983), 9.
3. See Padraig O'Malley *The Uncivil Wars: Ireland Today* (Belfast: Blackstaff Press, 1983). R. F. Foster in his study *Modern Ireland: 1600-1972* (London:

Allen Lane, 1988), 266, when commenting on 1790, noted that the 'old siege mentality' was still in evidence.

4. See for example Austin Clarke, 'Celebrations' in Maurice Harmon, ed., *Irish Poetry after Yeats* (Dublin: Wolfhound Press, 1981), 36f; Séamus Deane, *History Lessons* (Dublin: Gallery Press, 1983).

5. See Seán Ó Tuama, ed., *An Duanaire 1600-1900: Poems of the Dispossessed,* trans. Thomas Kinsella (Portlaoise: Dolmen Press, 1981).

6. Iain Crichton Smith, *The Exiles* (Manchester: Carcanet Press, 1984), 36.

7. See Patrick Corish, *The Irish Catholic Experience* (Dublin: Gill and Macmillan, 1985), on the use of the treatise method adopted in the early seventeenth century. The suspicion of Bible study was evident in the life and work of the very irenic 19th-century Roman Catholic bishop, James of Kildare and Leighlin, and in a wider context was the subject of concern to reverse this trend through the work of the Pontifical Biblical Commission and Papal Encyclicals throughout this century. See also John Barkley, *Ireland in Perspective* (London: B.C.C., 1989), on the Presbyterian 'controversies' of the nineteenth century; Clogher Diocesan Board of Religious Education, *How We Differ from Rome* (catechism); Roman Catholic Archdiocese of Dublin, *Apologetics and Catholic Doctrine: A Course of Religious Instruction for Schools and Colleges* (1939), and T.C. Hammond, *The One Hundred Texts* (Dublin: Society for Irish Church Missions, 1932), to cite but a few examples of this tendency.

8. See for example Elie Wiesel, *Night* (Harmondsworth: Penguin, 1988); Primo Levi, *The Drowned and the Saved* (London: Michael Joseph, 1988); Primo Levi, *Collected Poems* (London: Faber, 1988).

9. Quoted in *The Observer,* 17 July 1988, 15.

10. Milan Kundera *The Book of Laughter and Forgetting,* trans. Michael H. Haim (Harmondsworth: Penguin, 1983), 157. Cf my own 'A Visit to the U.S.S.R.' in *Doctrine and Life* 34 (10) 1988, 587-595, with particular reference to Lithuania.

11. Cited by Jean-Marc Ela, in Yacob Tesfai, ed., *The Scandal of a Crucified World* (New York: Orbis, 1994), 27.

12. See Max Thurian, *The Eucharistic Memorial,* trans. J. G. Davies, 2 vols (London: Lutterworth, 1960).

13 See Joachim Jeremias, *The Eucharistic Words of Jesus* (London: SCM, 1966).

14. Edwin Muir, 'The Annunciation' in *Collected Poems* (London: Faber, 1960), 117.

15. See Alan Warner, ed., *The Selected John Hewitt* (Belfast: Blackstaff Press, 1981).

Re-membering the Future

Lionel Chircop

In December 1993, I paid my first visit to Milltown cemetery in Belfast. There, names engraved on marble, accompanied by photographs, keep alive the memory of the departed. However, some names do not only recall particular persons but stand out among others in bringing to mind the sectarian violence that has plagued the North of Ireland. What arms put to silence, people try to keep alive in their memories and pass on to future generations. Why such a phenomenon? Do we recall the past so that we build up courage to raise arms against our persisting enemy? Are these memorials erected to serve as a catalyst for today's conflicts and resentment? Does memory offer the possibility of an escalating spiral of antagonism ... or peaceful reconciliation? Is memory simply a recollection of past facts ... or is *how* one remembers intrinsically linked to present facts and emerging future possibilities?

Perhaps our immediate reaction would be to forget all about the past and jump into a future of our liking. However, human history is not made up of clean breaks defining different periods but of an ongoing transformation that is rooted in the past, shaped in the present and tending towards a future that will always bring new surprises with it. This intergenerational perspective that considers humankind as a unity of past, present and future generations leads me to the conclusion that to forget the sins and mistakes committed in the past is a serious stumbling block to today's process of reconciliation. Why? Because what is forgotten cannot be healed, and that which cannot be healed easily becomes the source of greater evil. To prevent decline and the possibility of a worse disaster, we must recall the past that makes up human history and allow our memories to be healed and animated by hopeful futures. An Auschwitz that is forgotten is followed by a Hiroshima, and a forgotten Hiroshima may lead to the destruction of our world. By cutting off our common past, we risk paralyzing the evolution of a better future.

Back to the Future

While those who forget the past may be doomed to repeat it, just to remember the past is not enough. Simply to recall stark facts could be a source of resentment and irritation. One must have also a horizon of expectations and realistic visions. For it is this vision of future possibilities that influences the way we remember things and what we do with our memories in the present. What transforms memory into a positive catalyst is the horizon of future expectations that is borne in our minds and hearts out of a boundless love that hopes and renews all things. Just to recall past facts is like fixing our look on the rear mirror of a car, forgetting that our destination is elsewhere. A dynamic memory is more like glancing backwards in order to drive forward safely. The French have the imaginative expression 'reculer pour mieux sauter'![1] That captures in a nutshell what I understand by a dynamic memory and its role in building a better future of tolerance and peaceful coexistence. *How* we look backwards, coupled with the values and desires animating our foresight, determines the quality of our leap forward. I have always been perplexed by the fact that memories fomenting sectarianism are saturated with resentment about past conflicts and disputes about one's own identity to the extent that no breathing space is left for past and present day attempts at achieving peace and reconciliation. I strongly believe that genuine efforts at establishing peace in the past should become more memorable, perhaps not through photographs on graves and monuments but, by becoming alive once again in our hearts and minds.

The French writer André Malraux once made the shrewd observation that 'one day it will be realized that men (and women) are distinguishable from one another as much by the forms their memories take as by their characters.'[2] This remark drives home the point I am trying to make. How we live is not simply dependent on the events of our life, but also, and even more so, on the ways we remember these events. The way we place past events into our own personal history influences the way we live the present and anticipate the future. The present is not just a static impulse that ends the very moment it comes into existence, but a duration derived from the past and merging into the future.[3] We exist in the present, but we are truly alive because a past and a future are continually taking new shape in our consciousness here and now. This dynamic relationship between past and future times becoming reality in the present is nicely captured by Pentti Malaska:

Time flows to the present from two directions:
from the past and from the future.
From the past as our deeds accomplished, results materialized,
and from the future as our aims and visions,
ideas of hope or despair,
objectives targeted and committed to.
At the present the streams of time are moulded together,
and they cannot escape from becoming reality.
Men and women, all the same everywhere!
But their pasts and futures are different,
create diverse realities at the present
– a precious gift to humanity –
But why is it so strange to face,
and so difficult to tolerate?[4]

Befriending Wounding Memories

Most of our human emotions are closely related to our memories. Remorse is a biting memory, guilt is an accusing memory, gratitude is a joyful memory, and all such emotions are deeply influenced by the way we have integrated past events into our way of being in the world. We perceive our world with our memories. Our memory is crucial for the way we experience life.

When memories are undesirable and painful, our spontaneous reaction is to forget all about them. We want to forget the pains of the past and live as if they did not really happen. But we can never fully erase that which happens to us. Paradoxically, forgotten memories become tyrannical masters that can exert a crippling effect on us. A deeper analysis of our human experience would reveal that the past is not a dictator to be silenced or abolished but a voice to be listened to. It would be naive and harmful not to acknowledge unpleasant memories or past mistakes, for in the very germs of destruction lies the prospect of healing. The first step towards reconciliation is a contrite heart that celebrates its sorrow (not sadness) for the past shortcomings and grievances in front of an all loving God who turns *everything* to good for those who continually strive to love him and their neighbour.

It is not our mistakes that make us miserable but our inability to recognize them and to repent from repeating them. Without this inward conversion that dawns in our hearts as soon as we realize that we can do much better with the help of God's Spirit who strengthens us, our attempts at reconciliation and peaceful coexistence will be nothing more than temporary fragile ceasefires. Only those who face their wounded condition and make themselves open for healing, repentance and forgiveness can enter into a new way of living and become builders of 'the new heavens and the new earth'. Perhaps it is hard to realize that God is in the very facts of our human experience. We find it hard to believe that, like the prodigal son's father, God comes to greet us on our road to conversion not with condemnation but with a jubilation that melts away all our misery and saves us from self-condemnation. Whatever our situation might be, God always offers himself as an urgent need for the transformation of our present reality and makes out of our memory an active, grace-empowered, liberating remembrance that offers new hope for the future. By allowing our memories to become a 'sacred place' where the human marries the divine, we come to re-member the *whole* story, the story of humanity redeemed by the passion, death and resurrection of Jesus Christ.

'Remembering', says Max Scheler, 'is the beginning of freedom from the covert power of the remembered thing or occurrence.'[5] When we remember we create a space in which the wounded, wounding memories of the past can be reached and brought back into the light without fear. From a distance we tend to be more objective and detached from the hurts and motivations defining a particular situation, especially when we reflect on the history of past generations. Moments of solitude and reflection allow our memories to picture the whole story of humanity and to go beyond personal hurts and motivations.

Memories: A Sacred Space where the Human Marries the Divine

When the soil is not ploughed the rain cannot reach the seeds; and unless the leaves are raked away, the sun cannot nurture the hidden plants. So also, as long as our memories remain covered with fear, anxiety, or suspicion, the word of God cannot bear fruit. Our memory becomes compassionate only when, alongside the weeds, we cultivate the wheat and allow God to shower us with the gifts of the Holy Spirit, namely, 'love, joy, patience, kindness, generosity, faithfulness, gentleness, and self-control' (Gal 5:22). Only a memory that, in spite of its imperfection, is empowered by these gifts will recoil not only backwards but also forwards in a way that embraces both past happenings and the well-being of future generations. If our spine was meant to be ossified in order to keep us upright, our memory was meant to be dynamic and versatile in order to keep us alive and united as one family from generation to generation. We can easily become irritated by unresolved conflicts of the past if our memory is not constantly animated by a hopeful vision of what we would like the future to be. Our memory is not only a recorder of the past but a prophetic echo from the future. Without this prophetic dimension, animated by faith, hope and love, we easily drift to self-centredness and forget that we are called to live in communion with our brothers and sisters, no matter what their creed, origin or identity.

The great challenge in remembering is to constantly connect our human story with the divine story. We have inherited a story which needs to be retold time and again in such a way that the many painful wounds about which we hear day after day can be liberated from their isolation and be revealed as part of God's relationship with us. To remember faith-fully is to reveal that our human wounds are most intimately connected with the suffering of God himself. All human drama takes place in the pierced heart of the crucified Lord.

As Christians we are called to perceive reality with baptized eyes and minds and to constantly detect traces of the divine in our human situation. Our memory becomes sacred and truly alive when we reveal the connections between our small sufferings and Christ's passion, between our temporal life and the eternal life of God-with-us. Our human history should be a moving image of Christ's redemption from generation to generation.[6] It is only by lifting up our painful submerged memories out of the individualist or sectarian past and offering them on the table of the Lord that our pains can become a living sacrifice for the total and integral liberation of all humanity. Our painful memories on their own become too heavy a burden to carry. Only the 'suffering servant' who deliberately took upon himself our pains can transform our exhausting burden into a light yoke that is pleasant to carry. For to redeem does not primarily mean to take pains away but to reveal that our pains are part of a greater sorrow, that our experience is part of the great experience of him in whom 'we live, and move and have our being' (Acts 17:28). For people of faith, our identity in Christ is crucial in re-membering and interpreting our past stories, for as William Dryness puts it: 'without an informed memory of our past, and what God has done with that past, our openness to the future is ultimately without direction … In the end memory is the basis of real hope.'[7]

By connecting our story with the story of the suffering Messiah, we rescue our history from its fatalistic chain and allow our time to be converted from *chronos* to *kairos*, from a series of randomly organized incidents and accidents into a constant opportunity to explore God's saving activity in our lives. Christ's redemption gives not only depth to our memory but opens in front of us a horizon of hope that fills us with new courage and gives us a new identity that can never be confined to a sectarian ideology. Without this 'memorable' identity that is rooted and grounded in Christ, we have no firm ground on which to stand and we become pushovers for attractive ideologies, easily 'tossed to and fro and blown about by every wind of doctrine, by people's trickery, by their craftiness in deceitful scheming' (Eph 4:14). When as a community of the faithful we become too attached to our surrounding culture and circumstances and allow the memory of God's irruption into human history to fade, we begin to believe that our life depends upon circumstances rather than upon the grace of God. Then, along with memory, gratitude recedes into the background, and there is no strength or motivation to work for peace and reconciliation. We must be constantly reminded by word and sacrament where our true life lies; it is sinful to forget God's saving actions in the past. Thus the Passover story needs to be told over and over again. Our Eucharist is celebrated unceasingly. We need to know and to own our personal and corporate stories. Our personal stories take on new and deeper meaning as part of the larger and longer stories of our faith tradition, which are really memories of God's graciousness. In the Eucharistic assembly we hear Jesus' words, 'Do this in remembrance of me.' These words are an invitation for the worshipping community to appropriate the salvation Christ accomplished once and for all.

Forgiveness – Transforming the Accidental into the Eternal

If we convert to the way of the Lord and live our lives 'through him, with him and in him', we can truly forgive while fully remembering the hurts of the past. Every desert-ed past is transformed into a stream of life if we allow it to be irrigated by the divine gifts of forgiveness and the love that endures all. These same gifts of divine generosity can always be offered to our enemy. However, this does not amount to saying that we approve of any performed sinful actions. On the contrary, when we forgive we create space for conversion and tacitly invite the enemy to become our friend. To forgive is to reach out to the sinner in spite of the sin. To forgive is never to let the past have the final word on the other or on oneself. Commenting on the faith dimension of forgiveness, Kierkegaard said, 'Just as one by faith believes the unseen in the seen, so the lover by forgiveness believes the seen away. Both are faith. Blessed is the man of faith: he believes what he cannot see. Blessed is the lover: he believes away what he nevertheless can see.'[8]

Forgiveness never guarantees a truce, for it is not necessarily mutual. The one you forgive may remain completely hostile to you. But that is no reason to raise arms against your enemy again. On the contrary, it is this unilateral, unconditional expression of forgiveness by one part, the offended, which facilitates a change of heart and mind and behaviour on the part of the offender. 'Enlightened forgiveness', Mahatma Gandhi tells us, 'does not mean meek submission to the will of the evil doer, but it means putting one's whole soul against the will of the tyrant.'[9]

Breaking out of the walls of sectarianism and violence through repentance and forgiveness does not mean an immediate entrance into the promised land. Rather it involves a process of gradually learning to live tentatively, making allowances for the surprises that might come our way from our friends, our enemies and God himself. Such an open attitude encourages patience and joy, as the realisation dawns on us that we have enough time to do what God expects of us and that there is never enough time to do what God detests.

Love Hopes All Things

All our hope rests on the conviction that nothing, absolutely nothing, in our lives is outside the realm of God's forgiving love and mercy. By hiding parts of our story, not only from our consciousness but also from God's loving gaze, we claim a divine role for ourselves; we become judges of our past and limit mercy by our own fears. Thus we become numb not only to our own suffering but also to God's suffering for us. The challenge remains to see our unfolding experience as part of God's ongoing redemptive work in the world. It is through the marriage between our broken human past and God's redemptive activity in and through Christ that a new fellowship amongst us is created, a fellowship in which memories that formerly seemed only destructive are now reclaimed as part of a redemptive event.

No matter how adamant we are in defining our own identity against that of another in a way that foments conflicts and sounds only the voice of blood, it remains a fact that there is no memory that is complete darkness. Nor is their a memory of pure de-light. Our memories are wounded and loved at the same time. It would be completely miserable and inhuman to recall only our wounds and to forget the memories animated by love and forgiveness that nurture our day-to-day struggles. Our constant temptation is to throw to the power of darkness what we receive in the light. No matter how partial or incomplete are the impulses and insights that we receive in moments of inspiration, we should let them transform our darkness into shadows surrounded by bright areas, and let love gradually heal our wounds. For it is these healed wounds that give life to the otherwise insensible parts of our heart. Each healed wound becomes a sacred memory full of compassion and forgiveness. This mystery is deeply anchored in the biblical tradition. When Israel remembers God's great acts of love and compassion, she enters into these great acts themselves. To remember is not simply to look back at past events; more importantly, it is to bring these events into the present and celebrate them here and now. For Israel, remembrance means participation. The act of remembering serves to actualize the past for a generation removed in time from those former events in order that they themselves can have an intimate encounter with the great acts of redemption.

It is central to the biblical tradition that God's love for his people should never be forgotten. It should remain with us in the present. When everything is dark and fragmented, when we are surrounded by despairing voices, then we can find salvation in a remembered love, a love which is not simply a wishful recollection of a bygone past but a living force which sustains us in the present. Through memory, love transcends the limits of time and offers hope at any moment of our lives.

Called to be 'One in Mind and Heart' (Acts 4:32)

It was Thomas Hardy who said, 'If a way to the better there be, it exacts a look at the worst.' Only thus can we avoid repeating mistakes. However, as we have seen above, the interplay of how we interpret past events with our expectations for a better future is of crucial importance too. Through remembrance and foresight, coupled with prudence and responsibility, we can create a culture of peace that is responsive to the future, not merely driven by the past. A story which took place in the city of Sarajevo in 1992 illustrates the reality of a dynamic memory in the context of faith, hope and love. At four o'clock one afternoon in May, a mortar shell exploded in a square, killing twenty-two people who were waiting in line for food. The next day, at the exact same time, a cellist from the Sarajevo symphony came to the spot where the shell had exploded, set up his chair and instrument, and played Albinoni's 'Adagio'. He returned each day for twenty-two days to play the same piece, one for each of the twenty-two persons who had died. It was, one might say, a liturgical act, an act of consecration and remembrance so that the dead would not be forgotten. Cannot Albinoni's 'Adagio' become the hymn of contrition and liberation in the hearts of all parties involved in the peace process of Northern Ireland? Cannot arms be turned into ploughshares to dig new furrows in our memories where the seeds of justice, peace and reconciliation can grow from generation to generation?

Our memories are both the remembrance of past events and the re-membering of the common future of humankind. Rather than a collection of outdated fossils to be rejected, our memories consist of the many possible realities that can take shape in our life. Let not our memories be a graveyard of monuments, but a sacred space open to the eternal divine and its traces in the other. Let not our memories look for a justification of the past, but for a just future. Let not our memories be concerned with the sectarian question, 'Who am I in contrast to others?', but let our minds and hearts be invaded by the conviction that we are all one. As the new vision of tolerance and peaceful coexistence emerges, the dynamic memory of Jesus' own reconciliatory mission, expressed in his farewell prayer, may be coming closer to fruition: '... that they all may be one as you, Father, are in me, and I in you ... that their unity may be complete' (Jn 17:21-23).

Notes

This essay is mainly the fruit of a course I followed in Ecumenics given by Rev Alan Falconer, then director of the Irish School of Ecumenics. I am deeply grateful for his inspiration throughout the course and for his encouragement in writing this essay. I am also indebted to Dr Joseph Liechty for his critical reading and helpful suggestions to make this essay memorable and for assembling this new edition of *Reconciling Memories*. A word of thanks also to Fr Michael Hurley SJ, who, perhaps unknowingly, during a retreat in Ballyvaloo, inspired much of what I have developed about forgiveness.

1. 'Stepping back in order to the leap forward better'.
2. André Malraux, *Anti-Memoirs* (New York: Bantam Books, 1970), 125.
3. I am here handling time in the way Augustine proposed, namely, by assuming the coexistence of three qualities of time in the present: 'A time present of things past, a time present of things present, a time present of things future.' cf. A., Augustinus, *Confessions and Enchiridion*, trans. & ed. by A. C. Outler (Westminster: Philadelphia, 1955), 259.
4. Penttí Malaska, 'The Futures Field of Research', *Futures Research Quarterly*, (Spring 1995, vol 11/1), 80.
5. Max Scheler, *On the Eternal in Man* (New York: Harper and Row, 1960), 41.
6. For an account of the role of memory in redemption see Terence McCaughey, *Memory and Redemption*, (Dublin: Gill and Macmillan, 1993).
7. William Dryness, *How Does America Hear the Gospel?* (Grand Rapids: Eerdmans 1989), 78.
8. Quoted in R. Studzinski, 'Remember and Forgive', *Concilium* (April 1986), 17.
9. Quoted in G. Soares-Prabhu, 'As We Forgive', *Concilium* (April 1986), 65.

The Reconciliation of Memories

Mark Santer

Why is the category of 'memory' so important? Memory is important because of the crucial role it plays in relation to our sense of identity. A person with amnesia has lost his identity, except what can be reconstructed from other peoples' researches and memories. It is through our memories, through our recollection of the past, and through what others have told us about the past, that we identify ourselves as who we are.

Most of our memories are in some way social. We identify ourselves in relation to other people – our parents, our brothers and sisters, our friends and our enemies. We also identify ourselves as members of groups – this group over against that group, this family over against that, this church over against that. And so our identity is marked not only by what we ourselves, as individuals, can remember, but by the corporate memories of the group, and by what others have told us about the past we share if we belong to that group. To give a simple example, there are things about my early childhood which I can certainly remember for myself, but there are others of which I am not sure whether I really remember them myself or whether I *think* I remember them because I have been told about them.

Memory, whether individual or corporate, is always selective. We cannot remember everything. We remember the things we need to or want to remember, or things which have affected us so deeply that we cannot help remembering them. We remember things and people and events by telling stories about them. So we not only select, we also interpret, and interpret in the selecting. Some things, important to others, we simply will not notice or recall. Our choice is largely unreflective.

So it is striking how often two people, present at the same event, will give two different accounts of it. This is especially obvious when there has been a quarrel or some other breach of communication. We fall out with someone – and cannot even agree what it is we are arguing about. Commonly, if an injury is thought to have been done, it will be remembered and nursed by the party that thinks itself injured, while the party complained of may not even have noticed that hurt has been done. This is true of a family row; it is also true of communal grievances. So Irishmen have a story about what Oliver Cromwell did at Drogheda; it is important to their identity. Englishmen have no story about it at all; either it is not important at all or else it has been important to forget it. At all events, part of the Irish grievance is precisely the lack of English awareness.

We maintain our communal identity not only by stories, but also by festivals and rituals, and by stories embedded in ritual. That, after all, is what we do whenever we celebrate the eucharist. By remembering Christ's death, resurrection and coming again we remind ourselves of our identity as Christians. This remembrance is powerfully focused in the eating of bread and the sharing of a cup of wine in remembrance of his sacrificial death.

Similarly, the traditional Christian ceremonies of Holy Week and Easter are a powerful means whereby Christians identify themselves through their ritual remembrance of Christ's entry into Jerusalem, his last supper, his betrayal, his death and resurrection. This is wonderful for Christians. But the potential ambiguity of all such rituals of group identity comes out, when we remember what Holy Week could be like for the Jews of Eastern Europe. Then we see what happens when an in-group of the accepted requires an out-group of the rejected.

And so we naturally think of the rituals by which groups of divided Christians have marked themselves off from each other, and have kept the grievances alive which sustain their own identity over against their rivals. Thus Foxe's *Book of Martyrs* used to be Sunday reading for English Protestants. Guy Fawkes Day was, and in some places still is, an annual celebration of Anti-Popery. The Roman Catholics in England have fervently treasured the memories of their martyrs, put to death by a State whose religious face was the Church of England. I hardly need mention the Green and Orange martyrs of Ireland.

We all need our stories and our rituals. As I said at the beginning, without our memories we have no identity. But our memories are as subject to the effects of sin as the rest of our human condition. We abuse this gift of memory when we employ it for keeping ourselves in the right and others in the wrong, for keeping grievances alive and for perpetuating stereotypes which justify us in treating other groups in demeaning, or oppressive ways. Thus: women are irrational; Irish are stupid; criminals are animals; the unemployed are idle; you can never trust the Russians.

All of these points are important in thinking about communal conflicts of any kind. They have obvious relevance to conflicts between peoples and nations. But my particular experience is in trying to deal with religious conflict – conflict between groups which have rival accounts, rival stories, of why it is that they are divided. All conflicts produce histories – as we can see from the blossoming of history writing in the fourth and fifth centuries (celebrating the conflicts with paganism and between Orthodoxy and Arianism) and in the wake of the Reformation. The Protestant story had to be met by the Catholic story, and *vice versa*.

Let us notice a few things of which we must be aware in trying to move out of conflict towards reconciliation – points of which I myself have become aware through ecumenical work.

(i) Although doctrinal differences are of great importance, since our apprehension of the truth of the gospel is at stake, it is mistaken to think that our differences are simply matters of doctrine, or that it is theologians alone who keep Christians apart. The ecumenical task is not to reconcile theologies, but to reconcile the people and communities who use those theologies to identify themselves as distinct from each other. Theological differences become intractable when they become a function of one group's identity over against another, or have become the flags marking an institutional frontier. Once they have become badges of identity, such issues are kept alive by the need to tell a story which justifies the maintenance of the *status quo* of separation in face of the gospel demand for reconciliation. The attraction of doctrinal issues is that they appear to allow us to remain divided with a good conscience.

Thus Protestants keep justification by faith alive as an issue, precisely because their self-identity depends on a story which characterises Roman Catholics as people who do not believe in it.

Similarly, English and Irish Roman Catholics, who for centuries suffered persecution and disadvantage at the hands of a state which had identified 'Transubstantiation' as the litmus-paper of subversion, are reluctant to believe that there is nothing to argue about after all. It is not simply a matter of theology; it is a question of group identity.

(ii) Differences which we can live with within one communion become intolerable once there has been a breakdown of trust, and once this breakdown has become institutionalised, it becomes extremely difficult to persuade people that the differences do not justify division. The doctrine of justification by faith is a good example. In fact, disputes on justification, predestination, grace and good works raged in the pre-Reformation church and among both Protestants and Catholics after the Reformation. The issues are complex and by no means clear-cut. There is no doubt that there are differences of emphasis which one can broadly identify as Protestant and Catholic. Yet, as soon as one tries to show that on basic points we share a common faith, and that differences of emphasis should not be church-dividing, we are charged with papering over cracks, or of pretending that the historical disputes were simply a matter of verbal misunderstanding.

(iii) Once we are divided, we tend in our minds to pickle our opponents in the past. So a modern Protestant will imagine that, in dealing with the Roman Catholic Church, he must still be dealing with the abuses which outraged Luther. He will feel disorientated and upset if he is told that indulgences are hardly the issue today which they were 450 years ago. If a Roman Catholic tells him this, he will think that he is not a real Roman Catholic; and if I tell him, he will think that I have been deceived, either by Roman Catholic guile or by my own gullibility.

If we do not know a community at first hand, we tend to pin it down to its published documents, while making allowances for development and interpretation in dealing with our own. Thus Protestants who are suspicious of Roman Catholics will insist on reading ARCIC in the light of Trent as they themselves have traditionally understood it. They are reluctant to allow modern Roman Catholics to speak for themselves.

(iv) As I have already said, we often disagree as to what the argu-

ment is about. What seems to one party the crucial issue may not
be of interest to the other at all. Justification is a good example. For
the Protestant, that is what the Reformation was about; and if the
Roman Catholic has not even heard of the doctrine – and, far less,
regards it a matter for dispute – that, in Protestant eyes, is still further evidence of Roman Catholic error on the point.

Furthermore, even when we agree that there is an issue to be
resolved – and that is the case if only one party thinks that there is
an issue at stake – then we often disagree on how to approach that
issue. Purgatory and indulgences are a good example. They are part
of the Roman Catholic lumber, and Protestants keep reviving them
– not because they are important now, but because they *were* important 450 years ago and so are part of the story of why we are
Protestants. But then the question arises: how do we deal with
them? For Protestants, they belong in the context of justification;
for Catholics, their proper context is the doctrine of the church.

(v) No theological agreement exists *in vacuo*. It has to be received
by the communities which are represented by the theologians. If the
agreements are not received and accepted when they are made, the
work will have to be done again. Thus, for instance, the degree of
theological reconciliation achieved in the Anglican-Methodist conversations of the 1960s cannot be regarded as still on the table. The
communities which came so close have moved on. In fact, church
history is littered with agreements which have come to nothing because communities have failed to receive them – for instance, in the
fifth century, the christological agreement between the schools of
Alexandria and Antioch fell apart; in the fifteenth, the agreements
of the Council of Florence were repudiated by the Orthodox people of Constantinople; in the sixteenth, the agreement of Ratisbon
on justification was accepted neither in Rome nor in Wittenberg;
and so on. It is not sufficient for the theologians to learn to trust
and understand one another.

So what must we do? Three points:

(i) *Friendship* and *trust* at all levels are indispensable. We must
learn to talk to and listen *to* each other, and not just talk *about* each
other. As long as we just read about other Christians, we shall persist in our fantasies – just as, before the Wall came down, we could
persist in our fantasies about Eastern Europe if we never visited it
and talked to people who lived there.

Linked with friendship and trust is the matter of *will* and *desire.* If we do not desire reconciliation, we shall never have it, and it will be a comparatively easy matter to think of reasons of high principle for not being reconciled yet. We shall never get anywhere if we always demand change from the others, and never face up to the fact that repentance and change is also required of us.

Of course there will always be differences between Christians – as there are between husband and wife. But if we are committed to each other, we can face our differences as a shared and common problem, rather than use them as a reason for continuing to mistrust one another.

(ii) Part of our growth in trust is that we should listen to each other's stories. Thus, for instance, English Anglicans need to learn about the Catholic martyrs. We need to learn to share each other's celebrations, and to purge our own of those elements which depend on the denigration or misperception of our rivals. It is very good that when Pope Paul VI canonised the Forty English Martyrs, he did it in a way which included rather than excluded Anglicans. Again, in announcing the Pope's intention to beatify more martyrs on All Saints Day in 1987, both Cardinal Hume and Archbishop Runcie took care to see them as witnesses to the One Christ, in whose service both Protestants and Catholics have borne witness even to death.

Sharing each other's stories invokes sharing each other's festivals and rituals. Here the liturgical movement and the eucharistic revival are helping Christian people to recognise that what is being celebrated is a common faith. The increase in the practice of intercommunion, whatever the authorities may say, is a datum of theological significance.

(iii) Finally – does it need saying? – there was and is no reconciliation without the cross. Every time we celebrate the eucharist, we recall or remember the price of our reconciliation. We cannot recall the cross without recalling the sins which put the Lord on the cross – the sins by which we still crucify ourselves and each other. It is as we acknowledge our past – by bringing into conscious memory those things whose consciousness we have repressed – that the cross becomes the means of our healing. We have to forgive and let ourselves be forgiven.

Thereby we are united with Christ in his work of reconciliation. As ministers of reconciliation, we are not simply beneficiaries of the cross. We are called to share in Christ's work of redemption. That means receiving and bearing the fear and suspicions and even hatred of those who cannot bear to think of reconciliation. In asking people to look at their memories, we are threatening their identity. So no wonder they fight back. It is no good despising them. We need the gifts of patience and love. This is a real sharing of the cross. In working for reconciliation between Christians we are engaged in a fight with truly demonic powers, and we cannot expect to remain unscathed. But this is the point at which we show that we have a gospel, not just for the individual, but for the world. Those who belong to Christ are to live together in one communion as a sign that that is what human beings are made for. That is why theologians talk about *koinonia:* we are created, not to live apart, telling bad stories about one another, but to share a common life, whose image is both the simple table of the last supper, and the city of God whose gates are open to all the nations.

Myth and the Critique of Tradition

Richard Kearney

There has been much talk in recent years about reconciling traditions in Ireland. But before traditions can be properly reconciled, it is first necessary to understand how and why traditions play such an important role in our contemporary lives. What is their origin, their *raison d'être,* their end? Why doesn't the past just go away and let us get on with the future? Is it not time that sons buried their fathers and started living their own lives in a free and creative manner?

In addition to analysing the specific contents of our Irish traditions – social, literary, religious and political – it is perhaps necessary to offer a more philosophical account of the *form* of tradition in general. In this paper, I attempt to outline some aspects of such a philosophical account by looking at the central role played by myth in our understanding of tradition. Myth, I argue, is not some museum piece of the ancient past; it is a living dimension of culture which may serve either a negative *ideological* or a positive *utopian* function. Every tradition, I will argue, needs to be both demythologised and remythologised, for without such an ongoing process of critical and creative reinterpretation, there is, I am convinced, little hope for any realistic reconciliation of the different cultural traditions on this island.

I

A major question arising from the contemporary conflict between tradition and modernity is that of the role of myth. The modernist break with the past usually took the form of a *demythologising* project. While this project was a necessary corrective to the conservative apotheosis of tradition – the belief that the past constitutes some inviolable monolith of truth – it can also be pushed to extremes.

In the field of contemporary aesthetic theory, the 'textual revolution' has occasionally yielded excessive versions of formalism and nihilism. The impulse to deconstruct tradition, at all costs and in every context, has been known to result in anti-humanist celebrations of the 'disappearance of man'.[1] And in the process history itself, as the life-world of social interaction between human agents, is eclipsed. Being effectively reduced to a 'prison house of language', the very concept of history is drained of human content and social commitment. Deprived of memory, it falls casualty to the amnesia of the absolute text.

In the sphere of politics, the project of demythologisation has sometimes led to a full-scale declaration of war against the past. Marx anticipated such a move in *The Eighteenth Brumaire* when he distinguished between 1) the revolution which draws its inspiration from the past, 'calling up the dead upon the universal stage of history', and 2) the revolution which creates itself 'out of the future', discarding the 'ancient superstitions' of tradition and letting the 'dead bury the dead in order to discover its own meaning'.[2] The danger of the demythologising strategy occurs when it is pressed into the service of a self-perpetuating iconoclasm which, if left unchecked, liquidates the notion of the past altogether. Modern consciousness may thus find itself liberated into a no-mans-land of interminable self-reflection without purpose or direction. It is not enough to free a society *from* the 'false consciousness' of tradition, one must also liberate it *for* something. And this raises the question of 'memory' – and by extension 'myth' (understood in the broad sense of a collective symbolic project) – as a potentially positive and emancipatory force in its own right.

The attempt to erase historical remembrance can result in enslavement to the ephemeral immediacies of the present. It is a mistake to oppose in any absolute fashion the utopian impulses of modernity to the recollective impulses of tradition. A culture invents its future by reinventing its past. And here we might usefully contrast Nietzsche's 'active forgetting' of history (which so readily degenerates into the 'ludic disportings of disruption and desire') with Benjamin's more subtle notion of 'revolutionary nostalgia' - an active remembering which reinterprets the suppressed voices of tradition in a critical rapport with modernity.[3] It is this latter model which the Frankfurt School, and in particular Marcuse, had in mind when developing the dialectical notion of an 'anticipatory memory' *(vordeutende Erinnerung)* capable of projecting future images of liberation drawn from the past. The rediscovery of the subterranean history of the past as a 'presage of possible truth' can yield critical standards tabooed in the present. Recollecting the discarded aspirations of tradition thus triggers a liberating return of the repressed. The *recherche du temps perdu* becomes the vehicle of future emancipation.[4] Marcuse spells out some of the radical implications of this anticipatory memory as follows:

> Utopia in great art is never the simple negation of the reality principle (of history) but its transcending preservation in which past and present cast their shadow on fulfilment ... Forgetting past suffering and past joy alleviates life under a repressive reality principle. In contrast, remembrance spurs the drive for the conquest of suffering and the permanence of joy ... the horizon of history is still open. If the remembrance of things past would become a motive power in the struggle for changing the world, the struggle would be waged for a revolution hitherto suppressed in the previous historical revolutions.[5]

II

How does this relate to the dialectic of tradition and modernity which this paper has been exploring in the context of Irish culture?

In a 1978 commemorative address for Thomas Ashe (the 1916 patriot who died on hunger strike a year after the Easter rebellion), the late Sean MacBride, winner of the Nobel and Lenin peace prizes and a former Minister in the Irish government, accused 'many of our so-called intellectuals' of devaluing the 'concepts of Irish nationality and even the principles upon which Christianity is founded'. MacBride deplored the absence of idealism and the erosion of moral standards which were causing young people in Ireland today to despair and to be cynical of an insidious double-talk and the resurgence of the slave mentality which existed prior to 1916. 'It seems to me', MacBride concluded, 'as if we are at a crossroads at which the choice has to be made between idealism and possibly sacrifice or betrayal and an abandonment of our national tradition and goals.'[6]

MacBride is quite justified in reminding intellectuals of their obligation to respect the positive heritage of their tradition. He is also no doubt correct in warning against the fashionable tendency to summarily dismiss the very concepts of nationality, religion and cultural identity as so many outworn ideologies. (Indeed as even the Marxist critic Frederic Jameson remarked, 'a Left which cannot grasp the immense Utopian appeal of nationalism, any more than it can that of religion ... must effectively doom itself to political impotence').[7] MacBride is labouring under a severe misapprehension, however, if he rebukes all intellectual attempts to critically question or reinterpret tradition. Tradition can only be handed over *(tradere)* from one historical generation to the next by means of an ongoing process of innovative translation. And if tradition inevitably entails translation, it equally entails transition. The idea that there exists some immutable 'essence' of national identity, timelessly preserved in the mausoleum of a sealed tradition and impervious to critical interrogation, is a nonsense. Tradition can only be transmitted through the indispensable detour of multiple translations, each one involving both critical discrimination and creative reinvention.

Gone are the days, fortunately, when intellectuals were expected to serve the nation by parroting simplistic formulae such as 'Up the Republic' and 'Keep the Faith' – or, north of the border, 'No Surrender' and 'Home Rule is Rome Rule'. Gone also, one would hope, are the days when Irish intellectuals could be branded by a government Minister as 'pinko liberals and Trinity queers', or have their works banned because they raised questions which were better not discussed (a sorry phenomenon which prompted one distinguished commentator to cite 'anti-intellectualism' among the seven pillars of Irish political culture).[8]

The need to perpetually re-evaluate one's cultural heritage raises, once again, the central question of *narrative*. Narrative – understood as the universal human desire to make sense of history by making a story – relates to tradition in two ways. By creatively reinterpreting the past, narrative can serve to release new and hitherto concealed possibilities of understanding one's history; and by critically scrutinizing the past it can wrest tradition away from the conformism that is always threatening to overpower it.[9] To properly attend to this dual capacity of narrative is, therefore, to resist the habit of establishing a dogmatic opposition between the 'eternal verities' of tradition, on the one hand, and the free inventiveness of imagination, on the other. Every narrative interpretation, whether it involves a literary or political reading of history, 'takes place within the context of some traditional mode of thought, transcending through criticism and invention the limitations of what had hitherto been reasoned in that tradition ... Traditions when vital embody continuities of conflict'.[10] This implies that the contemporary act of re-reading (i.e. re-telling) tradition can actually disclose uncompleted and disrupted narratives which open up unprecedented possibilities of understanding. No text exists in a vacuum, in splendid isolation from its social and historical contexts. And tradition itself is not some seamless monument existing beyond time and space – as the revivalist orthodoxy would have us believe – but a narrative construct requiring an open-ended process of reinterpretation. To examine one's culture, consequently, is also to examine one's conscience – in the sense of discriminating between rival interpretations. And this is a far cry from the agonising inquest conducted by revivalists into the supposedly 'unique essence' of national identity. Séamus Deane is right, I believe, when he pleads for the abandonment of the idea of essence – 'that hungry Hegelian ghost looking for a stereotype to live in' – since our national heritage is something which has always to be rewritten. Only such a realisation can enable a new writing and a new politics, 'unblemished by Irishness, but securely Irish'.[11]

III

I will now examine the more specific hermeneutic context of the demythologising project which so powerfully informs modern thinking. Most critics of myth have focussed on its ideological role as a mystifying consciousness. Their approach has been termed a 'hermeneutics of suspicion' in that it negatively interprets (gr. *hermeneuein*) myth as a masked discourse which conceals a real meaning behind an imaginary one.[12]

The modern project of unmasking myth frequently takes its cue from the investigative methods developed by Marx, Nietzsche and Freud – the 'three masters of suspicion'. Nietzsche advanced a genealogical hermeneutic which aimed to trace myths back to an underlying will to power (or in the case of the Platonic and

Christian myths of otherworldly transcendence, to a negation of this will to power). Freud developed a psychoanalytic hermeneutic which saw myths as ways of disguising unconscious desires. Thus in *Totem and Taboo*, for example, Freud identifies myth as a substitution for lost primitive objects which provide symbolic compensation for prohibited pleasures. As such, religious myths are said to represent a sort of collective 'obsessional neurosis' whereby libidinal drives are repressed through a highly sophisticated mechanism of inhibition and sublimation. And thirdly, there is Marx who proposed a hermeneutic of 'false consciousness' aimed at exposing the hidden connection between ideological myths (or superstructures) and the underlying realities of class domination exemplified in the struggle for the ownership of the means of production (or infrastructure). Thus for Marx, the myth of a transcendental timeless fulfilment – whether it is projected by religion, art or philosophy – is in fact an ideological masking of the historical reality of socioeconomic exploitation.

Marx shares with Nietzsche and Freud the suspicion that myth conceals itself as an imaginary project of false values. It is 'myth' precisely in the sense of illusion, for it inverts the true priority of the real over the imaginary, of the historical over the eternal. Hence the need for a negative hermeneutics of unmasking. The critique of myth is, accordingly, 'the categorical refusal of all relations where man finds himself degraded, imprisoned or abandoned'.[13] And in this respect, Marx's denunciation of the mythico-religious character of the great money fetish in the first book of *Capital* constitutes one of the central planks of his critique of ideology. Moreover, it is this equation of myth with the fetishisation of false consciousness which animates Roland Barthes' structuralist critique of bourgeois 'mythologies' (where he argues that myth is an ideological strategy for reducing the social processes of History to timeless commodities of Nature).[14]

The negative hermeneutics of myth was by no means confined to the atheistic masters of suspicion. Many religious thinkers in the twentieth century have also endorsed the demythologising project. Indeed the very term 'demythologisation' is frequently associated with the theological writings of Rudolph Bultmann. Bultmann held that Christianity must be emancipated from those 'mythic' accretions whereby Christ became idolized as the sacrificial Kyrios of a saviour cult modelled on the pagan heroes of Hellenic or Gnostic mystery-rites.[15] Bultmann's demythologising is levelled against the mystification of authentic Christian spirituality. His critique casts a suspecting glance at all efforts to reduce the genuine scandal of the cross and resurrection to an ideological system wherein the newness of the Christian message is ignored or betrayed. Bultmann systematically exposes the manner in which the living word of the gospels often degenerated into cultic myths – e.g. the attempt to express the eschatological promise of the kingdom as a cosmological myth of heaven and hell; or the attempt to reduce the historical working of the Spirit through the church to a myth of triumphalistic power. To 'demythologise' Christianity is, for Bultmann, to dissolve these false scandals so as to let the true scandal of the word made flesh speak to us anew.

In recent years this work of theistic demythologisation has been effectively developed by the French thinker René Girard. Girard holds that the most radical aim of the Judaeo-Christian revelation is to expose and overcome the mythic foundations of pagan religions in the ritual sacrifice of an innocent scapegoat. Imaginatively projecting the case of all disharmony and evil on to some innocent victim, a society contrives to hide from itself the real cause of its internal crisis. True Christianity rejects the cultic mythologising of the scapegoat, deployed by societies as an ideological means of securing consensus. Only by demythologising this ideological lie of sacrificial victimage, by revealing the true innocence of the scapegoat Christ, can Christianity serve as a genuinely anti-mythic and anti-sacrificial religion.[16]

IV

What all these exponents of the hermeneutics of suspicion – theist or atheist – have in common is a determination to debunk the ideological masking of a true meaning behind a mythologised meaning. While confirming the necessity for such a demythologising strategy, we must ask if this critique is not itself subject to critique. In this way, we may be able to recognize another more liberating dimension of myth – the genuinely *utopian* – behind its negative *ideological* dimension. Only by supplementing the hermeneutics of suspicion with what Ricoeur calls a hermeneutics of affirmation, do we begin to discern the potentiality of myth for a positive symbolizing project which surpasses its falsifying content.[17]

But before proceeding to a discussion of the utopian horizon of myth we briefly rehearse the main ideological functions of myth – *integration, dissimulation* and *domination*. For it is only by smashing the ideological idols of myth that we can begin to let its utopian symbols speak. No contemporary consideration of myth can dispense with the critique of ideology. All remythologisation presupposes demythologisation. In an essay entitled 'Science and ideology' Ricoeur isolates three major traits of ideology:

1. *Myth as Integration.* Ideology expresses a social group's need for a communal set of images whereby it can represent itself to itself and to others. Most societies invoke a tradition of mythic idealization whereby they may be aligned with a stable, predictable and repeatable order of meanings. This process of ideological self-representation frequently assumes the form of a mythic reiteration of the founding-act of the community. It seeks to redeem society from the contingencies or crises of the present by justifying its actions in terms of some sanctified past, some sacred Beginning.[18] One might cite here the role played by the Aeneas myth in Roman society, the cosmogony myths in Greek society, or indeed the Celtic myths of Cuchulain and the Fianna in Irish society. And where an ancient past is lacking, a more recent past will suffice: e.g. the Declaration of Independence for the USA, the October Revolution for the USSR and so on.

Ideology thus serves to relate the social memory of an historical community to some inaugural act which founded it and which can be repeated over time in order to preserve a sense of social integration. Ricoeur defines the role of ideology thus:

> not only to diffuse the conviction beyond the circle of founding fathers, so as to make it the creed of the entire group; its role is also to perpetuate the initial energy beyond the period of effervescence. It is into this gap, characteristic of all situations *après coup,* that the images and interpretations intervene. A founding act can be revived and reactualised only through a representation of itself. The ideological phenomenon thus begins very early: for domestication by memory is accompanied not only by

consensus, but also by convention and rationalisation (in the Freudian sense). At this point, ideology … continues to be mobilising only insofar as it is justificatory.[19]

The ideological recollection of sacred foundational acts has the purpose therefore of both integrating and justifying a social order. While this can accompany a cultural or national revival, it can also give rise to what Ricoeur calls a 'stagnation of politics' where 'each power initiates and repeats an anterior power: every prince wants to be Caesar, every Caesar wants to be Alexander, every Alexander wants to hellenise an Oriental despot.'[20] Either way, ideology entails a process of codification, schematization and ritualization, a process which stereotypes social action and permits a social group to recollect itself in terms of rhetorical maxims and idealized self-images.

2. *Myths as Dissimulation.* If the schematic 'rationalisations' of ideology bring about social integration, they do so, paradoxically, at a 'pre-rational' or a pre-conscious level. The ideology of foundational myths operates behind our backs, as it were, rather than appearing as a transparent theme before our eyes. We think from ideology rather than about it. And it is precisely because the codes of ideology function in this indirect and oblique manner that the practice of distortion and dissimulation can occur. This is the epistemological reason for Marx denouncing ideology as the falsifying projection of 'an inverted image of our own position in society'.[21] Ideology is by its very nature an 'uncritical instance' and thus easily susceptible to deceit, alienation – and by extension, intolerance. All too frequently, ideology functions in a reactionary or at least socially conservative fashion. 'It signifies that what is new can be accommodated only in terms of the typical, itself stemming from the sedimentation of social experience.'[22] Consequently, the future – as opening up that which is unassimilable and unprecedented *vis-à-vis* the pre-existing codes of experience – is often translated back into the orthodox stereotypes of the past. This accounts for the fact that many social groups display traits of ideological orthodoxy which render them intolerant towards what is marginal, different or alien. Pluralism and permissiveness are the *bêtes noires* of such social orthodoxy. They represent the intolerable. This phenomenon of ideological intolerance arises when the experience of radical novelty

threatens the possibility of the social group recognizing itself in a retrospective reference to its hallowed traditions and orthodox pieties.

But ideology can also function in a dissimulating capacity to the extent that it conceals the gap between what *is* and what *ought* to be, between our presently lived *reality* and the ideal world of our traditional self-representations.[23] By masking the gulf which separates our contemporary historical experience from our mythic memory, ideology often justifies the status quo by presuming that nothing has really changed. This self-dissimulation expresses itself as a resistance to change, as a closure to new possibilities of self-understanding. Whence the danger of reducing the challenge of the new to acceptable limits of an already established heritage of meaning.

3. *Myth as Domination.* This property of ideology raises the vexed question of the hierarchical organization of society – the question of authority. As Max Weber and later Jürgen Habermas observed, social systems tend to legitimate themselves by means of an ideology which justifies their right to secure and retain power.[24] This process of legitimation is inherently problematic, however, in so far as there exists a disparity between the nation/state's ideological *claim* to authority and the answering *belief* of the public. Ideology thus entails a surplus-value of claim over response, of power over freedom, (or as Sartre would put it, of essence over existence). Put another way, if a system's claim to authority were fully and reciprocally consented to by those whom it governs there would be no urgent need for the persuasive or coercive strategies of ideological myths. Ideology operates accordingly as a 'surplus-value' symptomatic of the assymetry between the legitimizing 'ought' of our normative traditions, on the one hand, and the 'is' of our lived social existence, on the other. It is because there is no transparent or total coincidence between the claim to authority and the response to this claim, that ideological myths are deemed necessary to preserve the semblance of a united social consensus. (Such myths assure what Weber termed the 'charismatic' function of the social order.)

v

Myth is an ideological function. But it is also more than that. Once a hermeneutics of suspicion has unmasked the alienating role of myth as an agency of ideological conformism, there remains the task of a positive interpretation. Hermeneutics thus has a double duty – to 'suspect' and to 'listen'. Having demythologized the ideologies of false consciousness, it labours to disclose the utopian symbols of a liberating consciousness. This involves discriminating between the falsifying and emancipating dimensions of myth.

Symbolizations of utopia pertain to the 'futural' horizon of myth. The hermeneutics of affirmation focuses not on the origin *(arche)* behind myths but on the end *(eschaton)* opened up in front of them. It thereby seeks to rescue mythic symbols from the gestures of reactionary domination and to show that once the mystifying function has been dispelled we may discover genuinely utopian anticipations of 'possible worlds' of liberty and justice. A positive hermeneutics offers an opportunity to rescue myths from the abuses of doctrinal prejudice, racist nationalism, class oppression or totalitarian conformism, and it does so in the name of a universal project of freedom – a project from which no creed, nation, class or individual is excluded. The utopian content of myth differs from the ideological in that it is inclusive rather than exclusive; it opens up human consciousness to a common goal of freedom instead of closing it off in the inherited securities of the *status quo*. We shall return to this point below.

Where the hermeneutics of suspicion construed myth as an effacement of some original reality (e.g. will to power, unconscious desire, the material conditions of production or domination), the hermeneutics of affirmation operates on the hypothesis that myths may not only conceal some pre-existing meaning but also reveal new horizons of meaning. Thus instead of interpreting myths solely in terms of a first order reference to a pre-determined cause hidden behind myth, it discloses a second-order reference to a 'possible world' projected by myth. It suggests, in other words, that there may be an ulterior meaning to myths in addition to their anterior meaning – an eschatological horizon which looks forward as well as an archaeological horizon which looks back. Myth is not just nostalgia for some forgotten world. It can also constitute 'a disclosure of unprecedented worlds, an opening on to other possible worlds which transcend the established limits of our actual world' and function as a 'recreation of language'.[25]

The *epistemological* distinction between the two horizons of myth (i.e. archaeological and eschatological) also implies an ethical one. Myths are not neutral as romantic ethnology would have us believe. They become authentic or inauthentic according to the 'interests' which they serve. These interests, as Habermas recognized in *Knowledge and Human Interests* can be those of utopian emancipation or ideological domination. Thus the religious myths of a kingdom of peace may be interpreted either as an opiate of the oppressed (as Marx pointed out) or as an antidote to such oppression (as the theology of liberation reminds us). Similarly, it could be argued that the myths of Irish nationalism can be used to open up a community or to inure that community in tribal bigotry. And the same would apply to a hermeneutic reading of the Ulster Loyalist mythology of 'civil and religious liberties'. Moreover, our own century has also tragically demonstrated how Roman and Germanic myths – while not in themselves corrupt – have been unscrupulously exploited by Fascist Movements.

VI

The critical role of hermeneutics is therefore indispensable. But this does not mean that we simply reduce mythic symbols to literal facts. It demands rather that we learn to unravel the concealed intentions and interests of myth so as to distinguish between their inauthentic role of ideological 'explanation' (which justifies the *status quo* in a dogmatic, irrational manner) and their authentic role of utopian 'exploration' (which challenges the *status quo* by projecting alternative ways of understanding our world). Demythologizing as an urgent task of modern thought, must not be confused therefore with demythizing which leads to a reductionist impoverishment of culture.[26] The crisis of modernity is characterised by the separation of myth and history: a separation which desacralized tradition. But precisely because of this we need no longer be subject to the ideological illusion that myth *explains* reality. We should no longer expect myth to provide a true scientific account of our historical and geographical environment. 'Demythologization works on the level of the false rationality of myth in its explanatory pretension'.[27] Indeed it is the very demythologization of myth in this sense which permits the rediscovery of myth as utopian project. Having eliminated the ideological function of explaining how things are, we are free to reveal the symbolic function of myth as an exploration of how things *might* be. We begin to recognize that the 'greatness of myth' resides in its ability to contain more meaning than a history which is, objectively speaking, true. This is what Ricoeur calls the 'saving of myth' through demythologization.

> We are no longer primitive beings, living at the immediate level of myth. Myth for us is always mediated and opaque … Several of its recurrent forms have become deviant and dangerous, e.g. the myth of absolute power (fascism) and the myth of the sacrifical scapegoat (anti-Semitism and racism). We are no longer justified in speaking of 'myth in general'. We must critically assess the content of each myth and the basic intentions which animate it. Modern man can neither get rid of myth nor take it at its face value. Myth will always be with us, but we must always approach it critically … Only then can we begin to recognise its capacity to open up new worlds.[28]

What is required, then, is a hermeneutic dialectic between a critical *logos* and a symbolic *muthos*. Without the constant vigilance of reason, *mythos* remains susceptible to all kinds of perversion. For myth is not authentic or inauthentic by virtue of some eternal essence *in itself*, but by virtue of its ongoing reinterpretation by each historical generation of each social community. Or to put it another way, myth is neither good nor bad but interpretation makes it so. Every mythology implies accordingly a *conflict of interpretation*. And this conflict is, in the final analysis, an ethical one. It is only when *muthos* is conjoined with *logos* in a common project of *universal* liberation for all mankind that we can properly speak of its utopian dimension. Whenever a myth is considered as the founding act of one particular community, to the exclusion of all others, the possibility of ideological perversion immediately arises. Ricoeur makes this clear in the following passage from *Dialogues with Contemporary Continental Thinkers*:

> The original potential of any authentic myth always goes beyond the limits of any single community or nation. The *muthos* of a community is the bearer of something which extends beyond its own particular frontiers; it is the bearer of other *possible* worlds … Nothing travels more extensively and effectively than

myth. Whence it follows that even though myths originate in a particular culture, they are also capable of emigrating and developing within new cultural frameworks ... Only those myths are genuine which can be reinterpreted in terms of liberation, as both a personal and collective phenomenon. We should perhaps sharpen this critical criterion to include only those myths which have as their horizon the liberation of mankind *as a whole*. Liberation cannot be exclusive ... In genuine reason *(logos)* as well as in genuine myth *(muthos)*, we find a concern for the *universal* emancipation of man.[29]

We best respect the universalist potential of myth by ensuring that its utopian *forward* look is one which critically reinterprets its ideological *backward* look in such a way that our understanding of history is positively transformed.[30] The proper dialectic of *muthos* and *logos* observes both the need to 'belong' to the symbolic representations of our historical past and the need to 'distance' ourselves from them. Without the critical 'distancing' of the *logos* we would not be able to distinguish between the ideological deformations of myth and its genuinely utopian promise. For *muthos* to guarantee its *u-topos*, it must pass through the purgatorial detour of *logos*. But a due recognition of our sense of 'belonging' (i.e. that our understanding always presupposes an historically situated pre-understanding) is also necessary; for without it reason may presume to possess an absolutely neutral knowledge impervious to our embeddedness in a social community, historical epoch or cultural tradition. The claim to total truth is an illusion. 'Before any critical distance, we belong to a history, to a class, to a nation, to a culture, to one or several traditions. In accepting this belonging which precedes and supports us, we accept the mediating function of the image or self-representation'.[31] To renounce completely then the historical situatedness of the *muthos* is to lapse into the lie of a *logos* elevated to the rank of absolute truth. When reason pretends to dispense thus with all mythic mediation, it risks becoming a sterile and self-serving rationalism – an ideology in its own right which threatens to dominate our modern age of science and technology. Left entirely to its own devices, *logos* suspects everything but itself. And this is why the rational critique of myth is a 'task which must always be begun, but which in principle can never be completed'.[32]

VII

We return, finally, to the crucial question of national myth. How may we demythologize tradition while 'saving its myths'? Here we are confronted with the hermeneutic task of discriminating between the ideological and utopian function of national mythology. While it is absolutely essential to subject this mythology to a rigorous 'hermeneutic of suspicion' it would be foolish to conclude that all the myths of our tradition are reducible to the ideological function of mystification. We are obliged to respect the possibility that these myths contain a utopian horizon. As Tom Nairn rightly warns, even the most elementary comparative analysis shows that 'all nationalism is both healthy and morbid. Both progress and regress are inscribed in its genetic code from the start.'[33] Hence the limitations of the 'traditional Marxian negative hermeneutic for which the national question is a mere ideological epiphenomenon of the economic'.[34]

In the 'political unconscious' of Irish nationalism there also exists a utopian project which it is unjust and unwise to ignore. But this utopian dimension of our national mythology is only ethically legitimate to the extent that it is capable of transcending all sectarian claims (i.e. to be the one, true and only ideology) in a universalist gesture which embraces those whom it ostensibly excludes. At a political level, one might cite here the readiness of the Forum for a New Ireland (which took place in 1983-84 and to which all parties of Irish constitutional nationalism subscribed) to go beyond many of nationalism's 'most cherished assumptions' in order to respect opposing traditions and identities.[35] By thus demythologizing the myth of a United-Ireland-in-the-morning-and-by-whatever-means, it was possible to preserve the genuine utopian aspiration of the 'common name of Irishman' – a project which pledged to cherish all the children of the nation equally. At a literary level, we might cite the 'exploratory' narratives of James Joyce which demythologized the insularist clichés of Irish culture in order to remythologize its inherently universalist potential. Once a myth forfeits its power of ideological explanation, once it ceases to be taken literally as a force of intellectual hegemony, it ceases to mystify. And it is then that its utopian mystery is revealed. Myth no longer serves as a monolithic doctrine to which the citizens of the nation submissively conform; it becomes instead a 'bringer of plurabilities'. It is precisely the self-acknowledged *symbolic* nature of a myth's reminiscence and anticipation of collective harmony which commits it to a multitude of interpretations. 'In manifesting the purely symbolic character of the relation to men to the lost totality, myth is obliged to divide into multiple myths'.[36] The universality of myth is contained, paradoxically, in its very multiplicity.

Modern Irish culture provides us with many examples of this multiplication of myth. The old Irish myth of Sweeney Astray has been reinterpreted in a wide variety of ways by poets such as Clarke and Heaney, playwrights such as Friel and MacIntyre, the novelist Flann O'Brien (in *At Swim Two Birds*) and the film maker, Pat Murphy (in *Maeve*). Far from constituting a recycling of some immutable national vision, these rewritings of the Sweeney myth manifest a rich variety of different and often conflicting narratives. The retrospective allusion to indigenous myth thus opens on to the prospect horizons of a more universal culture. It is because our modern consciousness no longer believes in myth – at a literal level – that we can reinvent myth at a symbolic level. Without disbelief there can be no 'willing suspension of disbelief'. Without demythologization, no remythologization.

James Joyce powerfully exemplifies this dialectic in his modernist rewriting of the national myth of Finn. *Finnegans Wake* invites us to have 'two thinks at a time' – for as the title itself informs us, this narrative refers both to Finnegan's death (the term wake in Ireland means funeral ceremony) and to his rebirth (that is, Finn-again-awake). Joyce deconstructs the monolithic myth of Finn, the hero of Ireland's founding mythological saga, into an infinite number of myths. Joyce calls the *Wake* his 'messongebook'; and he thereby acknowledges that the 'national unconscious' – or the 'conscience of his race' as Stephen termed it – which expresses itself in his dreams *(mes songes)* of the legendary hero, may be interpreted either as an ideological lie *(messonge)* or as a utopian cypher *(message)*. Joyce was clearly aware that the Celtic myth of Finn and the Fianna had been invoked by the Irish literary revival and by many of the leaders of the new Republic (whose main national party was named *Fianna Fail*) in order to provide a renewed sense of cultural identity and unity for the Irish people. He saw the great potential of such myths as a means of animating the national unconscious. But he also recognised the possibilities of abuse. Joyce had little time for the sanctimonious romanticising which characterised aspects of the Celtic Revival. He disliked its tendency to turn a blind eye to the lived experience of the present out of deference to some sacralised fetish of the past. And he fully shared Beckett's disdain for a 'Free State' which proudly erected a commemorative statue of a dying Celtic hero in its General Post Office (where the Easter Rising began) at the same time as it introduced censorship laws which banned some of the finest works of its living writers. The recital of myths of the Motherland to legitimate a new intellectual orthodoxy was to be treated with critical scepticism; for such a practice was unlikely to foster a properly pluralist culture respecting the diversity of races, creeds and languages which existed in the nation. It was in defiance of chauvinistic stereotypes of the motherland that Joyce reinterpreted the ancient Celtic heroine, Anna, as Anna Livia Plurabella, whom he hailed as the 'Everliving Bringer of Plurabilities'. He thus opposed the 'one-minded' logic of ideological myth to the 'multi-minded' logic of utopian myth. *Finnegans Wake* features not *one* dominant personage but *many* interchanging personae who transform consciousness into a process of perpetual metamorphosis. Joyce's book explores a diversity of cultural myths (alongside the Celtic and the Judeo–Christian we find the Hellenistic, the Babylonian and the Chinese, etc.) In both its form and its content, *Finnegans Wake* is a 'manifesta' of multiple meaning.[37]

Conclusion

Joyce's literary model of myth as a creative 'bringer of plurabilities' has, I believe, immense implications for the reconciliation of traditions at both a political and religious level. It is not our purpose here to spell out these implications. Our task has been the more modest one of clearing some of the philosophical ground so that new debates might emerge. In conclusion, I can do no better than endorse Paul Ricoeur's plea that we 'maintain the tension between tradition and utopia. For the problem is to reactivate tradition at the same time as we try to move closer to utopia.'[38]

Notes

An amended version of this paper appears as ch. 8 of Richard Kearney, *Transitions* (Dublin: Wolfhound Press, 1987).

1. See in particular the structuralist and post-structuralist philosophies of Michael Foucault, Jaques Lacan and Jacques Derrida. For a detailed critique of this tendency see J.L. Ferry and A. Renault, *La Pensee 68: Essai sur l'anti-humanisme contemporain* (Paris: Gallimard, 1985). See Derrida's defence against such charges in my *Dialogues with Contemporary Continental Thinkers* (Manchester: Manchester University Press, 1984), 123-6.

2. Karl Marx, *The Eighteenth Brumaire of Louis Bonaparte* (1852) (London: Unwin Brothers, 1926), 24-6. See also Ricoeur's definition of myth in *Symbolism of Evil* (Boston: Beacon Press, 1967), 5.

3. See Terry Eagleton, 'Capitalism, Modernism and Post–Modernism', *New Left Review*, no.152 (1985), 64; and also Walter Benjamin, *Towards a Revolutionary Criticism* (London: Verso, 1981). See also Ricoeur's discussion of this same relationship between critical innovation and tradition in Note 9 below.

4. Herbert Marcuse, *Eros and Civilisation* (Boston: Beacon Press, 1955), 19, and also Barry Katz, *Herbert Marcuse: Art of Liberation* (London: Verso, 1982), 102, 153.

5. Herbert Marcuse, *The Aesthetic Dimension* (Boston: Beacon Press, 1978), 7.

6. Sean MacBride, quoted in *The Cork Examiner*, July 27, 1978.

7. Frederic Jameson, *The Political Unconscious: Narrative as a Socially Symbolic Act* (London: Methuen, 1981), 298.

8. Basil Chubb, *The Government and Politics of Ireland* (London: Longman, 1981), 21-3. See also Dick Walsh, 'Come on the Intellectuals', *The Irish Times*, June 20, 1985. 'Irish intellectuals have been accused of almost everything, from elitism to indifference and from subversion to being drunk and refusing to fight … Frequently these charges were trumped up because people in general, and their leaders in particular, did not take kindly to the idea of arguing with awkward customers about issues which, in the interests of peaceful existence, ought to be left alone. For the politicians and the Churches, such people were particularly troublesome … and the label 'intellectual' was tied to their names to show that they were at least boring and at worst dangerous.'

9. Walter Benjamin, 'Theses on the Philosophy of History', *Illumination* (London: Fontana), 57. See also Paul Ricoeur, *Time and Narrative*, vol.1 (Chicago: University of Chicago Press, 1984), 68-70.

10. Alasdair MacIntyre, *After Virtue* (London: Duckworth Press, 1981), 206.

11. Séamus Deane, *Heroic Styles: The Tradition of an Idea*, (Derry: Field Day pamphlets 4, 1984), 18.

12. See Paul Ricoeur, *The Conflict of Interpretations* (Evanston, Illinois, 1974); idem, *On Interpretation* (Yale: Yale University Press, 1970); and idem, 'The Critique of Religion', in C. Regan and D. Steward, eds, *The Philosophy of Paul Ricoeur: An Anthology of his Work* (Boston, 1978), 215. See also 'Ricoeur's Hermeneutic Conflict', *The Irish Philosophical Journal*, vol. 2, no. 11, 37.

13. Karl Marx and Frederick Engels, *On Religion* (Moscow, 1955), 50.

14. Roland Barthes, *Mythologies* (London: Jonathan Cape, 1972).

15. Rudolf Bultmann, *The Theology of the New Testament* (London: SCM, 1952), 295f, and also Rudolf Bultmann and Karl Jaspers, *Myth and Christianity: An Inquiry into the Possibility.*

16. René Girard, *Le Bouc Emissaire* (Paris: Grasset, 1982), in particular the chapter 'Qu'est-ce qu'un Mythe?', 36-7. See also my 'René Girard et le Mythe comme bouc émissaire', *Violence et Verité?: Colloque de Cérisy autour de René Girard* (Paris: Grasset, 1985), 35-49.

17. On this distinction between utopia and ideology see Karl Mannheim, *Ideology and Utopia* (London: Routledge and Kegan Paul, 1936); Frederic Jameson, 'The Dialectic of Utopia and Ideology' in Jameson, *The Political Unconscious;* and Paul Ricoeur, 'Science and Ideology', in J.B. Thompson, ed., *Hermeneutics and the Human Sciences* (Cambridge: Cambridge University Press, 1981), 222-47.

18. Mircea Eliade, *Myths, Dreams and Mysteries* (London: Fontana, 1968), 23: 'Myth is thought to express the absolute truth because it narrates a sacred history; that is, a transhuman revelation which took place in the holy time of the beginning ... Myth becomes exemplary and consequently repeatable ... By imitating the exemplary acts of mythic deities and heroes man detaches himself from profane time and magically re-enters the Great Time, the Sacred Time.'

19. Ricoeur, 'Science and Ideology', 225.

20. Ibid., 229.

21. Ibid., 227.

22. Ibid.

23. See Richard Kearney, *Myth and Motherland* (Derry: Field Day pamphlets 5, 1984), republished in *Ireland's Field Day* (London: Hutchinson, 1985).

24. Jürgen Habermas, *Legitimation Crisis* (Boston: Beacon Press, 1973).

25. Paul Ricoeur, 'Myth as the Bearer of Possible Worlds', *The Crane Bag*, vol. 2 (1978); reprinted in my *Dialogues with Contemporary Continental Thinkers*, 36-45.

26. On these distinctions between the 'explanatory' and 'exploratory' functions of myth and the critical procedures of 'demythologisation' and 'demythisatrai', see Paul Ricoeur, *The Symbolism of Evil* (New York: Harper and Row, 1967), and 'The Language of Faith, *Union Seminary Quarterly Review*, 28 (1973), 213-24; see also T.M. Van Leeuwen, *The Surplus of Meaning: Ontology and Eschatology in the Philosophy of Paul Ricoeur* (Amsterdam: Rodopi, 1981), 146-7.

27. Ricoeur, *The Symbolism of Evil*, 5.

28. Ricoeur, 'Myth as the Bearer of Possible Worlds', 39.

29. Ibid., 40-4. See also Mircea Eliade's perceptive account in *Myths, Rites and Symbols* vol. 1 (Harper, 1975), and in particular the section on 'The Corruption of Myths', 109-12, and on 'The Fallacy of Demystification', 120-3.

30. On this dialectic between ideology and utopia see my 'Religion and Ideology', 48-50; also the section on 'mythe et logos' in my *Poetique du Possible* (Paris: Beauchesne, 1984), 190-8; and my interview with Ricoeur entitled 'The Creativity of Language' in *Dialogues with Contemporary Continental Thinkers,*

29-30. Here Ricoeur suggests the possibility of a complementary dialectic between the retrospective horizon of ideology and the prospective horizon of utopia.

'Every society, as I mentioned earlier, possesses, or is part of, a socio-political *imaginaire*, that is, an ensemble of symbolic discourses. This *imaginaire* can function as a rupture or a reaffirmation. As reaffirmation, the *imaginaire* operates as an "ideology" which can positively repeat and represent the founding discourse of a society, what I call its "foundational symbols", thus preserving its sense of identity. After all, cultures create themselves by telling stories of their own past. The danger is of course that this reaffirmation can be perverted, usually by monopolistic elites, into a mystification discourse which serves to uncritically vindicate or glorify the established political powers. In such instances, the symbols of a community become fixed and fetishised; they serve as lies. Over against this, there exists the *imaginaire* of rupture, a discourse of utopia which remains critical of the powers that be out of fidelity to an "elsewhere", to a society that is "not yet". But this utopian discourse is not always positive either. For besides the authentic utopia of critical rupture there can also exist a dangerously schizophrenic utopian discourse which projects a static future without ever producing the conditions of its realisation. This can happen with the Marxist-Leninist notion of utopia if one projects the final "withering away of the State" without undertaking genuine measures to ever achieve such a goal. Here utopia becomes a future cut off from the present and the past, a mere alibi for the consolidation of the repressive powers that be. The utopian discourse functions as a mystificatory ideology as soon as it justifies the oppression of today in the name of the liberation of tomorrow. In short, *ideology* as a symbolic confirmation of the past and *utopia* as a symbolic opening towards the future are complementary; if cut off from each other they can lead to a form of political pathology.'

31. Ricoeur, 'Science and Ideology', 243.
32. Ibid., 245; See also Ricoeur's study of the Habermas/Gadamer hermeneutic debate on this question in 'Hermeneutics and the Critique of Ideology' in Thompson, ed, *Hermeneutics and the Human Sciences,* 63-100. See my application of the *muthos/logos* dialectic to *Irish culture in Myth and Motherland.*
33. Tom Nairn, *The Break-up of Britain* (New Left Books, 1977), 348, (cited in Jameson, *The Political Unconscious,* 248).
34. Jameson, *The Political Unconscious,* 298.
35. See John Hume's opening address where he declared that the Forum was not a 'nationalist revival mission' and that one of the reasons for our failure to resolve the national problem up to this may have been due to our inability to place the creation of a New Ireland 'above some of our most cherished assumptions'. Quoted in *Proceedings of the New Ireland Forum,* vol. 1 (Dublin Castle, 1984).
36. Ricoeur, *The Symbolism of Evil,* 168.
37. See the analysis of Joyce in my *Myth and Motherland,* and in my 'Mythos und Kritik', *Die Keltische Bewusstsein* (Munich: Dianos-Trikont, 1985).
38. Interview with Paul Ricoeur, *Le Monde des Livres,* February 7, 1986.

Reconciliation of Cultures: Apocalypse Now

Séamus Deane

The various attempts to reconcile the various ideas of culture in Ireland have been bound up with the requirements of different political situations. Oliver MacDonagh gives an account of one phase of this – from 1790-1820 – in his book *States of Mind* (1983). The spectacle of men in holy orders engaging in disputes about pre-Christian Ireland, the better to establish the continuity of their own religious and political tradition with that era, has a certain piquancy. But it also demonstrates the tragic impossibility of their seeing any hope of establishing continuity between the separated religions and traditions of the contemporary period. History and culture are brought in to supply the deficiencies of the present. So Catholic resurgence in the late eighteenth century takes the cultural form of presenting the Gaelic past as a noble and ancient achievement, the inheritors of which no longer deserve to be deprived of civil life under the Penal system. Protestant reaction after 1800 takes the line that the Celtic past is of no consequence, that its recent resurrection is a piece of romantic flimflam and that, therefore, Catholic claims to 'civility' are exaggerated or invalid. The story can be repeated with variations for the rest of the century and it extends, alas, into our own. Sir Samuel Ferguson, writing in 1833, appeals to the largely Protestant readership of the *Dublin University Magazine,* to 'learn to live back in the country we live in'; his attack on James Hardiman's *Irish Minstrelsy* (1831) is the opening shot in his campaign to recover ancient Irish culture for the Protestant as well as for the Catholic Irish of the day, although the bigotry of his attitude towards Catholics tends to make his campaign seem less ecumenical in its implications than it actually was. So too, the Young Ireland movement, led by Thomas Davis, sought a Celtic foundation for all Irish sects and divisions by envisaging the Irish-English problem as a battle between Celtic Romantics and British Utilitarians, a

theme which was to have a long run in Irish letters thereafter and
was to supply writers as various as Yeats, O'Grady, Pearse and Matthew Arnold with the dominating element of their thought about
Ireland.

Many of these efforts at cultural recovery and recuperation were
promoted by people who, like Ferguson, O'Grady and Yeats, were
trying to defend the interests of a class which was doomed to extinction, to try, that is, to give, through culture, an extension of a
life which had a diminishing political and economic future. Even
when Catholicism became politically triumphant in twentieth century Ireland, we find various writers – Sean O'Faolain, Austin
Clarke, Denis Devlin – attempting to re-attach it to a European or
to an ancient Irish past in order to rebuke and compensate for its
narrow and philistine contemporary manifestations. In other
words, culture has been used in Ireland for over 200 years (and
arguably much longer) as a category in which the deficiencies of the
existing state of affairs can be symbolically remedied. It is thus a
compensatory activity, a displacement into one area of problems
insoluble in another. Its history is both a dream of interpretation
and an interpretation of a dream. All through these various symbolic
narratives we find that key-words – Celt and Saxon, Gaelic and
Norman, Romantic and Utilitarian, English and Irish, Liberty and
Freedom – are either haunted by or correlative with the basic
disputatious religious terms, Catholic and Protestant.

To establish continuity is one thing; to do so in a triumphalist
spirit, validating one tradition as authentic, others as spurious, is to
reproduce the discontinuity the enterprise was designed to overcome in the first place. Whatever form our secular histories have
taken – linear patterns of progress, cyclic patterns of rebellion
against oppression, hypothetical patterns of what might have been
or revisionist patterns dedicated to the exploding of all myths other
than their own – it is surely true that no serious attempt has ever
been made to see within our own history a pattern that could be
described as essentially or structurally Christian, even though the
story of Christian sects and their battles is an integral feature of our
past and present. When I use the terms 'essentially or structurally
Christian', I mean a mode of thought that is governed by the great
historical typology of the Bible, one which has been more attractive

to the artistic mind than to others. The seven phases of progressive revelation in the Bible have been described by the literary critic Northrop Frye as Creation, Exodus, Law, Wisdom, Prophecy, Gospel and Apocalypse. (*The Great Code*, 1982). I cannot pursue his account here. Variations of it can be found in some of the great masterpieces of the past – in Dante, Spenser and Milton – and in modern times, in Yeats and Joyce. Belief is not a precondition of being able to use the Bible, although it sometimes seems to be a precondition of abusing it.

If we pause for a moment on the last phase, the Apocalypse, and its text, the Book of Revelation, we can elicit from it an example of the way in which we manage at regular intervals to use religion as a sanction for our failure or, indeed, refusal to reconcile cultures. Those seven-headed and ten-horned monsters, those dragons and horsemen, the Great Whore of Babylon and all the other allusions of the Old Testament which make up the fabric of that terrifying vision from Patmos, have been time and again used to ratify readings of history in which the downfall of the enemy – be it Catholicism, Protestantism, Communism or any other -ism – is foretold. This crudity is more often associated with Protestant fundamentalism than with any other sect, but it is true in a general sense that for many people, the Book of Revelation is an assurance that the truth, which is their truth, will prevail. This is exactly how one should not read a text of this kind. But it is also a lesson in how to create history as a story of eventual triumph. Misreading leads to rewriting, and the rewriting of the Book of Revelation is an outstanding example of the manner in which the Bible is recruited by Christians for sectarian and divisive purposes. As Northrop Frye points out in his discussion of Apocalypse, the Book of Revelation is not making a forecast, is not telling us that the great firework display is going to take place next Friday night or in the year 2000. Revelation, as the name implies, is an uncovering of what is happening now. It is a visionary formulation of the condition of our spiritual life. To read it as history is to suppress the spiritual, to make it subservient to the historical. The destruction described in Revelation is not the destruction of the world, but of man's exclusively secular vision of the world, the view which keeps us entrapped in time and space.

Mircea Eliade tells a story about a man who was collecting folk

material in Yugoslavia in the 1950s. In one village, he heard a standard folk-tale about a young man who was about to be married to a
local girl. Unfortunately for the young man, an enchantress had
also fallen in love with him and tried to persuade him to give the
girl up. He refused. As a consequence, on the night before his wedding, the enchantress lured him to a lonely cliff top and hurled him
over to his death. If she could not have him, neither would her
human rival have him. The collector asked when this had taken
place and was astonished to hear that it had happened only sixty
years before and that the bereft bride was still alive and still unmar-
ried. He went to her and asked for her account. She told him that
the death was an accident; that she and her betrothed were walking
in the mountains above the village on the night before the wedding
and he had slipped, fallen into a ravine and been killed. On talking
to the other villagers, he was told differently. One account claimed
that the bride was lying. She had killed her beloved herself because
he had taken her to the mountains that evening to tell her that he
was not going through with the marriage after all. Another version
had it that the problem was political. The two lovers were separated
by class and creed and the man had finally bowed to his family's
wishes and called off the marriage. For this she killed him. A variant
on this was that he had committed suicide in despair and that his
bride-to-be turned it into an accident to save her lover's name from
the disgrace of suicide and to deny to the members of his family a
triumph, however bitter, over her and him. Whatever the truth, the
collector ultimately decided that the story of the enchantress was
the only one into which all the others, so to speak, translated. She
was a symbol, created by the people to explain the mystery of the
man's death and also to take some of the harm out of it. It revealed
a tragic truth but it obscured the actual facts which, in their divis-
iveness, could not but be damaging in repetition.

On an awesome scale, the Book of Revelation works like that
folk story. It is a symbolic story, in code, of what is happening now.
It tells of the great battles of repression, anxiety and fear, the collision
between heaven and hell. The code can be read back into history. We
can see it as the retelling of a battle between Croats and Serbs,
Catholics and Protestants. But it is essentially a vision, not a myth.
Used as a myth, it ratifies a version of history in which the forces of

good overcome those of evil. There is a crucial, graded difference between, say, the biblical metaphor of the saving remnant and Yeat's mutation of it into the idea of the elite, and Ian Paisley's version of it as the doctrine of the elect and God's chosen people. A powerful metaphor of that kind is lethal when it is understood as fact, most especially as a fact in history, not of history. In other words, it is a fact, in this light, which will be the end-product of history, towards which it yearns. There is in such readings a disguised teleology. They look forward to the day that is to come, to the extinction of those who prohibit its arrival. It denies the present for the sake of the future. It says we are trapped now but will be free later.

Such literalism dominates our thought. In Ireland, the translation into literalism is appealing because, given our historical circumstances, we turn to literature (more than to the other arts) to find there the reconciliations we find nowhere else in our political lives. But then we translate from the literature back into the irreconcilable categories in which we are incarcerated. Art tells us that we are both free and trapped, both now and forever. It is the history of the spirit to be caught in this endless dialectic. It is the history told by the Bible. When the Bible refers to language, it does so in terms of a famous metaphorical opposition. On the one hand, we have the confusion of tongues, represented by the Tower of Babel; on the other, we have the 'pure speech' promised to the restored Israel, the counterpart to the gift of tongues in the Acts of the Apostles. The Temple of Jerusalem touched heaven; the Tower of Babel tried to touch it. The Tower is the prison-house of language, the false structure, entirely secular. The Temple is Christ, who is the cornerstone. Cultures are a Babel that can only become a Temple when their languages become the pure speech that Israel was promised. The confusion of tongues creates chaos, the gift of tongues creates reconciliation. Christians, who should know this best, pay least attention to it. In this respect, artists are more essentially Christian than the religious.

Finally, it has to be asked why it is so difficult to achieve a reconciliation of cultures in this (or in any other) country. The kinds of story, the forms of translation, the species of literalism at which I have glanced, seem to me characteristic of a culture (using this

word in its broadest sense) which has not reached or which has lost
its political maturity. A culture is not an entity which can safely or
enduringly base itself upon the grounds of race or religion or territory. These are childish and dangerous concepts. They did have
force, no doubt, at one time; but it is so long ago that it has almost
passed out of mind. Unfortunately, since the nineteenth century,
these concepts gained a new force and currency; in modern conditions, their effects were explosive. A mature culture is based on a
political idea, not on racial essence, religious faith, or nostalgia for
an historic territory. What Ireland needs is such a political concept.
Neither that of the Republic nor that of the United Kingdom suf-
fices any longer, because each is, by now, sectarianized. The
Christian religions play themselves false if they assume their fate is
bound up with the preservation of either. In doing so, they are mistaking the message of the Book of Revelation and misconstruing a
political for a spiritual apocalypse. Religious literalism breeds political fanaticism and prevents the emergence of either a true conception of religion or the possibility of a true political idea. It would
help the present situation if the distinction (not necessarily the separation) between church and state were acknowledged by the churches. Once admitted, then the churches could again become part of
our culture, rather than the translators of culture into literal and
lethal politics.

Reconciliation as Remembrance
'It takes two to know one'

Joe Harris

Introduction

The humanist project, the western tradition of rationalism in its various forms, which we are all heirs to whether we like it or not, is a project of self-assertion. It is carried forward on a number of pre-suppositions which it has taken us several centuries to even begin to see clearly, and we are well into another in the work of reconsideration and reconstruction of its implications. The major presupposition is that as human beings we have one task and that is self-preservation; but the human being referred to is a self, a knowing subject who is assumed to be motivated by the necessity to dominate and master both internal desire and external 'nature'. A sense of subjectivity comes about paradoxically through the disciplined repression of the anarchic desire for happiness, accomplished not just as a private venture, but through cultural forms, in particular the institutions of 'knowledge'. The self which is created and promoted through this cultural complex is the human subject of *knowing*.[1] This culture of knowing rests on an approved division (in which theory and practice are at one) between the knowing subject and the world as object.

A second feature of the enlightenment project is the generation of theories of 'language'[2] which support and embody the first major epistemological assumption. It has been bolstered by the philosophy of consciousness, some of the breaches in which have been exposed yet again in crisis, this time that of consumer capitalism.

The Demise of the Humanist Project

The demise of the humanist project, we might now say, is not unexpected given the contradictions set up between self, society, and the thrust to maintain communicative structures which, in evolutionary terms, fuels change and, in Christian terms, is the work of redemption in creation. Although mediated by 'knowledge' of God and having a name, the self is erased through the very logic of the project.

> Through the presentation of a consistent narrative of personal experience, the subject seeks to establish individual identity and to secure personal property. Such self-presentation is inseparable from recollection, representation and repetition. The temporality of the subject, however, subverts the identity, propriety, presence and property of selfhood. This subversion effectively dispossesses the subject.[3]

It is not unexpected, given the Faustian core, and in the case of atheistic humanism it is a

> struggle for domination (which) embodies the interrelated principles of utility and consumption which lie at the heart of technological consciousness. The psychology of mastery and the economy of domination represent efforts to deny death. This labour proves to be both narcissistic and nihilistic. Such self-assertion is finally self-defeating.[4]

We shall return to this question of how recollection, representation and repetition are linked and how 'memory' is subverted.

The inner meaning of the humanist project, as it has been exposed in its social forms, has been challenged in their different ways by Marx and his followers, by Weber particularly in his identification of the process of rationalization, and by the Frankfurt tradition[5] which has explored the disillusionment of the age at the dominance of instrumental reason. The intellectual and practical challenge thrown down by these analyses have been picked up by a growing critical sociological tradition.[6]

A Postmodern Context?

Are we in a post-modern age?[7] The sense of the breakup of orthodoxies in one way is stronger than it has ever been.[8] There is a play of discourses, few of which can listen to each other. In his analysis of a particular example, Castoriadis describes a culture which is a symptom:

> a culture which aims at (and largely succeeds in) dividing every-

thing between the algorithmic and the ineffable, between pure 'machine' and pure 'desire', and which drives into exile or makes unthinkable the essential core of what we are and what matters to us.[9]

Some regenerate the possibility of subjectivity (however anonymous) in cybernetic dreams, while others despair and plan to retreat from urban and social decadence either to the isolation and seclusion of the survivalists' wilderness or to the communal security of mindless affirmations of rightness and righteousness against the worldly legions of the devil. There is still plenty of life left in the fundamental desire as can be seen from ever renewed versions of the 'problematic individual' (Lukacs). One of the things that should concern us is the failure to communicate between all those who sense the distress of our accumulated history, on one side those who are still committed to the enlightenment project and on the other those who are claiming to dissociate themselves from its premises[10] and trying to be critical without being self-righteous – exceedingly difficult it must be admitted when so many forms of intellectual discourse are captured by the intellectual and political commitments of the university.

It makes all the difference whether or not we feel the failure of the enlightenment project, the domination of instrumental reason that is structured into our culture as competitiveness and consumption. Perhaps all of us to one degree or another live with 'a reified consciousness, comfortably adjusted to its alienation',[11] and we all share in Hugo Ball's feeling that 'this humiliating age has not succeeded in winning our respect'.[12]

To regenerate subjectivity will involve a break with accepted tenets of what reason is, through a restructuring of what we mean by thought and feeling, and a struggle to recover the wisdom of the notion that 'man is not an essentially intellectual creature'.[13]

Reconciliation as Transgression

In this context I think that reconciliation will mean 'transgression', for reconciliation is not about the repression of difference, but about us jointly transgressing the constraints, the boundaries that have solidified into our precious 'differences'. However, we would not be holding on to our differences and our boundaries did we not 'think' that it was worth the trouble. Experience suggests, therefore, that however joyful this transgression will become in our maturity, it will at first restimulate old fears and old distresses. To accomplish this task we need to recover 'memory' from the reductionist versions which hold sway in cybernetics and linguistics, let alone everyday speech. It seems to me to be fundamentally mistaken to conceive of memory as the capacity to recall and recollect things and events. We never do that, first because there is nothing there of that order to recollect and because recollection is not the name of the game. That is the positivist account of 'memory' structuring the activity of 'recollection'. What we have lost is the experience of constructing narratives, as a *shared* practice in the 'present'. In its place we have substituted descriptions which dissociate 'us' from the 'event'. It will therefore not be easy 'restoring judicious memory to its rightful place in the conversation of culture'.[14]

Something essential to our self-understanding as human beings is connected to the notion of memory; it is the pivot of culture.[15] Equally impressive is the rigid and repetitive force exerted against creativity by memory as deep cultural patterns of experience and language which we seem unable to steer. This volume provides insights into this, in particular the distortions involved in (but not caused as such) by the class of relationships referred to as those of collective responsibility. The distortions are the expression in cultural forms of the battle between unacknowledged memories and public remembrances. The question then becomes whether we are to be stuck with memories (and more memories) or can we engage in cultural remembrance which does not simply reactivate old rivalries and open old wounds.

The subtitle of this chapter comes from Gregory Bateson.[16] It reinforces the claim that there can he no 'cheap' reconciliation, for it challenges the assumption that knowing myself starts from a knower and works outwards in increasing rings of intersubjectivity. The proposal is that coming to know, if it is not to be the fractured epistemology of rationalism just outlined, is based on a relation, a connection, not simply between the knower and the known but in the wider context of knowing between connected knowers.[17] One of the most exciting intellectual moves to have taken place over the last forty years has been the recognition that, however astonishing

the exploration of 'nature' by what was defined as experimental 'observation', when we look at living and cultural systems or move to
the microscopic level we are into the realm of what Prigogine and
others have called *autopoiesis*.[18] The characteristic of such analysis is
that it gives a central place to the fact that systems are self-observ-
ing.[19] Of course they always have been, and much in philosophy
and social theory for a long time has been saying just that. The
space that has cleared now is based on recognising the nature of systems limits (a good example is Godel's work on undecidability[20]
and its disastrous implications for mechanistic systems thinking) and
that we do not have to pretend to be able to step outside a system to
be able to observe and be critical. The validity of our 'observations'
does not depend on that assumption about knowing. It is simply
radically different from how traditional science knows about (indeed creates) its world. From this point of view, consciousness[21]
takes on a different meaning as it moves from a knowing based on
'objectivity' to knowing based on participation. The validity conditions change as they find a basis in the nature of communication,
but in order to make this move we have to be clear that communication is not reduced to cybernetic information processing. Central
to this approach is a reconsideration of what we mean by 'memory'.

In this context we are talking about reconciliation of people,
subjects as embodied experience, and not just historical revisionism.
Reconciliation as communication between subjects has to encom-
pass the substance and the import of objective accounts open to
rational inquiry. Hence I find that I can no longer be satisfied just
with the recovery and rewriting of 'Irish' history as if that would
take care of and reconstruct memory. What I want is something more
fundamental which is heralded in the language of reconciliation.

The Economy of Experience – Being Protestant in Ireland

How did I come to this position? I was brought up in the part of
Belfast known as Sandy Row, and its extension into what is now
called (but was not in my childhood) The Village. This set of connections gave me structured, but as I shall claim, contradictory accounts of the world. One of these is the basic unionist-and-
Protestant ideology that we (read: no 'I' without a 'We') live in a
set-up the fundamental rightness of which is implicit in all we

think. Anyone who would dare to question this could only be in process of losing their wits. This is fitted into the language we use everyday and into the attitudes we are encouraged to adopt. I say fitted into language because there is a niggling sense of incompleteness, a hiatus, like a little wound, just enough to be troubling without being disabling, between the flow of experience and the managed 'use' of language. It is reinforced in my case by being brought up also in the Gospel Hall,[22] in which the bible, from Genesis to Revelation, is presented every day as the 'text' (and in this business 'texts' are vital) whose imagery interprets all memory and will therefore provide all I need to make sense out of the world, now and to come.

Alongside this patterning of my life, there is what I want to call 'experience'. At some level, I was experiencing something quite different which was constantly cutting across the account and the ideology presented to me as the one I should hold on to if I wished to retain a sense of family connections and to know who 'I' was. Part of this sense of cross-cutting experience was fed by the very evidence called in to support the ideology of biblical unionism. The whole of the biblical canon is offered as an indivisible unity, not open to fancy interpretation and individual picking and choosing, since the interpretation that does away with the need for further interpretation has been done.[23] However, there are parts of this total story which, when read through the very 'Protestant' codes of language, which were thought to have created and to buttress the 'correct' reading, keep running up against the public account of how I should feel and what values I should place on people and ideas.

To a person who has language (and the structure of mediation somehow forgot this) there are bits of the hallowed text which constantly disturb the monolithic version of life supposedly based on the text and the approved reading. I live, therefore, in a world in which I am enabled by some of the very resources which created the orthodoxy to challenge it. It certainly made life confusing and uncertain, but nudged me to pursue the valued but also dangerous thing which big people hinted at in talk about thinking for yourself. At this distance, I can only think that they were warning of the sense of isolation and fear that went with anything as dangerous as thinking, and it took me a long time to realise that many of them had indeed been impelled into this fearsome activity but had got stranded and given up, at least temporarily, rather than risk being cut off, as they must have imagined, from their birthright. It will take just a little imagination to picture what it was like living in Belfast, at a time when there was nothing like the rigid housing segregation that there is now, where you live close to people who are supposed to be of a different ilk from you, to think differently about the world, to look different (though when you look for the evidence you can find none), people whom you meet and together with whom you get on with fundamental things like playing games – until some crisis arises, or someone uses a particular word that sets the whole thing awry. I took it for granted that this was what the real experience of life was somehow about for everyone. In retrospect, it feels appropriate to say that I was fed by that experience. I assume it places me, as it does everyone else who reflects on the contradictions and connections in their life, in a situation where there is a gap between the public accounts through which the culture is negotiated and my experience as a subject which invites me (almost irresistibly) to start rewriting the accounts. It never occurred to me that political theorists might define my life as a narrow one, locked in what they patronisingly call the usual banalities of every day life. The present volume is about resisting that despairing stance.

Time for Finding Language

When we lived perpetually on the edge of crucial definitions about the categories through which 'identity'[24] is structured, the question which kept coming up then was what was I going to do with this discomfort. A number of routes were offered to me, partly in the process of a 'liberal' education. The first was that I should find a different language with which to work. In this regard, I need to say a little here about language and then later to develop the issue of language and memory. I feel it overstates the issue to say that language is all we have to keep us critical and aware. Language is crucial but is not itself the context. For that, communication is needed, the material context in which to string together forms of language in terms of information, utterance and understanding.

The danger is that we think of language in terms of a self-contained system that is opposed to the world.

> Expression is possible because its extra-linguistic correlate belongs to the world; if the referents were not connected, there could be no connection among the signifiers of language …
> The organisation of language is always based upon the organisation of the world, for it necessarily rests upon what is invisible in the visible.[25]

This quotation is an elaboration of ideas of Merleau-Ponty,[26] who had a strong sense of the relation between world and word and of the nature of language. The following paraphrases him: 'But it is also language itself that is expressed in expression. The being of language and the being-thus of language are expressed in every word of that language.'[27] Language is not a container of set meanings but the generator and carrier across seemingly impossible boundaries. Merleau-Ponty spoke of language being about 'parts' but each part was paradoxically a

> total part … representative of the whole, not by a sign-signification relation, or by the immanence of the parts in one another and in the whole, but because each part is torn up from the whole, comes with its roots, encroaches upon the whole, transgresses the frontiers of the others.[28]

A relation of the word and the word of this order releases us from the tyranny of a language digitalised and subordinated to ideas or 'reality', but equally from the view of language as our evolutionary talisman without which we would be dumb brutes. Either of these is to de-mean language and may help to explain why sincerity of intent, when based on faulty assumptions about the limits of language, has not proved a safeguard against the disintegration of reconciliation work.

Trying out different language meant that I had avoided the question of 'language'. All my 'languages' left me short of the point where I could grapple with the experience of hiatus, the missing bits, the knowledge of an erasure, a rupture, but also of access, of invitation, even of plenitude and of the possibility of integration and restart. As I see it now, this was being intimated in every day language. The blocks are not inherent in the system of language, communication and relations. They are identifiable in a particular cultural network and in the systems of subjective meaning through which social structure is managed by me, the person. It is such a relief to discover that this management is not controlled, though it is influenced, by the concepts inscribed in the social and psychic structure through which we each make do at any given time.

Writing an Uncensored History

A second route to resolve the contradiction between experience and cultural meanings was to learn more about the history, recover the censored facts. Then I would find encouragement to reach a consensus of some sort with those who differed from me. (At this stage it is easy to see that difference is treated as a problem rather than a resource.) This is surely an important task, for one way to release the imagination is to make available more of the social historical text in which consciousness is rooted. This 'text' is created in the actions of local times and places but the connections across time surpass these original actions and structure new patterns that are beyond the intentions of the original actors.[29] The gaps and blanks one comes across can be startling – at least from the point of view of the observer whose consciousness communicates with different gaps. A student, whose family, religion and schooling in the cultural context of the north of Ireland would lead one to assume particular knowledge, had not at the age of twenty heard about Daniel O'Connell. Discussion on the problems of teaching Irish history led to the student going home and asking parents why they had told their selection of Irish history. The story becomes more confused at this point because it is not clear whether or not 'information', let's call it, was available in school or whether the message from 'home' was to steer clear of controversial issues, disengage from a contentious history, for the sake of a supposed freedom from bias and indoctrination.

Parents appear to say they do not want to do to children what was done to them, that is set them up able to see the world only one way, enclose them in a language which cuts them off from other narratives and interpretations. It was an understandable mistake for parents to make; it was based on assumptions which a serious practice of reconciliation would have to challenge. The erroneous assumption is that by using a particular language we risk being trapped in the concepts, ideas and thought patterns which are used as the knowledge commodities of a rationalistic culture. This mistake derives from treating language as a conscious system, parts of which can be avoided as if contaminated, rather than the less instrumental version I have sketched above, in which human beings continue to create the world and the word – and therefore memory.

Total Parts

At some point, I came to the conclusion that it was not enough to work at retrieving the uncensored (rather than complete) history of our relations in the island of Ireland, however important an aspiration that is. Neither the search for a history nor a more sophisticated language could handle what was around – indeed they exacerbated the situation. For, travelling around Ireland, I find I am confronted by an experience of pain which I have come to interpret as being in touch with the experience of *the past* (that is what our language invites us to say), what is beyond my time, available in my time, an example of Merleau-Ponty's total part. The very act of looking on the land imaginatively and listening releases feeling which is this person, me, registering what is. It is not mystification in language or the fantasies of an observer projected unto an objectified world. When I became aware that I was being confronted by this kind of evidence that needed some kind of translation, I knew where to turn. It was to the messages that I recalled hearing long ago but did not know what to do with. I made the connection a couple of years back on the Twelfth of July at the 'field' in Garvagh, Co Derry, when I held on to my painful connection with all the people around me, and accepted that the same disturbance had happened when, as a child,[30] I used to go to the Orange parades and to the old field at Finaghy and could not understand my bond and my disconnection, or (as I thought) struggle to disconnect. What I had resisted all those years was a recognition of the intertwining of all the history of this land, the interlacing times of history[31] and the contradictions and confusions that must follow when we attempt to screen out these connections for the sake of a manipulable history. What I had to accept was that, in a creative sense, the history held me and that I needed to get out of the rivalry with its capacity to transcend me, and find out where there were resources to help. The crucial step was to see that we cannot recover memories as if there were such things. We can do something qualitatively different.

A Remembrance Version of Memory

The resource explored in this volume is a systemic version of memory, bringing remembrance back into the story as something more than the mere recall of information from the computing device in the head. Habermas talks, in the particular context of our understanding of 'science', of the need to 'deliberately marshall the analytical power of remembrance against those forces of repression in which scientism finds its roots',[32] as part of a more extended programme of retrieving effaced aspects of how we let ourselves know and the difficulty of admitting a central place to self-reflexion (sic).

It would not be surprising if many find this kind of talk confusing, given the kind of world we are faced with – one dominated by narrow rationalistic assumptions about thought and feeling. Some of us would write this kind of experience out of the story as a grand pathetic fallacy, a projection of 'personal' experience into an impersonal world. It would be a pity if we did this because it will obstruct the work of reconciliation by restricting the range of what has to happen. It would be possible for the work of reconciliation of memories to be displaced through glib formulae, or set apart from subjective experience in an alienated way, because we must keep our rational feet on the ground. I too aim for that but what I mean by rational is different, and I have tried to indicate something of what that is. It comes as a bit of a shock to have to give up the implied (but never very substantial) control of the thinking person in the way that it has been promoted through the liberal values that inform our education systems, in which we 'think' a lot about literature and art and display conceptual dexterity, but feel little. Witkin reflects a widely shared point of view when he says:

> The repression of subjectivity in our own age … has made of subjectivity a topic of special attention and study. This is all the more so because in the severe objectification of our existence the repression has taken a peculiar form. We have not denied the claims of feeling. On the contrary, we have solemnly endorsed

these claims. Our problem is that we have forgotten what they are. The task of remembering must begin again in earnest ...[33]

The resources are of course there for it, but the struggle, which is about re-evaluating the presuppositions of the enlightenment through which the culture is meditated, is resisted with both reason and innuendo. The visual arts, music, literature can leave us superficially ruffled, but there will be no new dream material, no stirring of the imagination, no experience of seeing, no excitement through the interrogation of appearances.[34]

Can we deliberately go about promoting the work of remembrance? I look back at myself and say that it was premised on holding on to the uneasiness and indeed queasiness of everyday life. It is helped along by actively filling in gaps, enlarging the horizon of vision by listening to the voices of the world – many of which we have to read off as confused and disillusioned, as part of a pact to narcotise us, and as deep cultural distresses projected into the structure of our every day lives. But other voices we should talk with, harmonize with, though there is no code book to tell us which. Reconciliation is intimate with these issues, both listening in general and the particular voices in our bodies which are the available evidence of our cultural condition. Once we assume that reconciliation is about world and word, and that this is possible only if we reject the rigid separation of analogic and digital modes of communication,[35] as we will always be struggling with amorphous, shapeless sentiments (not phantasies in the sense that the notion is used in psychoanalysis). This is what all our attempts at naming are about – the task of shifting the line between the conscious and the unconscious, which is imperative if we are to redeem the claim to subjectivity inscribed in our being separate in a social world. This range of feeling we cannot name too soon. Reconciliation appears to involve a commitment to *finding* language to talk to one another about experience and not look for shortcuts to knowing and naming.

The Data of Remembrance

A starting point would be the acknowledgement (in whatever form it would take), in face to face meetings where the trace of our history can only be avoided, that the history of this (these) island(s) is written in the bodies of all the human beings (other life forms I cannot consider here) who happen to be, or have been, living on the island(s). As for the time scales involved, I can only make a guess. It took me a long time to discover that I didn't live with just the particular selection of history that had been handed on to me as if it were from the outside. I came to realize that the history was revealed in its very delivery as partial, and that the strain of living was generated in the making of the narrative, because the assumptions about history did not acknowledge the complexity of experience, principally because the conception of language kept suppressing the analog dimension of experience. Koselleck seems to me to be on the right tack but is stuck with a distinction between linguistic and extralinguistic dimensions of experience.

> In the absence of linguistic activity, historical events are not possible; the experience gained from these events cannot be passed on without language. However, neither events nor experience are exhausted by their linguistic articulation. There are numerous extralinguistic factors that enter into every event, and there are levels of experience which escape linguistic ascertainment. The majority of extralinguistic conditions for all occurrences (natural and material givens, institutions, and modes of conduct) remain dependent upon linguistic communication for their effectiveness. They are not, however, assimilated by it. The prelinguistic structure of action and the linguistic communication by means of which events take place run into each other without ever coinciding.[36]

We can go further and acknowledge that the recollection of being comes with the body.[37] Dallmayr suggests that we need a notion of community that recognises the prior intersubjectivity of social life, and so far exceeds respect based on concepts of pluralism. This rests on a concept of the self and the individual based on an ontological 'intimate intertwining' of man and nature, self and other. We are all in that case living in a state of knowing about the deep nature of the world but have 'forgotten' our knowing. We therefore have to become involved in recollection, but not rationalist recollection; instead it is

> a probing of opacity or as an effort to decipher the signals of a precognitive or prereflective practice – a practice which is not

synonymous with individual or collective designs which seem
less akin to reason than to imagination (or to the poetic wisdom
discussed by Vico).[38]

This landscape is available *in the flesh* quite unlike the landscape of
memory in Dali's imagery (*The Persistence of Memory* of 1931) which
is untouchable, or kept at a distance by the eyes. We need a remembrance memory which can handle the notion of language as of the
world, not as another part of the world. Memory then is a
metaphor of the physical location (and language is physical and
analogic first) in which experience is 'written', and I do not have
any choice about what comes to me on the network. The notion of
'choice' may be retained in two senses: first about the limits of what
a person can decode of the whole (the prelinguistic and the linguistic – the world and the word) through the language available; and
second in the sense that whatever language is available, it always in-
jects the possibility of negation (different from refusal), and so I
may start to choose, without any suggestion of right or wrong,
what and how to read. This is where the view of language as carrying experiences as if in a container is exposed. The relation I have
suggested is if anything the reverse. Language is a part of the world,
and does not refer in an arbitrary fashion. However we are reluctant
to follow the specificity of its referrals because we want to know
them ahead of time. This desire to outwit language loosens the
hold that language gives us on the world as an *historical* world. It is
important to stress that this specificity is not the total knowing that
a rationalist version of understanding in language offers. Instead it
opens up an unending chain of specificities whose availability
depends on not formulating the meaning in advance.

> It is precisely because language is something other than a semiotic
> system, because the referral in language is virtually total, that it
> needs no more than a single point of contact with the world in
> order to be enmeshed in the generalised and non-chaotic trans-
> gression which brings it into being, and thus to be able to speak
> the world ... each language is a total cross-section of the
> world.[39]

I am therefore rejecting a notion of memory, language and understanding which gives priority to picking and choosing. It makes

sense to me to retain picking and choosing as the social structure in space and time closing off parts of the analog continuous and time-less world, making a selection appropriate to one dimension of time and space but not empowered to limit my horizon and turn boundaries, which are necessary to apprehending the amorphous, into barriers. The metaphor of the missing or erased tapes is helpful but should not be pressed too far, since it suggests the mistaken notion of the brain as a super computing device interfaced (!) with other forms of information appropriately translated. Even the most elaborate version of the computing device imaginable suffers from the limitation of an inbuilt gap between its digitalized functions and the capacity to read and give meaning. Bodily creatures like us do not suffer from that limitation, though our truncated account of language and knowing all but paint us into that corner.

The crucial thing to follow from this is that the accessibility of the analog continuum of world and word is not confined to people who live in a particular location in space and time. The tie-up is not of that order. While this is not an entirely novel notion, the predisposition of analytical thought constantly gets things back to front and screens out the richness of people's experience of space and time in cultural networks.

> In reality, every mutable thing has within itself the measure of its time; this persists even in the absence of any other; no two worldly things have the same measure of time ... There are therefore ... at any one time in the Universe innumerably many times.[40]

This suggests that access to the richness of history is not confined to those who have been located for a long time in one place and might claim in ways to have exclusive ownership of a tradition. I suspect that anyone who comes to live in a place can get access to the local *and* the extended history if they so wish, in spite of the suspicion expressed of those who would cease to be 'strangers'. Where I now live this suspicion is expressed in the word 'runners' to describe newcomers of up to twenty or more years residence. The crucial bit may be the willingness of a newcomer to penetrate and share a culture by testing the local boundaries and their deter-mination to keep out all but those born there. I can think of an English friend whose view of language and relations made it possi-

ble for him to listen and participate to the point of challenging
local exclusiveness.[41] Over fifteen years of living in Ireland, it was as if
the weave between language and the world took on another pattern
without losing the old – indeed he saw the old one as never before.
The competence at patterning and inquiry originally sustained by
his English locale was regenerated through engagement with the
local cultural material. I do not of course imply that he became
'Irish', or 'went native' as the saying used to have it. I am suggesting
something much more difficult, a willingness to let his language
and his experience of historical time be constantly recreated
through local social (and political) actions rather than be shaped
from what was affirmatively past and expressively present, his
English life. I would claim that he was involved with me in a new
venture in which 'memory' recedes in face of remembrances,[42] historical reconstruction of who we are, not who we think (even with
the support of sound scholarship) we were. In some basic sense,
those born (especially those born) in a place and time are shaped in
the flow and form of life but my suggestion is that this history, as
much as they can take, is available to all in a direct experiential
sense. It is resisting this that gives us headaches, as we refuse to see
and hear what we are seeing and hearing in our contacts with living
people every day.

The situation now, for me as a 'Protestant', is that I have *to go
through with* the experience of pain, not as regret but as grief, and
take responsibility for the bits for which I *might* take responsibility.[43]

Creation - The Context of Reconciliation as Remembrance

Finding this new language is something to be done with other
people. Reconciliation is a fundamentally social and communal
form of action. We must find at least one other person with whom
to create the comforting *(con-fortis)* physical context, for the real
work of remembrance is disconcerting, establishing boundaries and
connections while also simultaneously setting things adrift, de-
manding a new totality, a new order of context in which the new-
found and long-sought subject is in turmoil. This we locate in a
compelling and embracing narrative of history. In this we are not
concerned 'to secure presence and establish identity by overcoming
absence and repressing difference'.[44] This brings both peace and

disruption, unity and difference, as we cease treating each other as stereotypes and look for differences as the basis of communality. The change of emphasis towards difference and time means that we know the futility of the nationalist and racist myth of rediscovering the past in the present. Instead we are nurtured in the work of reconciliation through 'the possibility ... of seeing the present from the point of view of the past, from a moment when this present ... was entirely contingent ... not the reiterative unreality of reverie, which emptily rewrites history'.[45] The creative work is taking on ourselves again as the partial origin of our own history and becoming again the origin of possibilities, 'as having had a history which was history and not fatality'.[46]

Our recalling is to be done together, and I know of no re-calling that can be without grieving. From this will come much needed new images of reconciliation. In the Judaeo-Christian context, reconciliation as remembrance is the creation work of God in time, our time, the analog of then and now, bonded in my and your words, the cosmic time of creation.

Notes

1. This issue is central to social and philosophical debate and is renewed constantly. I have found the following delightful to return to: Majorie Grene, *The Knower and The Known* (London: Faber, 1966). The most prolific writer and the focus of much contemporary debate is Jürgen Habermas. A useful review is his *The Theory of Communicative Action*, vol. 1 (Boston: Beacon Press, 1984). On Habermas see Thomas McCarthy, *The Critical Theory of Jürgen Habermas* (London: Hutchinson, 1978).

2. Roy Harris, *The Language Makers* (London: Duckworth, 1980); idem, *The Language Myth* (London: Duckworth,1981); Anthony Wilden, *System and Structure*, 2nd ed. (London: Tavistock, 1980); Gordon P. Baker and P. M. S. Hacker, *Language, Sense and Nonsense* (Oxford: Blackwell, 1984).

3. Mark C. Taylor, *Erring: A Postmodern A/theology* (Chicago and London: University of Chicago Press, 1984), 14.

4. Ibid.

5. Aspects of the influence of the Frankfurt Tradition are discussed elsewhere in this volume.

6. Anthony Giddens, *The Constitution of Society* (Cambridge: Polity, 1984) is a useful starting point.

7. Robert Hughes, *The Shock of the New* (London: BBC, 1980) provides a constantly provocative and elegant commentary on this whole question.
8. A salutary reminder of others' 'revolutionary' times is provided by Marguerite Yourcenar, *The Abyss* (London: Black Swan, 1985).
9. Cornelius Castoriadis, *Crossroads in the Labyrinth* (Brighton: Harvester, 1984), 72.
10. The persistent struggle to grapple with the question of postmodernism is well exemplified in journals like *Telos, Praxis International, New German Critique, Theory & Society,* as well as a host of journals in the field of literary criticism, such as *Critical Inquiry.*
11. The phrase is Richard Wolin's.
12. Hugo Ball, of the Zurich Dada connection, quoted in Hughes, *The Shock of the New,* 63.
13. William T Bouwsma, 'Intellectual History in the 1980s: From History of Ideas to History of Meaning', *Journal of Interdisciplinary History,* vol. 12, no. 2 (1981), 279-91.
14. Fred Inglis, *The Management of Ignorance* (Oxford: Blackwell, 1985).
15. I find the work of René Girard important in this respect, as in many others. See his *Deceit, Desire and the Novel* (1976) and *Violence and the Sacred* (1977), both Baltimore, Johns Hopkins.
16. Bateson's work has been influential in many fields. See, for example, *Steps to an Ecology of Mind* (London: Paladin, 1973) and *Mind and Nature* (London: Wildwood, 1979). In this connection we should note Humberto Maturana and Heinz von Foerster.
17. See references in Note 1. Two other names should be added. Wittgenstein is in every part of the story now, and Gadamer is carrying on the work of a renewed hermeneutic tradition.
18 *Autopoiesis* – a Greek word: self-making, self-creating, self-organizing. See Ilya Prigogine, *From Being to Becoming* (1980), and Freeman, with I. Stengens, *Order out of Chaos* (New York: Bantam, 1984); Erich Jantsch, *The Self-Organising Universe* (Oxford: Pergamon, 1979). Influential but with a somewhat different set of assumptions is Niklas Luhmann, *Trust and Power* (Wiley, 1979). In a general sense the impact of the new physics is taking a long time to digest: see David Bohm, *Wholeness and The Implicate Order* (London: Routledge and Kegan Paul, 1980). The following quote is not untypical. As for its argument that is another matter. 'The existence, the life, and the warp and weft of interrelationships subsist in the Spirit: 'In *him* we live and move and have our being' (Acts 17:20). But that means that the interrelations of the world cannot be traced back to any components, or universal foundations (or whatever name we give to 'elementary particles'). According to the mechanistic theory, things are primary, and their relations to one another are determined secondarily, through 'natural laws'. But in reality relationships are just as primal as the things themselves. 'Thing' and 'relation' are complementary modes of appearance, in the same way as particle and wave in the nuclear sector. For nothing in the world exists, lives and moves *of itself*... So it is only the community of creation in the Spirit itself that can be called 'fundamental' ... The patterns and the symmetries, the movements and the rhythms, the fields and

the material conglomerations of cosmic energy, all come into being out of the community, in the community, of the divine Spirit.' P 11. Cf Jürgen Moltmann, *God in Creation* (London: SCM Press, 1985).

19. Ranulph Glanville is an excellent source on this. See for example, 'What Is Memory, That It Can Remember What Is It?' in R. Trappl, *et al*, eds, *Recent Progress in Cybernetics and Systems Research* (Washington, DC: Hemisphere Press, 1976).

20. One of the clearest expositions of the essence of Godel's work is to be found in Jean Piaget, *Structuralism* (London: Routledge and Kegan Paul, 1971). Castoriadis is also very clear and offers interesting connections.

21. Seyla Benhabib, *Critique, Norm and Utopia* (New York: Columbia, 1985).

22. The phrase 'Gospel Hall' refers generally to those groups within Protestantism who see themselves as holding on to fundamentalist principles. Specifically it refers to the connection of Assemblies in Britain and Ireland known as The Brethren, sometimes Plymouth Brethren (but not the Exclusives).

23. James Barr, *Escaping from Fundamentalism* (London: SCM, 1984).

24. Identity is a notion much bandied about in conversation in Ireland. I would like us to drop it at least for a while, since it has been captured in my view by a positivist outlook.

25. Castoriadis, *Crossroads*, 124-6.

26. Maurice Merleau-Ponty is usually associated with Phenomenology. Let that not put anyone off from approaching him. His best known work is *Phenomenology of Perception* (London: Routledge and Kegan Paul, 1984).

27. Castoriadis, *Crossroads*, 127.

28. *The Visible and The Invisible* (Evanston: Northwestern, 1968), 218.

29. Giddens, *The Constitution of Society*.

30. Nathalie Sarraute, *Childhood* (London: Calder, 1984) is suggestive of what might be done.

31. Moltmann, *God in Creation*.

32. Jürgen Habermas, *Knowledge and Human Interests* (London: Heinemann, 1972), 353.

33. Robert W. Witkin, *The Intelligence of Feeling* (London: Heinemann Educational Books, 1974), 1-2.

34. John Berger, *Ways of Seeing* (London: Penguin, 1972).

35. Anthony Wilden is a major source on this. This astonishing book is in a sense all about the distinction between, and the need to recover the connection between, analogic and digital modes of communication.

36. Reinhart Koselleck, *Futures Past: On the Semantics of Historical Time* (Boston: M.I.T. Press, 1985), 231.

37. See David Michael Levin, *The Body's Recollection of Being* (London: Routledge and Kegan Paul, 1985).

38. Fred R. Dallmayr, *Twilight of Subjectivity* (Amherst: University of Massachusetts, 1981), 251.

39. Castoriadis, *Crossroads*, 129.

40. Herder, quoted in Koselleck, *Futures Past*, xii.

41. Irish literature is replete with material on this, as one would expect given our 'colonial' history. See the works of Sommerville and Ross, and Molly Keane;

see also Anthony Wilden, *The Rules are no Game* (London: Routledge and Kegan Paul, 1986). The debate on ethnicity in the USA and Britain engages this question.

42. Walter Benjamin.

43. It is clear to me on reflection that I have to take responsibility for the 'total' parts. I had asked not to have to take on Cromwell, but a friend picked this up at once, and I am currently trying to understand what this is all about.

44. Taylor, *Erring*.

45. Castoriadis, *Crossroads*, 26.

46. Ibid.

Reconciliation: An Ecumenical Paradigm

Maurice Bond

Introduction

The central fear in much of our modern ecumenical and perhaps political debates is that of a loss of *identity* and this is as keenly felt here in Ireland as anywhere. It is not, for the most part, a fear of leaving the truth behind, because most of us realise that the truth moves out beyond our traditions, but one of being lost – the failure to preserve – something particular and important in our self-understanding. Our traditions are important to us, therefore, not simply because we believe them to be vehicles of truth but because they are our traditions – because they are vehicles of meaning. Truth claims are important – vital in terms of Christian belief – but in praxis they are often directed by our need to preserve that identity.

If our conception of identity and its preservation is static and reactionary then in a pluralist context it will also be conflictual.

The task in this paper will be to examine the nature of identity and its preservation by way of a more dynamic paradigm which, if given any credence, would demand *conversation* between traditions as a way of preserving those traditions themselves. I will attempt to examine these concepts by way of some recent developments in phenomenology and hermeneutical studies. The fundamental categories being *belonging, distance, conversation* and *fusion of horizons*. How these terms are being used can only fully emerge in the course of this paper.

I

The Ontological Reality of Pluralism

Martin Heidegger's work is central to this whole area. Heidegger's thesis is that ontology precedes and bases reflective understanding. Much of modern science proceeds on the assumption of a subject-object split in reality. Within such thinking the knowing subject examines objectivity or 'otherness' as that which exists over against subjectivity while for Heidegger thinking arises out of a context in which both subject and object are already bound together in being.

What is involved here can be seen clearly against the background of the philosophy of Descartes. Descartes begins with his famous *Cogito-ergo-sum* (I think therefore I am) which proceeds via the doubting of everything outside of the ego itself towards certainty which is based on the first principle of *Res cogitans* and moves forward by *Res existens*. This naked existing ego from which he begins is not first of all placed in being but rather can be shown to exist because it perceives itself as existing. In this way Descartes exemplifies the subject/object dichotomy of much of modern thought. The subject begins by distancing himself from that which he seeks to know. The first characteristic of his environment is its otherness in the form of dichotomy.

In contrast Heidegger seeks to explicate the reality of *Da-sein* (there-being). Our first and primary consciousness of ourselves is not of subject over against object but of inhabiting a world, a world which contains our traditions and those of others. In this way understanding is seen as being 'worldly' in that it arises from our recognition of being placed in the world. This givenness of the world we inhabit as a predetermined starting point is characterized by Heidegger as our facticity *(faktizitat)*. The world we inhabit is part of our self consciousness. The naked existing ego does not in fact exist at all but is rather an abstraction from existential reality. All understanding proceeds from and is directed by being itself – that within which we are what we are, i.e. our traditions. The explication of something as this or that is founded upon our forehaving, foresight and foreconception *(vor-habe, vor-sicht vor-griffe)*. All knowledge is anticipated by this basic pre-understanding of being placed.

Not only do we *reason* from our place (from within our tradition) but we reason back to it. This is the hermeneutical circle which, rightly understood, relates me back to my place in being with new possibilities, expanding that world itself. That world is not, therefore, expanded or challenged by an attempt to reason out of my place into that of another but is only meaningful in the existential sense if it returns and enlightens my world. It will never be academic in the sense of seeing itself as cut loose from significance for *Da-sein*. Understanding is always application in this sense. This will be of vital importance when we come to examine what it means to understand 'another' tradition.

It is Hans-Georg Gadamer who extends these observations and brings out their fuller implications as they apply to tradition and its authority. According to Gadamer, the overapplication of the modern scientific consciousness is in danger of alienating humankind from the fundamental recognition of 'belonging'. This is true in the fields of art, history and literature. Both art and language are historical realities, and humankind cannot meaningfully relate to history as an object over against humankind but only as that to which humankind belongs. Before we take hold of history, history takes hold of us. There is no objective knowledge of history but only that kind of knowledge which arises from and returns to the situation in which subject and object are already bound together in their being. Language is historical and our place within the context of our language is itself a central characteristic of our historicity. It also, therefore, lays hold of us before we lay hold of it as the medium of our understanding. Understanding can be described in this way as linguistic.

These observations prompt Gadamer to a reappraisal of what he calls *the enlightenment's prejudice against prejudice*.[1] which typifies the modern methodological division between bare subjective reason and 'objective being'. In so doing it attempts to reason from a non-place. Prejudice understood as pre-understanding or understanding funded *by our tradition* is a reality which cannot be suspended or denied because it is part of the forestructure of the process of understanding (as our place of reasoning). The enlightenment's attack on prejudice is aimed at what it considers to be the negative force of tradition: binding reason to dead and deadening convention and preventing it from meaningful progression. While Gadamer would agree that in a real sense we are bound up with tradition and that it has indeed such an effect when simply repeated, he would, as we shall see, reject the notion that the latter need be the case and would insist that interpretation as opposed to mere repetition is the one way in which we may have a real sense of belonging in our historically constituted world.

But how does tradition constitute itself as the place of reasoning – the context of understanding? Here he points to what he calls 'effective historical consciousness', the consciousness of being exposed to history as historical beings. This history to which we are exposed and in which we live is constituted by event, meaning and effect. Tradition includes all of this, and in our inhabiting tradition we ourselves are part of its history as it is part of us.

Gadamer sees his task as the rehabilitation of tradition as such, and it is not his primary task to examine how traditions might relate to each other within the context he describes. Nevertheless, it is not tradition with which we are bound up but traditions, not defective reason but reasonings, not only culture but cultures, not only language but languages. Not only do we inhabit the world but worlds. Within Christianity itself – and this is the nub of the matter for us – we are constituted in our being by and grounded in different traditions from which reasoning proceeds and to which it returns.

The importance of all this is not that it brings about a recognition that no interpretation of anything is without presuppositions. This is fact long since taken for granted in hermeneutical studies at least, if not yet in scientific research which often imagines itself to be in the world of objective knowledge or autonymous reason. Rather, the real importance of the works of both Heidegger and Gadamer lies in their explication of the nature of these presuppositions as predispositions which are grounded not just in epistemology but in ontology (not just what we know but what we are). They are not just a starting point from which we proceed to understand and evaluate, but what we are and that to which understanding brings us back with expanded possibilities for selfhood – 'our ownmost possibilities'.[2]

Thinking which is aware of its own historicity is thinking which is aware of its finitude and context. The related concepts of prejudice and effective historical consciousness belong to an ontology of finitude and contextualization. In that our way of knowing is bound up with our particular tradition and the prejuduce which being in that tradition entails, we cannot place ourselves in an ahistorical position which would give us an all seeing overview or an infinite perspective. Such a perspective would demand the finding of a nonexistent vantage point in being.

The question now arises, how is ecumenics to proceed – what can unity or identity mean amidst this pluralism? Do our prejudices and the effective historical consciousness which places us within our tradition mean that our place is fixed or static? On this basis ecumenical conversation would indeed be impossible and any attempts to converse would be a repeating of immobile positions across unbridgeable divides. This is why, for example, Protestant fundamentalists and Catholic ultra conservatives find ecumenics on anything more than a cosmetic basis impossible. If, on the other hand, we are forced forward from this static position by the needs of real conversation with our own traditions, then the same forward movement should involve the ecumenical conversation as well. We learn to assimulate differences in the encounter with our own traditions.

Having considered the phenomenon of belonging we must go on to say that this belonging displays an internal complexity. The way in which we belong to our traditions is described by Gadamer as the polarity of familiarity and strangeness. Our tradition is made up of texts and symbols, many of which are distanced from us in time and space – we belong to them and they to us within the tension of the near and the far. Many of these texts are historically intended in the sense of addressing a particular situation in a particular time. Effective historical consciousness means that we have a connection with the tradition out of which and to which these texts spoke and speak. Yet they are different from us in that we are now in a different situation which has new questions and a plurality of answers in the contempory context. This pluralist world is also part of our situation in being along with all its traditions – religious and political. We are, therefore, faced with two possibilities – an unreal and a real one. The unreal situation is that we may attempt to live in the past world which lies behind the text (written or oral) and our present situation. In this case there is no real communication with our tradition, much less with another, in a way which might provide us with the redemptive possibility of being challenged, and of challenging the contemporary perspectives of our time by the retrieval of meaning from these texts or history. We are content rather to ignore contemporary questions – including the pluralist question – and concentrate instead on a vain attempt at temporal regression,

condemning our future to the past. The real possibility is for a progressive interpretation which expands and enriches our tradition by
bringing its relevance into our situation and time. Here real conversation and communication are active not only within our own traditions *(intra-communication)* but also with other traditions *(inter-
communication)*. The human encounter with the world is a never
finished process and progression of meaning, and human experience gives rise to ever new encounters with our traditions and those
of 'others'.

The task of hermeneutics is to address itself to this tension of
belonging and distance or, to put it another way, these two senses of
belonging. If we are to *preserve* our traditions we must do so by
interpreting them in a dynamic way, what David Tracy would call
'radical belonging', which is radical in two senses – towards tradition
and by the retrieval of meaning via tradition towards the present for
the future. It is in this light that the concept of horizon assumes a
central significance for Gadamer.

We are constantly being re-informed. The hermeneutical circle
thus proves to be an expanding rather than a vicious one, a return
to self with enlarged vision and being. No disloyalty to our traditions is involved; on the contrary only thus can we really maintain
them. Thus, just as ecumenics is impossible on the basis of static
traditionalism, so is loyalty to our own traditions.

But can we go further still by explicating how this loyalty to and
preservation of our own tradition can demonstrate the inherent
necessity of and provide a model for the ecumenical task?

II

The Ecumenical Significance of the Concept of Belonging
For Heidegger and Gadamer the concept of belonging to tradition
is central to recognizing our place within being. We have further
noted the obvious fact that this belonging is pluralist – we do not
all belong to the same tradition. The Christian tradition is represented in different traditions.

Now Christians of all ages have at all times insisted that the
church has an essential unity. Once we have accepted the historicity
of our own positions and the finitude which this entails, we have
accepted that no tradition can have an ahistorical or absolute claim

to truth. The task remains therefore as one of explicating the reality of Christian unity from a pluralist standpoint. I have suggested that this need brings us back to the problem of how we interpret tradition as such and our own tradition in particular. The ecumenical spur is our common recognition that, despite the distance between us, the universal belief in the unity of the church entails common belonging as the body of Christ. This belief comes to us from the heart of our own tradition – whatever that tradition may be – and it is this tradition which informs our prejudices of the ecumenical compulsion of Christian being as part of the facticity of being 'thrown' into a Christian tradition. This has immediate implications in that it means that all the texts and symbols of whatever tradition belong to all Christians. But it goes further than this, for we belong to these texts and symbols at a distance. This distance, as we shall see, is not only temporal but in the case of other traditions contemporary. It is a question now not just of intra-communion but inter-communion. This concept of contemporary distance will need further explanation. At this point we can say that it results from our being placed with different traditions, and its reality is both an historical and contemporary fact. Nevertheless, just as our unity with our own traditions precedes our explication of it by laying hold of us before we lay hold of it, so also our essential unity which enfolds these traditions is a fact before we recognize it. It is already a fact, even if it is not yet pursued or exercised. If different Christian traditions are part of that to which we belong and if we are not to return to the subject-object dichotomy, it follows that we cannot treat these different traditions as objects over against us. We are dealing with that which is part of us within the effective historical consciousness of Christian unity (or Irish history?). In considering our essential belonging at a distance with the texts of tradition, Gadamer uses the I-thou analogy not in respect to any person-to-person appeal but on the basis of being addressed by the meaningful content of the texts and symbols themselves. We are involved in that which we seek to interpret. This analogy functions in a similar way with regard to the ecumenical encounter with the text, myths and symbols of other traditions.

Within our horizons we have this consciousness of unity which involves a two-fold tension of belonging and distance. I have

looked at what this belonging means and can now examine more
closely the other side of tension – distance.

These horizons have the 'near and the far' – our contemporary
self-consciousness and our relationship of belonging to texts and
symbols which are distanced in time from us yet part of us as effective historical consciousness. The same horizons include a consciousness of unity with other traditions, but again it is a unity with
tensions. Not only is there the temporal tension because we are
distanced from these 'other' traditions in time, there is the contemporary distance arising out of our 'different' places or being placed
within different traditions which, while they include each other, do
so as identity-in-difference. The relationship has the character of
being a dialectic which consists in these tensions. The aim of ecumenics is the explication and realization of Christian unity within
this dialectic. But how is this to be done? Does it consist in the
neutralizing of these tensions so that they disappear? I have suggested
that this is not only impossible but undesirable, because neutralizing would make it impossible for us to appropriate the Christian
faith adequately in relation to the diverse questions of human context and facticity. The real possibility lies, as with the interpretation
of our own historical tradition, in what Gadamer calls the 'fusion of
horizons'. If we take, for example, the South American Roman
Catholic Church we find that how it experiences its needs may
share certain similarities with the Western Church but also has differences. It is in a sense a tradition (South American) within a tradition (Roman Catholic) within a tradition (Christian) and shows
how despite greater awareness of each other in our contemporary
world the pluralist reality is heightened rather than lessened; no attempt at demolishing the differences between these traditions will
succeed, because such an attempt would fail to take account of the
ontological realities and questions which arise from 'there-being' in
that world – in that tradition. Nor can we in the West simply lift
their tradition and set it into our context. Nevertheless the ecumenical encounter is an imperative of being the Christian Church
and demands appropriation of the possible implications of Latin
American theology by way of a 'fusion of horizons'. Being
Christian demands that we appropriate the implications of 'other'
Christian traditions in order to 'realize' our unity. Being Irish demands a similar appropriation.

The Ecumenical Significance of
the Concept of the Fusion of Horizons

Two senses of 'preservation' can be distinguished but not separated. There is the way in which I preserve my tradition by rendering it meaningful to and in the contemporary context, which includes other traditions. The second form of preservation is the way in which even in this identity there can be no capitulation of one horizon to the other. For example, in interpreting the Christ event as it is portrayed through the gospels I preserve my identity with the core of Christian tradition, but it must be a real interpretation and cannot be on the basis of attempting to repeat a first century mind or situation. My own position as a 20th-century person asking 20th-century questions must also be preserved. Interpretation is not repetition any more than identity means being identical. Gadamer's 'fusion of horizons' promises to explicate a more dialectical approach to identity which can fully take account of these two senses of preservation. *It is not the forsaking of one place in order to be something else but an expansion of selfhood by way of being identified with and challenged by the 'other'.* The same is true of the ecumenical and political encounter.

Interpretation and identity as a 'fusion of horizons' follow on from what we have said about prejudice. It is important to emphasize again that horizons cannot be rightly seen as a set of fixed and static opinions which render us unable to evaluate 'otherness' – horizons are rather the basis of a dynamic and expanding self understanding which goes out of itself in order to find itself. We are characterized not just by what we are but by possibility – what we might be. Being reaches out in front of us so that ontology is a quest as well as a present reality. In this way the unity of the church partakes in the nature of being as such – it is already and not yet. As individuals and as communities we must constantly become ourselves in order to be ourselves. Each new experience of understanding must assimilate newness as otherness to what we are so that selfhood maintains a continuity in every new encounter with being. If our traditions are to enrich our present, they will do so by the process of retrieval of meaning for that present by hermeneutical interpretation of their otherness. The retrieval of projected possibilities out of the past calls us forward into the future without collapsing the present into the past in a way that would make the past our future.

The continuing tension of distance is not underplayed in interpretation as Gadamer is, in the end, inclined to do. For him it
would appear that to speak of horizons rather than horizon arises in
the context of an ontological fallenness and is necessary only as that
which is on its way to one horizon. Thus while he accepts the tension within the hermeneutical situation he does not allow it a continued existence within the fusion of horizons, which it must have
if it is to be truly dialectical as identity-in-difference. He is led at
times, due to his negative view of distance, to assert the formation
of one horizon. What is required is a more positive evaluation of
distance and difference which recognizes that, despite the fusion,
one horizon cannot be reduced to the other – the tensions cannot
be moved. One need not accept Nietzsche's radical non-commu-
nicative pluralism nor Gadamer's occasional tendency to accept the
non-hermeneutical position of a single horizon containing all
points of view – which runs against the main thrust of his thinking
– in order to realize that the fusion of horizons implies a tension between what is one's own and what is alien, between the near and the
far; and hence the play of difference is included in the process of
convergence. The *identity* which emerges from and in the fusion of
horizons is an *identity-in-difference*. The unity is unity in diversity,
within and between traditions.

At this point we can learn much from Hegel, who, despite this
concept of absolute knowledge or a single horizon, presents us with
a dialectical thinking that has a lot to teach us along the way. The
concept of 'negation' which plays such an important part in his dialectic is based on the proposition that any particular opens towards
the universal by calling forth the other as part of its definition. We
have already said that this is the case within any particular tradition
of the church in that it requires the concept of catholicity if it is to
be a credible Christian tradition – for Hegel identity is recognized
as it is and as it could be. An immobile self-contained selfhood or
static tradition is the height of subjective illusion. In his
Phenomonology of Spirit he gives a penetrating critique of 'sense
certainty' which is analogous to the enclosed selfhood which we
have rejected as a possibility. This sense certainty believes that it can
have a perception of the thing in itself – the particular shorn of its
essential relationships which are constitutive of the thing as it is.

Pure perception of anything breaks down because it fails to recognise that even the internal relationship of a thing to itself is a negative-in-positive relationship. G. R. G. Mure puts it in this way:

> If we recognise a finite thing so changing that it remains recognisably self same after change ... We will admit that it is ... a positive in negative, a concrete unity determined – that is negated – in and through the diverse phases of its temporal process.

Otherness within our own tradition

This is exactly what we have been saying about the hermeneutical relationship we have in preserving *our particular traditions*.

> On the other hand, otherness between the elements of one finite thing is their mutual determining of finite things ... The unique individuality of this thing breaks down as soon as we see that finite things, by virtue of the host of common characteristics which they share, and through the network of relations in which they stand, do deeply determine each other's nature.[4]

This is what we have been saying is the case between traditions, including Irish traditions or ways of 'being' Irish.

As Hegel sees it, this 'pure self perception' mode of reasoning cannot exist for long and passes to the other extreme in which it loses its conception of otherness. The tension between one finite thing or person and another is broken down by making otherness disappear into selfhood – his famous master-slave relationship is a good example. This also fails, because just as identity cannot be maintained on the basis of this one thing in the midst of pure and undialectical otherness, neither can it be maintained on the basis of a collapse of otherness into selfhood. Identity does not mean being identical. Selfhood which does not see itself as the whole demands *recognition by and of otherness.* Self-consciousness is a reflective reality which establishes identity in encounter with and appropriation of what is 'other' or different.

In Hegel's works all of this moves on toward absolute knowledge which is a denial of the finite. Nevertheless, it is, as we have said, the dialectical process itself and not Hegel's intentions which is important for us. What his dialectical description provides us with is the possibility of explicating the truth of wholeness and not the whole or absolute truth. His mistake was to confuse the two.

What he has shown is that in the realm of historicity the dialectic moves by way of negation and affirmation. A would appear to be in opposition to B but this absolute dichotomy breaks down and a fusion or synthesis appears. This synthesis is itself not without tensions – it is an identity-in-difference – and it in turn proves to be inadequate in the new situation, and so on. Any sense of identity we have will prove inadequate to a new situation. Having rejected Hegel's absolute synthesis, we can say that within an ontology of finitude any fusion is superior only in the sense of relative adequacy to the situation in which it comes about. There is no absolute superiority either behind us or in front of us. Any fusion will inevitably break down because of its internal tensions and relative inadequacy to new and different historical situations. Otherness may assume a new form and so may identity, but both will always be unsurpassable reality. Paul Tillich sums up the implications of this for our study very well.

> The ecumenical movement ... is able to heal divisions which have become historically obsolete, to replace confessional fanaticism by interconfessional cooperation ... but neither the ecumenical movement nor any future movement can conquer the ambiguity of unity and division in the Church's historical existence. Even if it were able to produce the United Churches of the World, and even if all latent churches were converted to this unity, new divisions would appear. The dynamics of life, the tendency to preserve the holy ... the ambiguities in the sociological existence of the churches, and above all, the prophetic criticism and demand for reformation would bring about new and, in many cases, spiritually justified divisions.[5]

Any glossing over this by attempts to bring about one visible organism as the church is an abstraction from the real ecumenical task of finding identity-in-difference. Identity-in-difference is the only kind available, within and between traditions.

III

Fusion and Critique
Gadamer's conception of tradition is in the end monolithic because it does not account for the encounter of traditions and the critique that a genuine encounter between them involves. If he were to take

such into consideration he would be forced to consider the possibility of certain facets of tradition being challenged and that challenge being sustained. Only within a positive evaluation of distance is this possible or probable – 'to see ourselves as others see us' implies distanciation as a productive force. This is why ecumenics and inter-tradition dialogue are so vital, so that we can view and be viewed within the perspective of belonging distance. We will never attain a true self consciousness or be challenged by fudged issues or blurred distinctions or as Vatican II puts it, 'Nothing is so foreign to the Spirit of ecumenics as a false conciliatory approach.'[6] Neither will a false conciliatory approach help with our Irish problems.

But must we go further still? It may well be that a retrieval of and fusion of horizons between the central instances of our traditions will expose our misunderstandings or even our individual traditional distortions, but what about those we may share? If ecumenics is not to be invoked at least in part in a fusion of illusions, a paralleling of distortions or an alignment of harmful interests, conversation must include a common critique. Consensus, even if it were possible, is no guarantee of truth. Here we are involved in the kind of debate which exists between Gadamer and Habermas.[7] If Gadamer is concerned with the renewal and interpretation of tradition and culture, Habermas is concerned to unmask their illusions and distortions by the 'pull of the future'. Gadamer will not allow, his rejection of distance cannot allow, the elevation of a critical moment to seriously challenge the authority of tradition. Habermas suggests that it is precisely this authority which must be challenged if we are to be freed – for his real interest is liberation – from its distortions of communication. For Gadamer hermeneutics is about understanding and unmasking misunderstanding; for Habermas this displays a traditional innocence and an innocent tradition which history does not bear out. For Gadamer it is the authority of the past which predominates, for Habermas it is the 'pull of the future'. Neither of these men are concerned with ecumenics or our Irish situation but they are concerned with hermeneutics. We have seen why Gadamer's conception of tradition, while it is in many ways fundamental, is in the end inadequate to the ecumenical reality and task. When we approach the problem of critique, this inadequacy is at its most obvious. Can Habermas help? We are concerned with

possible distortions in our traditions: we are, as an eschatological
faith, concerned with the pull of the future, and we recognize the
ambiguity of all our ecclesial existence and traditions. Without
therefore following Habermas in detail, it may be concluded that
what he suggests is missing in Gadamer's hermeneutics is, at least in
part, necessary in our ecumenics with regard to our own traditions
and Christianity in general. Were not Tetzel's actions a distortion of
the faith and of human dignity, was it not based on economic interest? Was not the Reformed Church of South Africa practising a distorted ecclesial life based on racism and racist interests? Is not the
entire Christian tradition guilty of a distortion of the Jewish question
– a distortion possibly going back even into the New Testament
itself? Are we capable of treating women as equals merely on the
basis of the authority of the Christian tradition? All our traditions
contain distortions. Does an answer to these questions mean that in
finding it we will have had to leave a conversation with our traditions behind and be guided instead by the future? The answer is
'yes' if by leaving behind we mean we must not repeat, but it is 'no'
if we mean by leaving behind that our traditions have no further
relevance. All of our Christian traditions present us with models of
liberation – Exodus, Resurrection, etc. – models of how to begin
again, models of discipline and the denial of self interest – models
of reconciliation. Critique is also a tradition and this is nowhere
truer than in the Christian faith. Where are we to find the resources
to envisage our future if not in encounter – in conversation – with
our past? While the past must not take the future prisoner, neither
can it breach all the bounds. It is a radical belonging which promises
freedom. Again, as Ricoeur so aptly suggests, 'perhaps there would
be no more interest in emancipation, no more anticipation of freedom, if the Exodus and the Resurrection were effaced from the
memory of mankind.'[8] Nevertheless we must address the future,
and sustained address demands that we also address the possible
distortions in our past. Emancipation cannot simply be based on
the past anymore than can consensus. One cannot speak with
Gadamer of a common accord which carries understanding without assuming a convergence of traditions which does not exist,
without hypostatizing a past which is also the place of false consciousness, without ontologizing a language which has always only

been a distorted 'communication competence'.[9] This is indeed an overstatement of the case and was not written regarding ecumenics – but it could have been.

Conclusion

To sum up, we have suggested that we must recognize identity as a dialectical rather than a static or conflictual reality and that its preservation demands a mutual learning process between 'our' and 'other' traditions. For the most part we have not directly addressed the political questions, but in that there is no absolute dichotomy between theological or political questions – particularly in Ireland – such questions and the direction of our thinking upon them is fairly obvious.

One of the problems, however, in any political analogies is that one section of the Irish people has an inadequately developed sense of 'belonging', i.e. the 'Protestant people of Ulster', and it is only if this belonging can be fostered and nurtured that any genuine fusion can take place.

Perhaps only the 'pull of the future' can make this possible, a pull in which all our traditions must be transformed into living, liberating praxes. Here again it is as we accept the distance between ourselves and the myths, symbols and events of our past traditions, that such a liberated belonging is possible.

Notes

At the time of first writing this chapter, in 1987, I was much less aware of the phenomenon which is characterized as the 'postmodern condition', with its emphasis on the time and place determination of all our different reasonings. In fact there is no such thing as autonomous reason as an entity but only different reasonings. However, the concept of the fusion of horizons, in its own way, implies this. Acceptance cannot be achieved by attempting to arrive at one fixed position and neither can any appreciation of self or self-consciousness. Whatever the longer term judgement may be on postmodernism in general and deconstructionism in particular, they have emphasized again, at least, the elusive and volatile nature of all identity. If any identity is possible, it can only ever be one in which difference and deference are seen as of the very nature of selfhood or self-consciousness as identity-in-difference. The implications for both Church and Irish identity are enormous. There is no reasonable position we can all arrive at, only positions from which and to which we reason. Our only hope is if these places of reasoning de-

mand 'the other' in order to be 'self', as does our intra-tradition encounter itself
demand the assimilation of otherness, in the form of other times and places of reasoning, if it is to have any form of historical identity. This has been the basic contention of this paper. Otherness is the unsurpassable shape of identity as the fusion
of horizons.

1. Hans-Georg Gadamer, *Truth and Method* (London: Sheed and Ward, 1976),
    241-5.
2   Paul Ricoeur, *Hermeneutics and the Human Sciences,* ed. and trans. John B.
    Thompson (Cambridge: Cambridge University Press, 1981), 93.
3. *The Philosophy of Hegel* (Oxford, 1965), 14.
4. Ibid.
5. *Systematic Theology,* vol. 3 (London: SCM, 1963), 169.
6. *The Documents of Vatican Two,* ed. Walter M. Abbott SJ (London: Geoffrey
    Chapman, 1967), 354.
    For two recent surveys of this debate, see Ricoeur, *Hermeneutics,* ch. 2, 63-100
    and also Richard Kearney, 'Religion and Ideology: Paul Ricoeur's Hermen-
    eutic of Conflict', *Irish Philosophical Journal,* vol. 2, no. 1 (Spring 1985), 37-
    52.
8. Ricoeur, *Hermeneutics,* 99-100.
9. Ibid., 87.

Reconciliation of Histories

Margaret Mac Curtain

The historian in a sense is the social psychologist of the past. He studies how individuals behave and what made them behave as they did; he studies groups of individuals, the interaction of groups, their growth, development and, in some cases, their dissolution. Unlike the psychologist, however, he finds no direct application in his discipline to human affairs, and few historians would claim that their knowledge of past events enables them to predict with any certainty the course of future events. On the contrary, it seems to imbue them with a more heightened awareness of the indeterminacy of human behaviour, with a greater insight into the transitoriness and relative instability of apparently solid and permanent institutions, and with a sense of the intransigence and paradox in human behaviour.

Report of The Teaching of History in Irish Schools.[1]

1966 was an important year of re-assessment of their historical past for Irish people. The national television station, RTÉ, carried a series of documentaries commemorating the fiftieth anniversary of 1916. Professor Francis Shaw wrote a powerful, immoderate article on 'The Canon of Irish History' – a challenge which seriously undermined the Pearse myth. Such was the mood of the time that the article was not published for six years. The study-group which presented the Report to the Minister of Education began in January 1966 and had ten sittings. The study group was chaired by Professor John Mc Kenna whose years of teaching and clinical experience in the field of child psychology gave an added dimension to a group of seven people, four of whom had a professional interest in history. To one participant, looking back over a distance of some twenty years, the mind and influence of Professor T. D. Williams permeates the thinking expressed in substantial sections of the

Report. Quintessentially, Desmond Williams was the historian of reconciliation. Notably in the fifties, he guided students and readers of his reviews, which appeared weekly in the pages of *The Irish Press* and *The Leader,* through the wastelands of historical positivism and placed them on the *terra firma* of historical objectivity. Invariably he directed the seeker to look for the purpose of history. History, he argued, is not what actually happened, but what historians, on the basis of available evidence (which is never complete), say has happened.

Section 5 of the Report, 'History Teaching for International Understanding and National Identity' was, in the main, his contribution to the working party's deliberations. Here is in evidence his style of thinking aloud and his detachment to see as many sides of the problem as his researches enabled. Here too were expressed some of his favourite themes:

> While the fact that history should be used as a vehicle for promoting international understanding may not be universally accepted, there is little doubt that most people are agreed that history teaching should not be used to implant stereotypes, prejudices and irrational hatreds of other peoples. However, in our anxiety to minimise the irrational destructive forces which may be stirred up by strongly biased history teaching, we should not make the mistake of being unduly evasive by suppressing the truth and modifying the facts in such a manner that they become meaningless. (282)

Misunderstanding between nations, Professor Williams argues, falls into four categories. It is further exacerbated by prejudice and bias in history books and through teaching. The four categories enumerated are: 1. traditional international enmities between countries; 2. religious divisions between ethnic, social and national groups; 3. the assumption that western culture and civilization and Christianity, on which they are based, is the only culture and religion which is of value; 4. misunderstanding between ex-colonial powers and former subject nations giving rise to the conviction that white races are superior to all others. To former students of Desmond Williams, this particular section of a long-forgotten Report puts them immediately in touch with his convictions about the nature of the historical process, and what the role of Irish history could become; indeed it is remarkable how much his philosophy has influenced the current debate on the true nature of revisionism in Irish history.[2]

The middle years of the sixties were ones of relative security for society in the Irish republic. The visit of President John F. Kennedy of the United States to stay with President de Valera gave a fillip to a sense of being Irish in the wide world. The cordiality of the exchanges between the Taoiseach and the Prime Minister of Northern Ireland seemed to set the barometer at 'set fair'. The modest success of the republic's ambassadors at the United Nations was a visible indication of foreign policy incorporating and enhancing a real position on neutrality.

In hindsight, what is strikingly absent from that 1966 Report was an awareness of a need for some reconciling dimension in the relationship between the official history of the southern state and the development of Northern Ireland in the fifty years since 1916. The previous year a dialogue of north-south historians took place at Ballymascanlon outside Dundalk. The topic under discussion was 'Bias in the teaching of History'. The host planners were the committee of the European Society. To that dialogue came Professor J. C. Beckett of Queen's University Belfast and Professor T. D. Williams from University College Dublin. Professor Patrick Lynch, the economist, took the chair on this occasion. How hopeful and vigorous it all seemed with three such distinguished reconcilers speaking from diverse perspectives. Much of what J. C. Beckett said on that occasion is contained in his essay, 'The Study of Irish History' (*Confrontations: Studies in Irish History,* 1972). In that essay, as at the Ballymascanlon dialogue, Professor Beckett warned the student of Irish history to be prepared for an element of discontinuity in the study of the past. The history of Ireland can never be formulated simplistically as the struggle between native and foreigner. Nor can it ever be unified schematically in the mould of English or French history. Implicit in a scrutiny of England's past is 'a natural and overriding unity' which reaches back to the eleventh century. As for France, J. C. Beckett points out that there is a hierarchy of rank for national histories and French history is central to Europe and to the world as well as possessing patterns of unity and continuity.

The land of Ireland supplied the element of continuity, the matrix of all other relationships, in his estimation. Its influence on the inhabitants of the island was a thread that runs through the history of Ireland. Cogently he points out:

> But the writing of history can never be simply teleological; it is influenced, but not governed, by the end to which it moves; the process is more important than the conclusion. And to find any process of historical development that connects resistance to Anglo-Normans in the twelfth century with resistance to the Black-and-Tans in the twentieth, one must not only ignore the evidence that does exist, but invent evidence that does not exist. (16)

Not for nothing was J. C. Beckett's collection of essay's entitled *Confrontations*. With inexorable logic he points out that, for a large portion of settlers, their relationship with Ireland remained ambiguous, and to a greater or lesser extent they resisted its influences in the realm of traditions and institutions, and in turn their ideas, tradition, and institutions profoundly influenced the earlier inhabitants of the island. He was, of course describing the settlers of that troubled century, the seventeenth, and his conclusions were indeed prophetic in the light of the violence that erupted in Northern Ireland after 1969. 'It is by studying the way in which the settlers were influenced by the conditions of Irish life, and the way in which they themselves modified the influence of those conditions in the earlier population, that we may well be able to identify the distinctive characteristics of Irish history, and build up a framework round which that history may be written.' (25)

Professor Desmond Williams approached the topic of bias from a different angle, that of a twentieth century historian with an intimate knowledge of Germany. Much of what he said was incorporated into the section he contributed to the Report the following year. The need for a continuous reassessment of possible prejudices in history teaching had resulted in the promotion of international studies of history teaching and a flow of textbooks. Notably after World War Two, Unesco had endeavoured to set up an exchange between French and German historians. The 1951 Unesco Commission on the teaching of history for international understanding instructed historians to examine such areas to which the attention of teachers should be drawn in order to bring their teaching into concord with the facts established by scientific research. In the sixties there were courageous attempts to produce a 'European' textbook: in these attempts the European schools which accompanied the growth of the consciousness of the European Community reported on their limited success, limited mainly because of the retention of traditional prejudices and interpretations. Prejudice, according to Desmond Williams, was the single most obstinate element which impeded the progress of modern research from filtering down into the textbooks. With prejudice can be associated the magnetic attraction of stereotypes.

Can histories be reconciled? Is truth so harsh that it threatens with fragmentation the illusory reality which, in a multiplicity of fragile structures, envelopes not just our personal identity but the past identities of our communities? Does the seemingly unassailable fortress of each particular establishment on this island, Unionist or Republican, Protestant or Catholic, remain impervious to the persuasion of rational analysis of our shared past? Specifically, what is the position of the founding myths of the modern state(s) of Ireland?

Identity is at the core of reconciliation. Crucial to an understanding of our present *impasse* is the realization that the inability to discard those elements of a national identity which make it a caricature and even grotesque identi-kit leaves the communities on this island in a kind of trapped stasis. There is, for instance, the top-of-the-morning, beer-swigging, stage Irishman who has been with us a long time, the 'fictional' Irishman, a construct whose nationality poses no threat to the ethnic divisions that run through Irish society.[3] More subtle in ways is the ultra-nationalist whose defensiveness against the outside world is an assertion of anti-English sentiments, one who balances Gaelic antiquity against the English intruder, Gaelic spirituality against materialism from outside the island, and whose 'national' literature is a form of alienation of the colonised.

There is, then, a high degree of integrity demanded of the historian who makes the decision to retain processes of reflecting, writing and presenting Irish history in the first language of the state, Irish, aware that, as the twentieth century draws to a close, this is to render him speechless to whole sections of the population

of the island, and not listened to by groups who profess to think
and speak in Irish. It is a predicament not unknown to the Dutch
historian, Pieter Geyl. In his essay, 'The National State and the
writers of Netherlands History' he examines the conflict that arises
between the history of a linguistic group, Flanders, which is at least
potentially a national group, and the modern states established in
that area, Belgium and the Netherlands. Geyl considers the ability
of the nation states to change their attitudes as an important factor
in bringing about unity: 'The Catholics now pull their full weight
both in the political and cultural life of Holland. The Protestant
conception of Dutch nationhood, which had been decaying for so
long already, has become frankly untenable. Meanwhile in Belgium
the Flemish Movement obtained the redress of most of the old
grievances'.[4] Geyl's conclusions are as valid for Ireland today as they
were for the Netherlands after World War Two, in the final para-
graph where he speaks so tellingly of the historian's obligation to be
aware of the existence of a problem. It is that of the mind-set which
allows no freedom to cross 'the boundary' of one's sentiments or prejudices and, adds Geyl, it has often been fostered by the modern state
'with its high claims to total allegiance, and with its efficient machin-
ery to assist, but at the same time gently to guide, the historian'.

History as an academic discipline in Britain and Ireland is over a
hundred years old if we accept Ranke and Acton as its founders. In
that span of over a century, little acknowledgement has been ges-
tured towards the changing role of memory, or indeed towards the
impact of psychology on our understanding of memory, and how it
works. Despite our growing dependence upon information systems
and our recognition of the computer-like components of the
human memory, at times it appears as if popular Irish history functions in a mysterious continuum that has more in keeping with the
storing capacity of the bardic memory of four hundred years ago
than it has with the Unesco recommendations on the teaching of
history to young people. One of the contemporary movements of
today's historians is to be interested in the cluster of attitudes and
psychological traits that create a mentality, or a collective mentality
within different levels of a particular society. We are a memory-car-
rying people who know all the tricks of keeping race-memories
alive through song, music and ballad.

And one read black where the other read white, his hope
The other man's damnation:
Up the rebels, to Hell with the Pope
And God Save – as you prefer – the King or Ireland

Louis MacNiece 1938

Historians are asking (and endeavouring to answer their own questions) if there is a general *Weltanschauung* or collective set of attitudes which remains obdurate to any imposition of formal, conscious beliefs and constitutes a certain temper or mentality.[5] Memory as history was 'invented' by Renaissance humanism and developed as a handmaid of the emerging nation-states of Europe in the following centuries. Machiavelli's reflections on the connection between history and power suggested that history could be made by an act of resolution on the part of the ruler. He also implied that the spoils of victory gave to the victor the right to render the 'official' history and thus please the Prince. As for the vanquished, they retained their memories and out of them narrated their own version of what happened, passing it on orally to future generations in a variety of media.

We go to history, as to economics – where formerly we went to religion or the classics – to find a meaning for life. Each generation has then an obligation to write its own history. But first memories need to be reconciled. Hurt memories cry out for healing. Distressful memories can keep a myth like Ulster's Bloody Massacre of 1641 trapped in a dismal recurring record. One way to deal with an uncomfortable past is to carry out an operation on the brain, to anaesthetize the pain of the past. One way of presenting Irish history is to execute some kind of cosmetic alteration on its face, to clean up those sad, dark places where the human spirit droops from the weight of its history, and offer a bland synthesis of the 'good old times'. But this kind of forgetting or deliberate disremembrance is to render Ireland's past a kind of leprechaun land, or if we are dealing with the twentieth century, a Disneyland. The sanitization of Irish history – what a theme for a futuristic television series.

'National memories and ideological instincts cannot be disregarded' was, according to Desmond Williams, axiomatic for the direction of foreign policy on the part of governments.[6] Equally he could have placed the Irish Civil War in that context. An authority on the Irish civil war, he once lectured for two hours and twenty minutes on that topic, holding an audience comprised of survivors, diplomats, people who had not spoken to each other for over a quarter of a century. When he had finished in an atmosphere of hushed silence, the applause that broke out was tumultuous. More important for the historian, his objectivity and fair-mindedness were commended. With that lecture there commenced a new era of approaching Ireland's recent past in history writing. A path-breaking series of radio lectures on the years between Easter 1916 and the first years of the new Irish state, edited by T. D. Williams, made their appearance in book form in 1966. It was titled *The Irish Struggle* and within its covers were a collection of well-researched essays by leading experts. There, for the first time, readers had access to the Williams analysis of the Irish civil war.

The eruption of violence in Northern Ireland since 1969 has long since shattered any complacency the Irish republic may have experienced fifty years after the 1916 Rising. The task of writing recent Irish history has not been easy over the last thirty years. In the eighties and nineties a new reproach was hurled at those historians who were engaged in writing political history of the twentieth century; they were 'revisionists' and they wrote 'revisionism', not history.

It is too soon to assess the consequences of the hostility that the writing of Irish history by a younger generation has provoked, or to gauge the effect of the word 'revisionism' in terms of linguistic evolution. If the usage persists and leads to clarity and accuracy, then it will ultimately facilitate the writing of history; if on the other hand, 'revisionism' is used as a term that fudges or obfuscates significant areas of historical understanding, we must conclude that unconscious assumptions are getting in the way of receiving correct information.

Sometimes it is not prejudice that freezes people into a mindset, it is fear. The 'crime' of Galileo was that he proposed for consideration an obvious truth, that the earth is not the centre of the universe; he challenged an article of faith, one upheld by church and state, shrouded in tradition, rooted in language. The myth-level of a society has a volcanic dimension, however deeply embedded in the unconscious it appears to be. In a sense both Richard

Kearney and Séamus Deane rendered the topic under consideration here, 'Reconciliation of Histories', a service when they drew
our attention to the myth element in a culture. Is it possible to demythologise national myths and yet preserve the country's myths?
To put it more starkly, can myths become conduits of destruction
that necessitate demolition?

From time to time there sweeps over practitioners of the craft of
Irish history feelings of being maimed or scarred by our history. It
remains disconcertingly present below the surface. With it goes as a
nagging accompaniment a sense of being 'losers' in the panorama
of world history. Some countries have similar wounds – Poland, the
Lebanon, Mexico. To possess a history of discontinuity is no disgrace. Meaning and pattern are concealed in that discontinuity.
What matters is not the validity of the question: why did our history
happen this way or that?, but what role has our memory played in
keeping us victims of our past, or inheritors of our future?

Notes

1. 'Report on The Teaching of History in Irish Schools', *Administration*, vol. 15
   (1967), 268-85.
2. The author is indebted to the late Professor T. D. Williams who suggested a
   re-examination of the Report in the light of the Ballymascanlon Dialogue. His
   untimely death prevented further discussions with him on the theme. The
   weaknesses in this paper are mine, the illuminations his.
3. For an interesting development of this idea, cf J. T. Leerssen, *Mere Irish and
   Fíor-Ghael* (Amsterdam: 1986), 85-168.
4. P. Geyl, *Debates with Historians* (London: Fontana, 1962), 228-9.
5. See, for example, G.E. Aylmer, 'Collective Mentalities in Mid-Seventeenth-
   Century England: The Puritan Outlook', *Royal Historical Transactions,* fifth
   series, no. 36 (London, 1986), 1-25.
6. T.D. Williams, 'The Primacy of Foreign Policy', *Nonplus* 2, 1960, unpaginated.
   I am grateful to my colleague, Dr Michael Laffan, History Department,
   UCD, for having drawn my attention to this seventeen-page essay.
7. Further to Civil War archives and the Thirty Year rule see R. Fanning, 'The
   Great Enchantment: Uses and Abuses of Modern Irish History', in *Ireland in
   the Contemporary World. Essays in Honour of Garret Fitzgerald*, ed. J. Dooge
   (Dublin: Gill and Macmillan, 1986), 136-7.

Testing the depth of Catholic/Protestant enmity: The case of Thomas Leland's *History of Ireland*, 1773[1]

Joseph Liechty

When explaining some aspect of Catholic/Protestant conflict, many interpreters of Irish history, ranging from propagandists to professional historians, develop some variation on a deep-rooted theme: that the relationship between Catholic and Protestant communities is naturally and normally, or at least frequently, peaceful. According to Oliver MacDonagh, from at least 1800 all Irish nationalism was characterized by 'blind assumptions that Ireland was one and indivisible politically, and that religion was a false divider of Irishmen, used as such by British governments intent on maintaining control of the island',[2] and these have remained as unifying creedal statements for followers of both Tone and O'Connell. But the theme is by no means the exclusive property of nationalism. In David Hume's eighteenth-century account of the Irish rebellion of 1641, he was willing to acknowledge 'the inveterate quarrels' to which Ireland was subject, but he believed that 'during a peace of near forty years' these had 'seemed, in a great measure, to be obliterated', so that on the eve of the rebellion the pacific effects of English policy seemed to have 'bestowed, at last, on that savage country, the face of a European settlement'.[3] In this assertion Hume did not innovate, he only granted the imprimatur of philosophical history to John Temple's history of the rebellion, the standard Protestant account. In a very different context, historian Desmond Bowen has employed his own variation on the peace theme at the heart of *The Protestant Crusade in Ireland, 1800-1870*. By his telling, 'the radical divisions of the two peoples which marked Irish society after the 1820s had not been found' from 1800 to 1822, when 'religious peace existed generally'.[4] O'Connell, Tone, Hume, Temple, Bowen: they are men with little enough in common, yet each has found it useful to assert or assume the existence of peace between Catholics and Protestants.

The assumption of peace seems to be the enemy of sound history. It encourages highly selective versions of history, allowing national-ist propagandists to ignore the real concerns of real Protestants by creating more congenial fantasy Protestants, and allowing Protest-ant propagandists to ignore the justice of Catholic grievances and their own share of guilt. The assumption of peace is usually accom-panied by far too simple accounts of why this peace does not exist at any particular moment. Thus Tone and O'Connell pinned all blame for sectarian tension on the British, Temple and Hume found in the perversity of Irish Catholicism the sole explanation for the rebellion of 1641, and Bowen argues that religious conflict began 'abruptly in 1822 with a declaration of war' in a single ser-mon.[5] The tension between assumed peace and actual conflict tends to produce either outright self-contradiction or, as the price of apparent consistency, huge gaps in the historical record. Conor Cruise O'Brien has demonstrated that when James Connolly's hist-orical writings treat of Irish Protestantism they suffer both maladies, self-contradiction and selective silence, but perhaps the silence is most striking: Belfast and its obstreperous Protestants simply disap-peared from Connolly's account of nineteenth-century Ireland.[6] Bowen's *Protestant Crusade* is a prime example of self-contradiction. Bowen asserts that 'religious peace existed generally' between 1800 and 1822, and he provides a couple of pages of documentation. But throughout the book he either modifies or undermines his own thesis, admitting at one point, 'most Protestants, most of the time ... were not only anxious, but actually fearful of a sudden storm di-rected against them.'[7] Yet despite his contradiction of his own thesis, Bowen closes by nostalgically regretting a lost 'state of religious and social peace'.[8]

Put simply, the assumption of peace, in all its variations, is at odds with good history because it is a matter of crying peace where there was no peace. The cause of sound scholarship would be far better served by an opposite point of departure – that the funda-mental state of Catholic/Protestant relations was enmity, whether latent or manifest. Then historians are more likely to assess realistic-ally the formidable task facing those historical movements that hoped to effect some kind of mutual accommodation, or even rec-onciliation. We are also more likely to appreciate the fundamental questions each community needed to answer for itself to allow even a possibility of genuine accommodation. For instance, a study of eighteenth-century Protestantism exposes a set of entwined questions that included at least the following: Are Irish Catholics human? Or do they simply need to be civilized? Are their actions subject to rational explanation? Or is accounting for Catholic behaviour a subject for demonology? Can Irish Catholics change? Or, for example, does the nature of the 1641 rebellion forever fix the Protestant response to them? Should Protestants attempt to convert Catholics? If so, how? What is the role of coercion? Of education? Of evangelism? Do Protestants accept guilt for present or past treatment of Catholics? What does that guilt consist of? Is the Catholic Church authentically Christian? If not, can individual Catholics be Christians? These questions, and others like them, arose naturally for Protestants as a result of the internal logic of the Reformation, their view as settlers of the native population, and their feelings of vulnerability to the Catholic majority. No doubt this set of questions varied from one generation to another, new ones emerging and others disappearing, with some questions always present but periodically shifting in importance or even meaning. Historians, then, need to ask: Which of these questions were being asked, and how were they being answered? Which were suppressed or left unanswered? If a particular scheme seemed to promise accommodation but attempted to skirt these questions, how did it propose to do this, and what effect did it have? In fact Protestants proposed very few sets of answers to these questions that could bring a genuine accommodation with Catholics even into hailing distance. Answers acceptable to Catholics were unacceptable to Protestants, and vice versa.

A history based on the assumption of peace will always be unlikely to raise these fundamental questions. The cause of sound history will not be served best, however, by simply exchanging one set of inadequate assumptions for another. Historians will do far better to subject their working assumptions to the most rigorous scrutiny, a task which might well begin by paying some attention to what we mean by peace in various situations. Overuse has so drained the word 'peace' that it has become an empty vessel capable of being filled with the most incompatible meanings, ranging from a peace that means little more than a lull between battles to the peace of full and deep-rooted harmony. More fundamentally, historians must test the extent of peace and the depth of conflict in case study after case study.

What follows is just one such effort. It perhaps bears a special significance, however, because both the historical circumstances and the personalities involved seemed to make possible an accommodation between Catholics and Protestants. That such hopes were disappointed suggests the depth of Catholic/Protestant enmity.

By the 1770s the fields of Irish history were long since ripe for harvest. In an essay on eighteenth-century Irish historiography, Jacqueline Hill demonstrates that by mid-century significant points of convergence between three major interpretations of Irish history – patriot, liberal Catholic, and Gaelic enthusiast – seemed to make possible a synthetic general history of Ireland.[9] By the 1760s, however, the basic assertions of these three schools had drawn counter-claims, and now 'everyone (or so it seemed) was waiting for the 'philosophical' history of Ireland which would identify the *real* lessons of Irish history.'[11] The Anglo-Irish community, with its peculiar position as neither fully English or Irish, seemed best situated to produce the necessary historian, and in the 1760s the obvious man for the task was Thomas Leland, a fellow of Trinity College Dublin.

Leland's classical scholarship had made him the best known and most widely respected of Irish scholars.[12] Furthermore, he seemed to have the temperament and approach necessary to produce a philosophical history of so contentious a subject as Irish history.[13] Perhaps the most important of these personal qualities was his 'superiority to bigotry, civil or religious', which found expression in friendships with men ranging from Quakers to Catholics.[14] Probably the closest of these friends was a Catholic, Charles O'Conor, the leading Irish antiquarian, a writer on behalf of Catholic rights, and a man of great liberality and integrity. Beginning with an academic correspondence, their relationship became a warm personal friendship. Leland bent rules to grant O'Conor access to Trinity's rich collection of Irish manuscripts, invited O'Conor to spend a summer with him in his summer home in the Wicklows, and drew O'Conor into Dublin Protestant society to an unprecedented extent.[15] In the preface to his *History of Ireland,* Leland acknowledged a debt, 'above all, to the zealous friendship and assistance of Charles O'Conor'.[16] Indeed the story of their friendship is an essential part of the story of Leland's effort to write a philosophical history of Ireland.

By 1767 O'Conor was urging a mutual friend to encourage Leland to take up a history of modern Ireland. The literary gap was shameful and Leland the man to fill it, for he was 'a philosopher, as well as a Christian', who would not 'permit religious zeal to extinguish the lights of philosophy'. Should Leland hesitate, 'let him feel the reproach that if we do not exhibit a Hume or a Robertson in our island, it will be his fault'.[17] O'Conor wrote to a Catholic friend that he had indirectly encouraged Leland to write a history of Ireland from Henry II to 1688, 'to us the most important of any' historical undertaking. 'It is a pity that a man who distinguished himself thro' Europe by writing the life of a monarch of a remote country and age, should not bestow part of his abilities to adorn (and what is better) instruct and reform his own country.'[18]

Others were encouraging Leland, also, and by 1769 he had clearly taken up the challenge.[19] His progress must have seemed most promising to O'Conor. Leland told O'Conor that such work must be written 'with a liberal indifference to all parties, English & Irish, civil & religious', and he requested O'Conor's help with certain thorny problems.[20] Leland's scholarship promised much, for he was proving to be an eager examiner of primary sources.[21] The relationship between the two men steadily deepened, culminating in 1772 with Leland's inviting O'Conor to spend the summer with him, that they might 'eat, drink, walk, and ride' together.[22] Such close friendship could only have made it more difficult for Leland to disappoint O'Conor's hope that a philosophical history would promote 'reform' – that is, greater Catholic rights.

O'Conor must also have been pleased with Leland's developing interpretation of the sorest of points in Irish historiography, the rebellion of 1641. Each October 23, the anniversary of the Irish rebellion, brought many a cautionary sermon from Church of Ireland pulpits. But the most important of them was delivered in Christ Church cathedral, an event described by historian Walter Love as the traditional occasion of rejoicing in the protestant ascendancy and of memorialising the black treachery of catholic rebels; it was a yearly reminder of the supposedly incorrigible disloyalty of the Irish catholic population, and the sermon in Christ Church was always preached in a tone appropriate to the governors from Dublin Castle and all their fashionable train.[23]

A sample of Irish rebellion anniversary sermons suggests that Love did not exaggerate – their primary purpose was to burn ever more deeply into Protestant consciousness the conviction that Catholics could never be trusted.[24] But when Leland delivered this sermon in 1770 he took a radically different approach.

In a sermon customarily used to flail Catholics, Leland concentrated on Protestant guilt. To be sure, he did not take the approach of some Catholic historians and simply stand Protestant accounts on their heads.[25] But he did make sure that Protestants accepted a full share of guilt for the savagery of 1641. Although disdainful of Catholic teaching – 'popish superstition',[26] he called it – he acknowledged that Catholics had just grievances. 'Let truth itself bear witness,' he said, 'how far the iniquities of our forefathers contributed to exasperate, to confirm, and to perpetuate' Catholic rancour. 'When the gradual progress of their arms had extended their power and possessions, were the old natives, a spirited and haughty race, conciliated by kindness, by equity, or by justice? Or were they treated, where they could be so treated, like beings of an inferior order?'[27] Such sins were not mere memories. 'If we should consider the condition of our poor, or the conduct of their superiors, the manner of common life, or the characters and pursuits of those more exalted, we might possibly find abundant matter for an odious parallel.'[28] This theme Leland developed at length before concluding that 'papal superstition' was the 'the great and leading cause of this day's calamity'.[29] Nonetheless, he urged his powerful audience to 'charitably hope that Popery, at this day, hath been softened by a kind of tacit reformation. While we cautiously guard against all possibility of danger, we may the less scruple to indulge such sentiments.'[30] He hoped that by examining 'the errours [sic] and iniquities of our forefathers', Protestants might, 'taught by their example, ... reform our own conduct, and avert the return of God's judgments'.[31]

In 1772 O'Conor must have been further cheered by a historiographical essay Leland published. His performance showed him to be all that a philosophical historian should be: sceptical of exaggerated claims, capable of close and fine reasoning, disinterested, and free from provincialism. And best of all, Leland's judgments leaned, in a moderate way, toward the Irish interpretation of things.[32]

During the year and a half that Leland's *History* was kept in the printer's shop by various delays and illnesses, O'Conor and his close friend John Curry, another Catholic historian and activist, were perhaps less than fully philosophically serene as they waited to see the results. First Curry got from the printer's shop oral reports of Leland's content, which suggested that Leland had written a strongly Protestant account, and later he actually managed to obtain sheets of Leland's work as they came off the press. He was more and more upset. The worst blow was Leland's account of Islandmagee, a massacre of innocent Catholics by Scottish soldiers. In a projected historical work, Curry hoped to base his account of 1641 on an argument that Islandmagee was the first massacre of the rebellion, thus inciting the Catholic response. But now Leland maintained that it had been a slaughter of thirty families, not 3000 people as Curry argued in his *Historical Memoirs,* and it had happened not in November, 1641, but in January, 1642, as a Protestant response to Catholic killings. Curry wrote furiously, 'is Temple, Borlase, or Hume as dangerous an enemy as your friend? – I am really sick.'[33]

In October 1772 O'Conor read the illicitly attained sheets for himself. He found Leland guilty of both prejudice and sloppy scholarship – Leland had resigned 'his literary merit, and all credit with impartial men'.[34] Finally published in June 1773, *The History of Ireland* was greeted by mixed popular and critical reactions, and so it has continued down to the present day.[35] What may be said with certainty is that Leland's *History* never sold well and that it never achieved anything like the reputation of Hume's work on England or Robertson's on Scotland. But why this was so is very far from clear.

To examine Leland's scholarship fully is a task well beyond the scope of this sketch. What we may reasonably ask is how Leland treated Irish Catholicism, why he chose this stance, and why it disappointed so many of his supporters. His detractors put forward four main explanations of what they viewed as Leland's failure to treat Irish Catholicism fairly, all of them advanced by O'Conor even before the book was published: Leland was a poor scholar, he was prejudiced against Catholics, he wanted to sell lots of books, and he hoped for a clerical preferment.[36] The last three charges fall within our boundaries, and each is difficult to accept. All of them require us to believe that Leland's contemporaries completely misjudged his character, for he had a high reputation for integrity and liberality – this is the man O'Conor had earlier described as 'a philosopher, as well as a Christian', a writer destined for 'a superior orb', where 'religious zeal' does not 'extinguish the lights of philosophy',[37] as 'one of those persons whose benevolence is too well rooted by nature to be extirpated by education'.[38] The latter two accusations – of selling his scholarly soul in return for popularity and advancement in the church – require us to believe that Leland was not only a knave of the first order for acting with such base motives, but also a fool of equal standing, because he misjudged his audience so badly that he wrote a party history that appealed to no party.[39] Leland won neither popularity nor promotion.

A simpler and more fruitful line of inquiry is to work with Leland's self-understanding: he was a Protestant clergyman doing his best to write a history 'executed with a liberal indifference to all parties, English & Irish, civil & religious'.[40] From this vantage point, Leland's failure to satisfy any party does not indicate personal inadequacy. Instead it exposes the wide gap between Protestant and Catholic views of Irish history, even as those views were expressed by men of Leland's and O'Conor's high character. Leland failed, at least in part, because he had a nearly impossible task.

In discussing Leland's stance towards Catholicism, we will be justified in focusing our attention where most of Leland's readers seem to have turned first: his account of the rebellion of 1641. A comparison with Hume's treatment of 1641 in his *History of England*, which had become the prestigious standard for English history and for philosophical history generally, will help to explain the scholarly context in which Leland wrote.

Leland was keenly aware of the precarious position occupied by an aspiring historian of Ireland. Explaining in his preface the failure of eighteenth-century Irish Protestants to produce a history of

Ireland, Leland concluded that lingering 'prejudices and animosi-
ties' were principally to blame.

> Time, and reflection, and an increasing liberality of sentiment,
> may have sheathed the acrimony of contending parties; and
> those at a distance may look on their contentions with indiffer-
> ence: yet, even at this day, the historian of Irish affairs must be
> armed against censure only by an integrity which confines him
> to truth, and a literary courage which despises every charge but
> that of wilful or careless misrepresentation. [41]

The image of a sword of acrimony, sheathed but lying close at
hand, must have seemed increasingly appropriate as he pondered
the mixed responses to his work.

Throughout the *History* Leland was casually dismissive, even
derisive, of Irish Catholicism. In the Reformation period, Leland
believed, any attachment to the Catholic Church was based on ignorance – an ignorant clergy and an ignorant laity were 'in proportion to their ignorance, abjectly attached to the papal authority'.[42]
Hume's attitude was much the same. Commenting on the reformation period, he said that for Irish Catholics, the 'ancient superstition, the practices and observances of their fathers, mingled and
polluted with many wild opinions, still maintained an unshaken
empire over them'.[43] A favourable assessment of Catholicism, especially Catholicism in Ireland, was not among the distinguishing
characteristics of philosophical historians.

When it came time for Leland to account for 1641, he paused to
issue an aside. It sounded very like his reflections in the preface and
showed him to be fully aware of the delicacy of his task. 'It is difficult, if not impossible,' he said, 'for a subject of Ireland to write of
the transactions now to be explained, without offending some, or
all of those discordant parties, who have been habituated to view
them through the medium of their passions and prepossessions.'
His general task he understood to be 'to form a general narrative
upon the best information to be obtained, with an attention steadily
confined to truth, without flattering the prejudices, or fearing the
resentments of sects or parties'. Specifically, he must 'trace the causes
and occasions of a rebellion, whose effects have been important and
permanent; and do not cease to operate even at this day, after a
lapse of one hundred and thirty years'.[44]

In his account of the rebellion's causes, Leland steadily developed two themes: the pernicious influence of Catholicism on the
Irish, and the follies of English policy. His treatment of
Catholicism was harsh and conventionally Protestant, but his judgment of English policy was of a different nature. Leland cited two
particular examples of English mismanagement. The Old English
had been treated badly, which created dangerous tensions and resentments; and plantation, however laudable its goals, had been
handled poorly at every step of the way, thus augmenting Irish
Catholic discontent.[45] Hume, on the other hand, acknowledged no
English guilt. In his account, the rebellion seems to explode from
nowhere. The seventeenth-century English plan for Ireland, said
Hume, was 'by justice and peace to reconcile that turbulent people
to the authority of laws, and, introducing art and industry among
them, to cure them of that sloth and barbarism to which they had
ever been subject'.[46] The method for achieving these selfless goals
was plantation, which Hume believed had been highly effective.[47]
On the eve of the rebellion 'the pacific plans, now come to greater
maturity, ... seemed to have operated with full success, and to have
bestowed, at last, on that savage country the face of a European settlement.'[48]

To describe the course of the rebellion, both Hume and Leland
employed violent and dramatic language, and both saw Catholic
doctrine and clergy as fomenting massacre. But here the similarity
ends. To the extent that Hume acknowledged causes at all, he at-
tributed all blame to the lethal combination of the Irish people and
the Catholic religion, while Leland assigned guilt to both Irish
Catholicism and English policies. Hume described the rebellion in
Ulster as 'an universal massacre', while Leland chided settlers for
forgetting that 'their suffering brethren had in several instances,
been rescued from destruction, and protected by the old natives'.[49]
Hume described the Irish as inhuman, Leland saw them as ignorant. Hume depicted the settlers as entirely passive victims, while
Leland criticised them for their 'violent and indiscriminate' response to the cruelties they had suffered, which 'transported them
to the very brutal cruelty which had provoked their abhorrence'.[50]
Perhaps most important of all, Hume memorialized the rebellion as
'an event memorable in the annals of human kind,' characterized

by 'cruelty ... the most barbarous, that ever, in any nation, was
known or heard of' and 'worthy to be held in perpetual detestation
and abhorrence.'[51] This was precisely the role that the rebellion had
always played for Irish Protestants. In contrast, Leland's account
was noteworthy for the absence of eternal verities.

Hume and Leland diverged even more in describing later stages
of the rebellion. Hume paid little attention. He did note that Old
English Catholics feigned loyalty to England and detestation of the
rebellion, but this was merely a ploy to obtain arms. Then, drop-
ping all pretense of loyalty, 'and, joining the old Irish', their
Catholic compatriots, they 'rivalled them in every act of cruelty towards the English protestants'.[52] Leland's account was very different. He pointed out the impossible circumstances of those
Catholics who wished to remain loyal. One example was the Earl of
Clanricarde, who, despite his extensive efforts to keep the peace in
his area, 'was a roman catholic, and therefore hated and suspected
by the state. Every assistance was denied him, and every occasion
seized to mortify and disgust him.'[53] Searching for an explanation
of English failure to quash the rebellion, Leland concluded that the
chief governors simply did not want the rebellion to end too early –
Irish fury must spend itself fully so that those in power would gain
from new forfeitures of property.[54] He also condemned them for
indiscriminate use of torture to 'supply the want of legal evidence',
citing the abuse suffered by the aged and innocent Patrick
Barnwall.[55] While Leland placed most of the blame for the immediate outbreak of the rebellion on Irish Catholics, he placed most of
the responsibility for its continuation on the Irish administration.

Such was philosophical history as written by the best qualified
member of the Anglo-Irish community. The two main Protestant
interpretative stances toward the rebellion of 1641, which were
often quite contradictory, might be called royalist and parliamen-
tarian. Although Leland incorporated elements of both, his work
was definitely within the royalist camp, which had always been
more sympathetic to Catholic claims. Where he innovated was in
his recognition that Catholics had been abused and provoked prior
to 1641, a point almost entirely ignored or denied by both parlia-
mentarians and royalists. The obvious source of this argument, although he did not acknowledge it in his notes, was John Curry's

work on the Irish rebellion. The result was a more complex than usual account of Irish history, but it was also quite useless to all contemporary lines of interpretation.

The most bitterly disappointed readers were surely those liberal Catholics and their supporters who had the most inflated hopes. Philosophical history, O'Conor expected, would not merely tell the Irish story more honestly than before, it would 'reform us as much',[56] perhaps to the extent of eroding support for the penal laws.[57] Given the written opinions of Hume, the preeminent philosophical historian, this seems rather naive. It seems even more naïve, or at least desperately hopeful, when we examine the various forces acting on Leland.

An immediate and towering barrier to O'Conor's reforming expectations was Leland's understanding of his task as an historian. History is 'philosophy teaching by example', said Lord Bolingbroke,[58] and his maxim captured a central tenet of philosophical history. But in a perverse way, Ireland has long been an island filled with philosophical historians who are only too willing to read their philosophy into history and then learn from the resulting example. Leland rejected this aspect of philosophical history and settled on a narrower task – to narrate events and explain their causes as faithfully and impartially as possible. Reforming the nation was conspicuously absent from his conception, and throughout the *History* he consistently eschewed anything approaching policy prescriptions. Any education and example would only be implicit in his text.

Leland might have served O'Conor's reforming purposes by reversing the usual Protestant interpretation, thus implying that Protestant fears behind the penal laws were groundless. Again, an immediate barrier: Leland's reading of Irish history simply did not support the notion that the usual Protestant understanding could honestly be reversed. His contentious account of Islandmagee, for instance, was based on a careful reading of manuscript evidence and is now the accepted version of modern scholarship. But even beyond this, taking this option would have been almost impossible for any Protestant, and indeed nothing was really pushing Leland in this direction.

Of course Leland's Protestant tradition was steeped in anti-

Catholicism. For a Protestant he was unusually liberal in the extent of his personal contacts with Catholics and his apparent willingness to extend at least some civil rights to Catholics, but he shared his community's traditional contempt for much of Catholic doctrine and for what they perceived as the domineering role of the Catholic clergy and the subservience and ignorance of the Catholic masses. None of Leland's many published sermons had an attack on Catholicism as its theme. In fact he rarely mentioned Catholicism at all, which makes the tone of his few casual references all the more significant. As just one example, in a sermon on miracles Leland used the illustration of 'a man skilled in mechanicks [sic], acquainted with the magnet or the electrical fire, versed in the experiments and processes of the chemical art, [who] might in a crowd of savages, or perhaps in a congregation of ignorant Popish bigots, easily pass for something more than human'.[59] The reference to 'ignorant Popish bigots' was an utterly gratuitous aside, but in this and similar instances one has the impression that Leland was not so much seeking to offend Catholics or attack Catholicism as he was simply drawing an image from the treasury of shared Protestant understanding.[60]

Prevailing trends of progressive thought did little more to promote a positive assessment of Catholicism. In the mid-eighteenth century, some degree of anti-Catholicism was a feature of virtually every major system of thought. Penal laws had the sanction of John Locke, the patron saint of English liberalism, and while more radical modes of enlightenment thought might regard all forms of religion as more or less equally suspect, in Protestant lands Catholicism was a more judicious target – hence Hume intended his criticism of Catholicism's role in the rebellion as an implicit criticism of all religious enthusiasm.[61] Ironically then, his account of 1641, if sprinkled with a few scripture references, could have passed for an Irish rebellion anniversary sermon, which neatly illustrates the unlikely convergence of traditional Protestant historiography and philosophical history. The enlightenment was never likely to give an Irish Protestant clergyman a positive view of Catholicism.

The one possible influence on Leland toward a more favourable assessment of Catholicism might have been his contact with liberal

Catholics like O'Conor. But O'Conor and company, in their desire to advance the cause of Catholic rights, had conceded many points. They had accepted the idea that primitive Irish Christianity was free of Roman influence, they accepted a Protestant church establishment, they protested against their exclusion from civil rights on the grounds that this was 'popery', and they distanced themselves from the kind of liberal and crusading political ideas that Protestants found in the Catholic tradition and worried about in contemporary Catholics.[62] A man like O'Conor remained a staunch Catholic, but what he displayed most visibly for the Protestant world was what he had conceded, not what he retained. Leland's relationship with O'Conor probably helped him acknowledge the possibility, even the likelihood, of what he called a 'tacit reformation' in Irish Catholicism, and it may have helped him to see that seventeenth-century Irish Catholics had just grievances, some of which remained down to his own time. But it did not create in Leland an appreciation for Catholicism as such, especially not one that could be applied retroactively to Catholics of the Irish rebellion era.

Leland might have met O'Conor's reforming hopes in a second way, much more subtle but also more fundamental, by acknowledging that Protestant fears were founded on a more or less accurate reading of the past, but arguing that no eternal principles could be drawn from ancient events, no matter how horrible. In fact Leland seems to have favoured this approach. He developed it, however, not in his *History* (that would have violated his brief as narrator), but in his Irish rebellion anniversary sermon of 1770. It was here that Leland did his historical philosophising, and given O'Conor's profound disappointment with Leland's *History*, it is ironic that Leland's applications of his historical viewpoint in the sermon included a condemnation of contemporary treatment of Catholics by Protestants and a strong implicit criticism of at least some of the penal laws. This he accomplished by a two-pronged approach. First, he humanized Catholics by depicting them as not only sinning but sinned against, and he desanctified Protestants by exposing them as not only sinned against but sinning. But the way he dealt with the meaning of the past was at least equally important. In an earlier historical essay, Leland had expressed astonish-

ment that the Scots should think it 'a matter of the least importance to the honour and dignity of their nation at this day', whether
they derived their blood from Irish emigrants, or the native savages
of Caledonia'.[63] In his sermon, he applied something of the same
historical approach to the much more recent and contentious subject of the rebellion. Hume spoke for the Irish Protestant tradition
when he said the rebellion was 'an event memorable in the annals of
human kind, and worthy to be held in perpetual detestation and
abhorrence', and ironically, men like John Curry were locked into
the same general view of the rebellion's significance – the extension
of Catholic rights in the eighteenth century depended on exonerat-
ing Catholic participants in a seventeenth-century rebellion.
Leland cut through this knot by acknowledging the possibility that
'Popery, at this day, hath been softened by a kind of tacit reformation.' In a tentative way he had broken free from the pervasive Irish
inclination to draw immediate and direct political implications
from the past, working instead with a view of history that acknowledged the possibility of genuine development and change. Leland
indulged in liberal and potentially reforming reflections on Irish
history, along the lines that O'Conor had hoped for, not in the
History of Ireland, but in an Irish rebellion anniversary sermon
preached in Christ Church cathedral.

Although Leland's *History* was sorely disappointing to liberal
Catholics, it cannot be shouted too loudly that there was equally
little in it for Protestants seeking support for the penal laws.[64]
O'Conor and Curry were disappointed that Leland had not reversed Protestant understandings of 1641, but from a Protestant
perspective he had failed equally to uphold them. Leland spread responsibility for the rebellion among Catholics and Protestants,
which was of little use to someone looking to history for justification of the penal laws. For such purposes they needed an account
like Temple's, or Hume's, in which Catholics were perfect savages
and Protestants perfect innocents.

If Leland's *History of Ireland* disappointed just about everyone,
including some close friends, the response to it must have been
equally disappointing to him. Although he was at the height of his
powers, Leland never wrote another scholarly work. In the autumn
of 1773, he obtained his first parish ministry,[65] and it was that work

to which he devoted most of his energies for the rest of his life. He died in August 1785, remembered as a man of high character, a fine classical scholar, a devoted pastor, and a competent historian who did not quite succeed in writing a philosophical history of Ireland.

Leland's 'failure' and O'Conor's disappointment raise the issue of what may reasonably be expected of historians. Modern understandings of the historian's primary task seem to have settled less with Hume and the philosophical historians than with Leland and his goal of narrating events as fully and faithfully as possible. While denying the possibility of absolutely objective, value-free history, historians generally seek to keep personal perspectives and values firmly under the control of scientific historical methods and disciplines. In the dialogue between historians and interpreters of history (and it is a dialogue that sometimes goes on within one head), the historian's function might almost be seen as making life difficult for the interpreter by insisting on a rich and complex account of history which stubbornly resists the imposition of too simple interpretive schemes. Historians provide the raw materials worked by interpreters, who may be philosophers, ethicists, theologians, or indeed anyone else who wishes to try a hand at understanding the meaning of history. If historians choose to confine themselves to faithful narration they are not to be despised, for they have performed their fundamental and indispensable task. If they take up interpretation as well, however, they are to be welcomed, because they will know more intimately than anyone else the contours of the historical landscape being surveyed.

In Leland's circumstances his apparent failure was less a sign of personal failing than of the well-nigh impossible task he had undertaken. If success meant writing a history of Ireland as widely acceptable in Ireland as Hume's history was in England, Leland was required to provide nothing less than an entirely new conceptual framework for interpreting Irish history, an intellectual revolution he was no more capable of generating than were his peers. In fact his interpretation probably went as far in a Catholic direction as could reasonably be expected of a mid-eighteenth-century Irish Protestant clergyman. He wrote a history that altered Protestant understandings not by negating or reversing them, but by adding elements of the Catholic understanding. The result was a strikingly different picture of the rebellion and, in a general way, of the relationship between Catholics and Protestants. Catholics and Catholicism were, as usual, depicted as villains, but they were not inhuman, or demons, they were human beings whose actions could be rationally explained. And the charges of villainy were spread around, because one of his explanations for Irish Catholic behaviour was the provoking folly and injustice of English policy toward them. Leland's was an understanding of Irish history that knew very little of innocence. But even at full stretch his efforts failed to meet the hopes of his understandably disappointed friend and counterpart, Charles O'Conor, who from his Catholic standpoint had extended himself perhaps even farther than Leland had. If any two men could have bridged the gap between the Protestant and Catholic communities, they were Leland and O'Conor. Their failure is a powerful testimony to the depth of Catholic/Protestant enmity.

Notes

This paper was first published in *Archivium Hibernicum* and is used by permission.
1. I am especially grateful to Jacqueline Hill for her comments on drafts of this essay.
2. Oliver MacDonagh, *States of Mind: A Study of Anglo-Irish Conflict, 1780-1980* (London, 1983), 23.
3. David Hume, *The History of England, from the Invasion of Julius Caesar to the Revolution of 1688* (first published, 6 vols, London, 1754-61; this edition, 8 vols, Dublin, 1780), vol. 6, 430.
4. Desmond Bowen, *The Protestant Crusade in Ireland, 1800-1870* (Dublin, 1978), x.
5. Ibid., xi.
6. Conor Cruise O'Brien, *States of Ireland* (London, 1972), 89-98.
7. Bowen, *Protestant Crusade,* 132. For documentation of his thesis see 84-5; for modifications see 48, 83, 96, 131, and 141.
8. Ibid., 310.
9. Hill, 'There was an Englishman, an Irishman, and a Scotsman: Perceptions of Irish History, 1690-1790', unpublished essay, 5-10.
10. Ibid., 10-19.
11. Ibid., 19.
12. For an English assessment of Leland's classical work, see *The Monthly Review,* vol. 49 (September 1773), 205.
13. For Leland's approach as a controversialist, see *The Monthly Review,* vol. 31 (August 1764), 118-30; vol. 31 (October 1764), 305-07; and vol. 32 (March

1765), 191-4, which describe his pamphlet battle with Bishop Warburton. The reviewers recommended Leland's authoritative yet fair-minded and polite 'manner of writing ... as a pattern for all the dealers in theological controversy' (March 1765), 194.

14. N. a., 'Life of the Author', in Thomas Leland, *Sermons on Various Subjects* (3 vols, Dublin, 1788), vol. 1, xliv.

15. For an account of their relationship, see Walter D. Love, 'Charles O'Conor of Belanagare and Thomas Leland's "Philosophical" History of Ireland', *Irish Historical Studies,* vol. 13, no. 49 (March 1962), 1-25.

16. Thomas Leland, *The History of Ireland from the Invasion of Henry II, with a Preliminary Discourse on the Antient State of that Kingdom* (3 vols, Dublin, 1773), vol. 1, v.

17. Charles O'Conor to George Faulkner, 15 September 1767 and 13 June 1767, in Catherine Coogan Ward and Robert E. Ward, eds, *The Letters of Charles O'Conor of Belanagare* (2 vols, Ann Arbor, Michigan, 1980), vol. 1, 226, 215.

18. Charles O'Conor to Chevalier O'Gorman, 1 September 1767, in Ward and Ward, *Letters of Charles O'Conor,* vol. 1, 222.

19. Among those strongly encouraging Leland was his good friend Edmund Burke. See Edmund Burke to William Markham, ca. 9 November 1771, in *The Correspondence of Edmund Burke* (10 vols, Cambridge, 1958-78), vol. 2, 285.

20. Thomas Leland to Charles O'Conor, 5 January 1769, in Ms. B.I.2., Royal Irish Academy (hereafter, RIA).

21. For Leland's use of sources, see four 1771 letters between Leland and Dr Ducarel, librarian of Lambeth Library, in John Nichols, *Illustrations of the Literary History of the Eighteenth Century* (8 vols, London, 1817-58), vol. 3, 547-9, and also, Love, 'Charles O'Conor and Thomas Leland', pp 5-6. However, a later review of Leland's *History* did criticise him for inadequate use of primary sources ('Memoirs of the Life and Writings of Thomas Leland, D.D.', *Anthologia Hibernica,* vol. 1 (March 1793), 165-7.

22. Leland to O'Conor, 9 May 1772, in Ms. B.I.2., RIA.

23. Love, 'Charles O'Conor and Thomas Leland', 8.

24. For representative samples, see Edward Wetenhall, *A Sermon Setting Forth the Duties of the Irish Protestants, Arising from the Irish Rebellion, 1641, and the Irish Tyranny, 1688, etc., Preached Before his Excellency, the Lord Lieutenant and the Lords Spiritual and Temporal, and Divers of the Commons, in Christ Church, Dublin, Oct. 23, 1692* (Dublin, 1692); Edward Walkington, *A Sermon Preach'd in Christ Church, Dublin, on Saturday the 23rd of October, 1703, Being the Anniversary Thanksgiving for Discovering the Irish Rebellion, Which Broke Out in the Year 1641* (Dublin, 1703); Ralph Lambert, *A Sermon Preach'd to the Protestants of Ireland, Now Residing in London, at Their Anniversary Meeting on October 23, 1708* (London, 1708); St George Ashe, *A Sermon Preached to the Protestants of Ireland, Now in London, at the Parish-Church of St Clement Dane, October 23, 1712* (London, 1712); Edward Young, *A Sermon Preached in Christ-Church, Dublin; on Sunday, October 23, 1763, Being the Anniversary of the Irish Rebellion: Before His Excellency Hugh, Earl of Northumberland, Lord Lieutenant General and General Governor of*

Ireland: and the Lords Spiritual and Temporal in Parliament Assembled (Dublin, 1763); and James Traill, *A Sermon Preached in Christ-Church, Dublin; Before the Right Honourable the House of Lords: on Monday, the 23rd of October, 1769; Being the Anniversary of the Discovery of the Irish Rebellion* (Dublin, 1769). More than forty such sermons were published. Later specimens exhibited somewhat greater moderation than early ones, but all justified Love's description.

25. Jacqueline Hill finds that the Abbé James MacGeoghegan's *Histoire de l'Irlande* (3 vols, Paris, 1758-62) presents an account of Anglo-Irish relations that is a 'mirror-image' of David Hume's ('There was an Englishman', 18), and John Curry's work, *Historical Memoirs of the Irish Rebellion in the Year 1641* (London, 1758) and *An Historical and Critical Review of the Civil Wars in Ireland, from the Reign of Queen Elizabeth to the Settlement under King William* (Dublin, 1775), often exhibits the same tendency.

26. Leland, 'On the anniversary of the Irish rebellion', *Sermons*, vol. 3, 5.

27. Ibid., 6-7.

28. Ibid., 19.

29. Ibid., 11.

30. Ibid., 17.

31. Ibid., 17-18.

32. Thomas Leland, *An Examination of the Arguments Contained in a Late Introduction to the History of the Ancient Irish and Scots* (London, 1772).

33. For their agonising wait, see Love, 'Charles O'Conor and Thomas Leland', 10-15. The quotation is from Curry to O'Conor, 12 October 1772, in Ms. B.I.2., RIA.

34. O'Conor to Curry, 31 October 1772, in Ward and Ward, *Letters of Charles O'Conor*, vol. 2, 30.

35. For the immediate response, see *The Monthly Review*, vol. 49, 205; Sylvester O'Halloran, *Ierne Defended: Or, a Candid Refutation of Such Passages in the Rev. Dr. Leland's and the Rev. Mr. Whitaker's Works, as Seem to Affect the Authenticity and Validity of Antient Irish History, in a Letter to the Antiquarian Society* (Dublin, 1774); John Curry, *Occasional Remarks on Certain Passages in Dr. Leland's History of Ireland, Relative to the Irish Rebellion in 1641* (London, 1773); John Wesley, journal entry for 5 July 1773, in *The Works of the Rev. John Wesley* (14 vols, London, n. d.), vol. 3, 501; and Love, 'Charles O'Conor and Thomas Leland', 224. For critical opinion of the later eighteenth and nineteenth centuries, see Edmund Burke to Richard Burke, 20 March 1972, in Burke, *Correspondence*, vol. 7, 104; N. a., 'Life of the author', in Leland, *Sermons*, vol. 1, xliv; James Wills, *Lives of Illustrious and Distinguished Irishmen* (6 vols, Dublin, Edinburgh, London, 1840-7), vol. 6, 148; Charles Read, *The Cabinet of Irish Literature* (4 vols, London, Glasgow, Edinburgh, Dublin, 1880), vol. 1, 306; 'Memoirs of the Life and Writings of Thomas Leland', *Anthologia Hibernica*, vol. i (March 1793), 165-7, which was reprinted as 'Dr. Thomas Leland', *The European Magazine, and London Review*, vol. 36 (August 1799), 75-7; Francis Plowden, *A Postliminious Preface to the Historical Reviews of the State of Ireland*, 2nd ed. (Dublin, 1804), note on 13-14; and Leland's entry in the *D.N.B.* For opposite reactions of modern scholars,

see Walter Love, 'Edmund Burke and an Irish Historical Controversy', *History and Ideas,* vol. 2, no. 2 (1962), 182, where he calls Leland's *History of Ireland* 'another piece of anti-catholic propaganda', and Francis G. James's much more positive assessment in 'Historiography and the Irish Constitutional Revolution of 1782', *Éire/Ireland,* vol. 18, no. 4 (1983), 10-12.

36. O'Conor to Curry, 31 October 1772, in Ward and Ward, *Letters of Charles O'Conor,* vol. 2, 29-30.

37. O'Conor to Faulkner, 15 September 1767, in Ward and Ward, *Letters of Charles O'Conor,* vol. 1, 226.

38. O'Conor to Curry, 12 February 1772, in Ward and Ward, *Letters of Charles O'Conor,* vol. 2, 9.

39. In 'There was an Englishman', 20, Jacqueline Hill identifies as a central feature of Leland's work 'his reluctance to draw instant conclusions which would align him with any of the contemporary models of Irish history'.

40. Leland to O'Conor, 5 January 1769, in Ms. B.I.2., RIA.

41. Leland, *History of Ireland,* vol. 1, 2.

42. Ibid., vol. 2, 160.

43. Hume, *History of Great Britain,* vol. 5, 393.

44. Leland, *History of Ireland,* vol. 3, 86.

45. Ibid., 88-9.

46. Hume, *History of Great Britain,* vol. 6, 430.

47. Ibid.

48. Ibid.

49. Hume, *History of Great Britain,* vol. 6, 437; Leland, *History of Ireland,* vol. 3, 128.

50. Hume, *History of Great Britain,* vol. 6, 437-8; Leland, *History of Ireland,* vol. 3, 128.

51. Hume, *History of Great Britain,* vol. 6, 437-8.

52. Ibid., 443.

53. Leland, *History of Ireland,* vol. 3, 138.

54. Ibid., 132.

55. Ibid., 164.

56. O'Conor to Faulkner, 13 June 1767, in Ward and Ward, *Letters of Charles O'Conor,* vol. 1, 214.

57. Love, 'Charles O'Conor and Thomas Leland', 4.

58. Henry St. John, Viscount Bolingbroke, *Letters on the Study and Use of History* (2 vols, London, 1752; reprint New York, 1970), vol. 1, 15, quoted in James, 'Historiography and 1782', 6.

59. Leland, 'Proof of Christianity from Miracles', *Sermons,* vol. 1, 83.

60. For other examples, see Leland, *Sermons,* vol. 3, 5, 49.

61. Hill, 'There was an Englishman', 14.

62. Ibid., 8.

63. Leland, *Examination,* iv.

64. Even John Curry, in his *Occasional Remarks,* acknowledged that several reviewers had found Leland dangerously pro-Catholic in his treatment of the rebellion.

65. N. a., 'Life of the Author', in Leland, *Sermons,* vol. 1, xlix.

Reconciling the Histories of Protestant and Catholic in Northern Ireland

Frank Wright

The theme of this paper is that reconciling the histories of Protestant and Catholic in Northern Ireland is the reconciling of two opposed national histories. It is therefore a work with few precedents, because by and large national communities that coexist on the same soil develop in rivalry and antagonism with each other. It is more common for them to eventually separate from each other than to become reconciled. Reconciling of histories is therefore not an academic exercise. It is the uncovering of stories that are only important when they are of service to some pre-existing reconciling purpose. In the first section I deal with the question of why reconciling moments of history are likely to look like tangents to a history of antagonism. In the second section I look at the place of British responsibilities. Any effort by Britain to create the long term foundations for intercommunal trust, such as I believe the Anglo-Irish Agreement might be, will be greeted with mistrust which must be recognised as a fact rooted in the historical experience of British power and not made the basis for repudiating responsibility.

In the third section I will try to elucidate the process whereby the antagonistic histories and histories of antagonism have rubbed away any reconciling edges. Any lasting peace in Ireland, or even moves toward such a thing, would depend upon both communities recognising how they had been trapped in antagonism with each other.

As an introduction to this discussion, here are unionist and nationalist stereotype views of the Famine that I have drawn up impressionistically from discussions I have heard.

The Famine didn't affect the North much. Protestants are hard working and they got along OK even if Catholics in some parts of Ireland didn't. Maybe England didn't do much, but then you couldn't have expected it when there was Famine in England and Scotland at the same time.

There were grain ships leaving Ireland in the middle of the Famine. Emigration and even starvation suited British purposes very well. It is still going on today in the North, where Catholics are three times as likely to emigrate as Protestants. Otherwise there wouldn't be a unionist majority here.

Neither of these summaries contains any totally indefensible statement, but they reflect antagonistic perceptions of the role of British power in Ireland. This historical selectivity is an unsurprising consequence of the history of national antagonism. Whatever is 'remembered' has a fairly direct bearing on the things that preoccupy people today. Opposing communities do not need to speak different languages in order to be different nations. The Orthodox Serbs, Catholic Croats and Moslems of Bosnia all speak Serbo-Croat and are distinguished as separate national entities by their different religions. Just as Irish Catholics often speak of Ulster Protestants as 'fellow Irishmen', so Serbs often spoke of Croats as 'brother Slavs'. These formulae could mean either brother (with implied separate national identity) or little brother (who had to be taught that he really was a 'slav' or an 'Irishman'). Both Croats and Ulster Protestants, in order to rebut claims that they are really only subdivisions of the 'other' nation, emphasise their religion as that which marks them out as different. National groups coexisting on the same soil tend to develop their nationality in rivalry with each other, and the features of their histories that are most important to them are therefore the things that have clearest bearing on that antagonism.[1]

At first sight this statement may not seem to be fair comment on Irish nationalism, which emphasises the more avowedly non-sectarian strands of its own history. But because it sees Britain as the main enemy, it largely ignores Unionism itself. It takes notice of Unionism only ephemerally and then only at moments of heightened antagonism, making the point that it is somehow an artificial product of British or sectarian manipulation. Unionism is treated as a one-sided repudiation of the 'non-sectarian' Irish nationalist tradition; and even if it is admitted that Catholic clerical strands of nationalism may have helped to encourage it, it is seen nonetheless as an unjustifiable anti-national deviation. The United Irish rebellion of 1798 demonstrates that Ulster Protestants are 'really' Irish, and would (or will) become so again if only certain British entanglements are undone. While conversely unionist histories tend to emphasize religious divisions, they too can use 'non-sectarianism' in the same way. Ignoring the experience of Northern Catholics, some stress the economic benefits of the link between the North and Britain, and see Catholic rejection of such liberal 'non-sectarian' arguments for the union as proof of their irrationalism. 'Non-sectarian' gambits can easily be used as a means of self-justification and to cut off any effort to empathize with the experience of the 'other'.

It is, however, possible to build up entirely reputable defences of either position without any serious distortion of historical fact. All that is required is that the standpoint of the observers reflect the direction from which threats of physical violence, humiliation and denigration are converging toward them. Both will focus upon moments of antagonism because these are also most significant to both positions. The relatedness of the histories of the two national communities depends upon this forced relationship between them. The more locked into rivalry they actually became, the more the things which defined them were products of the rivalry itself. Rivalry uproots any legitimate authority and gradually proliferates actual dangers which end up being the source of identity. As this happens, the space for neutrals or doubtful members of each bloc contracts. Eventually memories of any less malignant inter-communal relationships are either belittled (shown to have merely concealed things that would blossom into malignancy), hijacked (to show how one community displayed a trust not reciprocated by the other), or forgotten (because ultimately they had an 'insignificant' effect on the present).

What then would count as a reconciling of histories? First, if it were possible for either community to inflict a lasting defeat on the other, the mere fact of successfully eradicating the risks of further violence would tend to enshrine the 'history' of the victor community. Apart from my dislike of this prospect, I am also sure it is impossible in this situation. So, putting this possibility aside, we are left with two communities trapped in an antagonism. It is inconceivable that anything like a peace, a reconciliation of histories or memories, could ever be generated that did not recognize the mutual threat relationship as a fact. If it is not recognized as a fact, it will always re-emerge as a spiral of accusations. How are fact and accusation to be distinguished? It can only be by recognizing that 'we' and 'they' have been trapped so that we have become part of the threat to each other. As national rivalries escalated, the justifications of 'our' side made the 'trap' look like a righteous cause.

The obstacles standing in the way of reconciliation of histories might then be as follows. The most important is that reconciling moments of past history are intrinsically uninteresting unless they serve some current reconciling purpose that is there before them. Secondly, historians looking for such moments find their work incomplete unless they also explain why these moments had so little effect upon present day realities. To do their job properly they are obliged to tone down the significance of whatever they unearth to reflect its current 'insignificance'. Thirdly, if the substance of national antagonism is the impairing or breakdown of mutual trust, many of the countervailing tendencies in the past – innocent of this distrust – did not even seem important enough for contemporaries to record. Fourthly, once antagonism has crystallized, people who are condemned to live in it often soften it in ways that attract very little attention. It is therefore difficult to disentangle all the factors which contribute to make better moments of the past invisible, unimportant, insignificant, etc. But without the hope or faith that there will one day be a better future, searching through this supposedly 'insignificant' past is like searching a pile of old bricks for cornerstones that the builders of nations have rejected.

To illustrate the second problem as I experienced it: While I was writing about nineteenth-century history of the North of Ireland, I often came across people who are now largely forgotten and was strongly tempted to create 'if only' myths about how they might have changed the shape of what actually happened, had certain 'extraneous' things not occurred. This was a rivalry with reality. I did no service to those such as James McKnight (of whom more later). I was trying to turn into retrospective challengers notorious figures such as the Rev Hugh Hanna. I was failing to grasp how far Hanna's significance arose from his proximity to violence. As René Girard shows in his analysis of Dionysius of the Bacchae, the most significant in a vortex of antagonism are those who can both threaten

violence and control the threat simultaneously.[2] It is only thinking
about the subject of this paper that helped me to see that I had been
imposing upon McKnight and others almost a retrospective guilt
for lack of 'achievement'.

The third and fourth problems suggest a different kind of difficulty. Who is to judge what, out of the virtually hidden things,
count as reconciling and why? Once we grasp the moral chaos generated by thinly veiled or blatant force fields, the chair of the impartial observer disappears. Uncertainty of motive is the rule rather
than the exception. (That may be true everywhere but it becomes
glaringly so in a field of potential violence.) It is possible that novelists
are better able to penetrate these zones than any supposedly scientific researchers, because they do not experience the same pressures
to secure an 'impartial' standpoint or to make proposals about what
ought to be done. William Faulkner in *Intruder in the Dust* – a
story that looks more like a political statement about the American
South than any of his other novels – leaves us in doubt about how
far he himself is speaking through Gavin Stephens. Stephens says
that the South (in 1948) is defying the North in order that it should
free the Blacks in its own time; but Faulkner shows us that
Stephens has blind spots about what it means to be Black and cannot empathize with Blacks.[3] Rebecca West in *Black Lamb and Grey
Falcon* cites a Croatian's summary of the Serbo-Croat conflict:

> Nothing here has any form. Movements that seem obvious to
> me when I am in Paris or London become inconceivable when I
> am in Zagreb. Nothing matters except the Croat-Serb situation.
> And that, I own, never seems to get any further.[4]

By resisting the temptation to second guess him, she leaves this despairing judgement to confront the reader directly.

A reconciling function of history may be to find episodes that
demonstrate the difference between knowing national conflict is a
malignancy and mistaking it for a righteous cause. Such history will
not have any visible thread or continuity, but will look rather like a
series of tangents intersecting the history of antagonism. It will be
partial, subjectively chosen and disconnected. It will have to be prepared to announce the importance of the 'insignificant', 'unimportant', and 'ineffective'. But we need have no reason to be ashamed
of any of this. Martin Noth wrote of Christ:

World history at the time took no notice of him. For one short moment his appearance stirred men's minds in Jerusalem; then it became an episode in past history and people had to concern themselves with what seemed like more important things.[5]

The short moment lasted while followers and opponents held the mistaken belief that he would attempt to 'deliver now' (i.e. politically). It is only the miracle of the resurrection that makes whatever else Christ did and said visible to us. So, when we engage in debate about the resurrection, whether it was an intervention of a divine superpower or a fraud or whatever, our debating rivalry over these questions serves to obscure the miracle – that somehow Christ is visible, though he would otherwise rank among the 'insignificant' and 'ineffective'. The effort to reconcile histories is both necessary and fragmented. Necessary in order that we can recover the simple truth that we are made different by experience and not by inherent qualities. Fragmented, because in the middle of a preoccupying antagonism we know that the proof of this is everywhere; but we can only grasp hold of little bits of it.

At this stage it is necessary to explain how I see reconciling possibilities in the North of Ireland, and the part Britain has to play in them, because all such judgement is necessarily political. When it seems possible that nothing will work, then we must admit there is only a relative relationship between political judgements made from different standpoints. This is all the more true because national conflicts do not, by and large, end up with reconciliation of antagonists. More commonly they are concluded only by victories or mutual separation. For reasons I cannot go into at length here, I am convinced that neither of these outcomes will generate a 'peace'. Victories would not be final and the intensified separation would not dispel the antagonism. I cannot comment on the sincerity of those who believe otherwise, except to say that I disagree. The conflict is corroding not just British authority but authority as such, and without authority all justifications for violence spread like a hydra. The only possible authority – one which can be seen to place all peoples in Northern Ireland in a symmetrical relationship toward State power – is something approaching a joint sovereignty of Britain and the Irish Republic. The danger with moving toward this arrangement is that if it fails, it will prove rather conclusively that the external guarantees of both communities cannot bring tranquillity, and will in fact lead to a degeneration into renewed tensional separation as the only remaining means of letting violence burn itself out.

For present purposes what matters is that Protestants cannot be expected to comply with an arrangement in which State power's legitimacy rests ultimately upon a nationalist majority; and Catholics cannot be expected to comply with an arrangement in which State power's legitimacy rests ultimately on a Protestant majority. Neither community could in the long run contain the confrontational pressures within them if placed in these situations. That is what either side's history of the experience of antagonism shows. But for an arrangement, such as the Anglo-Irish agreement might be, to work, it will become increasingly necessary for its basis to be explained and taken responsibility for. Part of our problem is that before witness to Christian unity can be meaningful, it is necessary to recognize that the 'religious' communities are, for better or worse, national communities. The use of religious-political rationales for conflict will be encouraged if the real reasons for conflict are not spelled out. To separate Christianity from tribalism will not be possible if a superior attitude is taken toward the very real experiences that make 'tribalism' a quite normal response to the world as it seems to be.

The ongoing division between Protestants and Catholics in the North of Ireland has been shaped by the presence of Britain, from which the descendants of most of the Protestants came as settlers in the seventeenth century. Even if 'divide and rule' was once a conscious strategy, as the antagonism began to involve ever wider sections of the population, there was no means of ruling that did not regenerate division. Internal tranquillity, whenever it prevailed, ceased to be peace and became more like a 'truce' of communal deterrence. British power might contain the worst manifestations of antagonism (though it equally might choose not to) but communal deterrence meant that the potential for antagonism endlessly recharged itself.

This is scarcely unique to Britain in Ireland. Its relationship to Ulster Protestants was not unlike that of the German Reich towards Germans in its Polish border lands (Posen/West Prussia), or of the Austrian Empire toward Germans in its Czech border lands (Bohemia/Moravia). Faced with simple choices between retaining support from Protestants or Catholics in the North (or from Germans or Czechs in Bohemia), the central states, however reluctantly, had to align themselves with their 'own' people.[6] The frontier defiance actions, such as the overthrow of the Badeni decrees in Bohemia (1897-1901), or the enforced modification of the Asquith Home Rule Bill to include partition (1912-1914), illustrated the limited flexibility of the central state in dealing with their frontier nationals. These defiance actions threatened to produce Imperial-nationalist disturbance in the core areas of nations and to dislocate the functioning of the state apparatus; and if all other methods of breaking accommodative relationships between the central state and the 'other' nation in the frontier failed, defiance actions worked. Each defiance action that worked increased the alienation of the 'other'.

In the long run, the different paths of Ulster on the one hand and Posen/West Prussia or Bohemia on the other, depended on the outcome of the first world war. The doctrine of self determination applied in 1918-20 contained no means of resolving the problems of mixed nationality zones. No nation was prepared to have its own national minorities left under the rule of the nation it had developed in rivalry and antagonism with. And therefore all self determination claims were mutually contradictory. Austria and Germany lost Germanic areas to Poland and Czechoslovakia because the peace treaties were written by the victors. By contrast, the British retained Northern Ireland and the maximum land mass that contained a workable unionist majority. Had Britain lost the whole of Ireland, it seems likely that Ulster Protestants would have been made a cause celebre of British nationalism in the manner of the 'lost' Germans. Despite the creation of a system of devolved government at Stormont, the distance that has developed between Britain and Ulster Unionism since 1920 probably owes more to the fact that Britain never 'lost' Northern Ireland than to the institutional arrangements themselves. If this judgement seems counterintuitive, consider who would have predicted British enthusiasm for the 'fantastically loyal' Falkland Islands before the Argentinian invasion of 1982.

The distance of Britain from Unionism today certainly has some positive effects. It ensures that Britain makes more of an effort to behave neutrally between opposed blocs than it would if it treated the North of Ireland as a test or touchstone of British nationality. Its efforts to preserve positive British-Irish relations in spite of the conflict in Northern Ireland are probably Northern Ireland's best single asset. It is the absence of any comparable accommodation between Israel and Syria over Lebanon, and between Turkey and Greece over Cyprus, that has made these places what they have become. But the desire to keep a distance from Unionism has also prevented Britain from taking full responsibility for reforming Northern Ireland for fear of being unable to shed that responsibility if the effort failed. For example, an effort might have been made to respond to the Civil Rights movement in 1968-69 by reconstructing the North within the UK between 1968-71 on the lines of the US reconstruction of the Southern States – both were then faced with civil rights demands rather than nationalist alienation. But the refusal to override or abolish Stormont before 1971, though keeping Northern Ireland at a convenient distance from British politics, meant that British power eventually got stuck again in its 'normal' posture of supporting Unionism against Nationalism. The effects of the 1971 internment on the legitimacy of British power have been lasting. Thus the posture of 'neutrality' has often been a screen to diminish responsibility for something which Britain is very much part of.

The volatile and inconsistent behaviour of British governments toward internal antagonism provides nationalists and unionists with very good though opposed reasons – illustrated by popular histories – for distrusting British power. This is now simply a fact from which there is little chance of escape. The best service Britain could do for people in Ireland is to make it possible for the different national groups to recognize the validity of each other's mutual mistrust. Only when that is possible is it also possible to create trust. Unfortunately, the path to any such outcome involves taking actions which – in the immediate future at least – increase mistrust of British intentions. It means attempting to place both national groups in a symmetrical relation to state power in the North of Ireland. As that means institutionalising the guarantor role of the

Irish Republic on behalf of Northern Catholics, it also means that Britain must eventually be able to fulfil the same role in relation to unionists, despite their present dislike of the British moves to institutionalize the Republic's role in the Anglo-Irish Agreement. Movement toward this goal will be difficult and will encourage distrust of British intentions, but we will undermine the process altogether if we respond to such distrust with moralizing statements about 'bigoted and intolerant Irishmen'. The way in which the Anglo-Irish Agreement is defended will also affect what it will mean in practice and whether it will ultimately work or not.

Ethnic frontier national conflicts, by destroying the sacred properties of the law and uprooting democratic principle, help to illustrate what nations actually are. People in the metropolis, for whom these things may seem unproblematic, are allowed to ignore the fact that nationalisms are not merely 'like' religions – they are religions. They are, as Girard shows all religions are, built upon the sacrifice or expulsion of scapegoats. In religions we are all united under the sign of a scapegoat, and in the case of nationalisms the scapegoats are non-nationals. The nation state looks like a rational entity while internal disturbers of the peace can be isolated (i.e. criminalized) and the vengeful aspect of the judicial system more or less concealed from view, and while the conduct of antagonistic relations with non-nationals is monopolized by the state. The relationship between transcendental or universalistic religions and nationalisms seems uncomplicated while the problem of vengeance is concealed from view. 'Give unto Caesar that which is Caesar's' has a relatively straightforward application. In frontier zones, where the law relates differently to one community than to the other and where democratic rules are mere procedures in a battle whose results are never accepted (i.e. all self determination claims are intrinsically in contradiction with each other because no one trusts the 'other' with power over minorities of our people), the religious claims of nationalism are much more clearly visible. The scapegoats of each national religion are immediately present and cannot be scapegoated, so violence against scapegoats is never expelled. Metropolitan fascisms are only a variation on this. In their case, national vigilantes carve out for themselves a 'right' to attack aliens and 'traitors', often in fact using 'lost' frontier people as their pretext for doing so (as

Nazism with regard to the Polish frontier or Italian Fascism with regard to Fiume). In these situations the religious claims of nationality corrode the transcendental religions. Whereas in Ireland the nationalities are denominated by branches of Christianity and not by language, this danger is especially severe because the line between the transcendental (Christianity) and the national is so thin. It is somewhat easier for Catholicism to keep its distance from Irish nationalism, because it is not an article of Catholic faith that the political unity of Ireland is sacred. It is more difficult for Protestantism because, if unionist self-description as British is repudiated, unionist self-definition is forced back upon Protestantism. Unless Unionism is recognized as an assertion of Britishness, and not simply as a perverse distortion of Christianity, there is no prospect of freeing Protestant Christianity from worldly (nationality) religions. These claims to Britishness may create severe political difficulties. It is certainly politically impossible to uphold them in the way that the majority of unionists presently want them upheld. But if we do more than point out that Christianity cannot be subordinated to any particular national cause without ceasing to be Christianity, if we suggest that a nationality is 'false' because what distinguishes its members happens to be their religion rather than their language, then we encourage people whose nationality has been defined by their religion to make that religion a tool of secular politics and help to drag the transcendental down into the world of the purely political.

Let us now turn to the dynamics of the internal antagonism of which British power is the pivot. René Girard in *Violence and the Sacred* argues that much of our inability to understand sacrifice stems from our inability to credit it with any real purpose.[7] He argues that its purpose is to contain the dangers of vengeance. In most metropolitan societies the supremacy of the judicial system has cancelled the risks of circles of vengeance so thoroughly that we imagine we are too rational, too advanced or whatever to need to consider the prospect. In ethnic frontier societies, not only is no such cancellation possible, but each outbreak tends to increase the risks of future outbreaks; the mechanisms that reduce the risks never abolish them. That is one reason why many people can be found in the North of Ireland who know histories of the conflicts in their own localities in great detail, stretching back a long way. To demonstrate this point it may help to speak of a period in Northern history which looks outwardly fairly tranquil, between about 1837 and the 1870s.

In Southern Ulster during the 1790s the British state adopted the Orange Order, which had grown out of sectarian contest between Protestant and Catholic weavers, as an auxiliary to suppress the Catholic Defenders. After the Act of Union in 1801 the Orange Order continued to be tolerated or encouraged as a deterring force in these areas, until the 1830s when the Whig-O'Connellite administration extended the centralized magisterial and constabulary system into the North. During the Under-Secretaryship of Thomas Drummond (1836-39) something like normal law and order was imposed in the North. Although it ensured that some districts remained largely free of sectarian aggravation, in many areas it was rather a tranquillized form of communal deterrence than a peace.[8] Orange landlord-magistrates and priests kept restraint over their followers, knowing that so long as tranquillity prevailed, the centralized law and order system could and probably would criminalize those who struck first blows. Unless secular power can be relied upon to criminalize (i.e. isolate) any act of violence, it is likely to find itself intervening against acts which are already part of a circle that has generated reasons for itself, such as 'reprisal', 'deterrence action', 'pre-emptive strike' and so on. It then becomes powerless to eradicate pretexts for violence, and must either accept that powerlessness as a fact or become tacitly or actually partisan in order to secure at least somebody's support and compliance.

Communal leaders seeking to preserve tranquility, had to ensure a sufficient degree of control over their own following to be sure that they could prevent any violence from emanating from their 'own' (except of course where they judged that after a confrontation they could expect the state to need compliance from their camp rather than the other). And that meant showing enough sympathy with the 'provoked' amongst their own people to keep influence over them. The success of the Drummond system, therefore, probably depended not so much upon creating a tabula rasa of sectarian dangers but rather on providing a framework within which local leaderships could successfully accommodate each other and restrain their followers. Obviously such leadership positions

could be used for either tranquillizing or for confrontationalist purposes, but the serious danger was (and is) that it is impossible to be
absolutely clear what intentions lie behind these kinds of leaderships. We cannot for example be sure, when an Orange leader
preaches 'readiness' against 'Catholic power' and 'charity' toward
Catholic neighbours, whether the first injunction is intended to
prevent actual aggression (and therefore restraining) or whether it
makes nonsense of the second injunction. Until the 1870s, the
build-up of Catholic society in some areas of the North (schools,
churches, etc.) depended in the last analysis upon the protection of
the centralized law and order system. Law and order authority in
Dublin Castle was responsive to pan-Catholic pressures at Westminster. It was therefore possible for Catholic clergy to reinforce
moral arguments for Catholic restraint with strong arguments from
expedience. Confrontationalism could jeopardize any recourse to
the law. When a plainly reciprocal aggravation ended up in local
courts, advantage would fall to Orangemen.

In the 1860s Fenianism appeared in the South of Ireland, challenging both British power and Catholic clerical accommodation
with it. In the North, Fenianism itself had very limited support,
partly because it was a manifestly unrealistic political strategy, but
there was nonetheless sympathy for Fenian prisoners. The revival of
Orange marches as a counterblast to Fenianism made it increasingly
difficult for Northern priests to prevent Catholics from engaging in
confrontationalism with Orangeism. And between 1867 and 1872
the Drummond system broke down.

The decision of the British government to permit marches (after
1872) because it could not prevent Orange marches, is an early instance of a successful defiance action. As centralized control over
law and order receded, a greater initiative fell to the local magistrates. Orange magistrates who took the leadership of the Order
were acting as a balancing wheel between Orangeism and British
power. Toward British power the tolerance of Orange processions
was represented as their price for keeping control of Orangeism; as
magistrates they used their powers to both legitimize and restrain
ritual displays of deterrence toward Catholics. Their leadership
functions depended upon arbitrating the relationships between
Orangeism and British power, representing both to each other.

Most of the nineteenth-century history of the North of Ireland is unimportant from the standpoint of the present day. What is very well known is that in the 1880s politics and religion seemed to become one, and this was reinforced when the Home Rule question polarized unionists and nationalists against each other. Before then it may have been incipiently so, but enough energy was being put into preventing this from happening to see why it did so. When forced to choose, many people did so reluctantly. In 1840 when O'Connell attempted to secure the Repeal of the Act of Union, his reception in Belfast showed just how little Protestant support and how much strong opposition there would be to an Ireland ruled by the kind of forces he mobilized. But as I shall outline in a moment, his campaign subsided in 1843 and anyway had limited effect in the North. In my description of the system of communal deterrence in the intervening years, I have stressed that the potential for polarization was never very deeply buried in some areas. But insofar as it was buried, it depended upon centralized law and order power acting as a moderating force upon potential conflict. At this time it was still possible publicly to call the threatened antagonism the malignancy it was, and to act in ways that visibly contradicted it. From these efforts, countervailing possibilities of mutual trust developed, even if their foundations look distinctly feeble from a present day perspective.

So long as Northern Catholics under clerical leadership relied upon central state power and largely eschewed reprisal against Orange provocations, Northern Protestant liberals viewed Orangeism as the major local menace to tranquillity and supported Catholic demands that it be restricted. But when confrontationalism became more reciprocal in the 1870s, not only did clerical restraint weaken but Protestant liberals who remained critical of Orangeism found themselves increasingly powerless. By slow degrees Orangeism ceased to be looked upon as provocation, and its ranks expanded as a defence against the very opponent it helped to provoke. Liberalism slid away from its outright opposition to Orangeism and toward approval of the more restraining forces within it. This process was already visible in the aftermath of the 1872 riots in Belfast and crystallized after the Home Rule crisis of 1886.

It would be absurd to attempt to make some kind of golden age

out of the thirty years preceding 1886. From the point of view of a
post-1886 nationalist, earlier clerical accommodation with British
powers and Northern Protestant liberalism looked like weakness –
i.e. a failure to match Orangeism. Indeed, not only nationalists but
also some Protestant liberals, who became prominent unionists
after 1886, began to rewrite the forgotten years as a kind of inter-
lude in an ongoing battle. But the forgetting of these years was also
a move toward abolishing the memory of everything that was not
confrontation.

When people live in the shade of violence, they also live in fear
of the worst things said and done in their name, because they know
they are in danger of being held responsible for them by the 'other'.
It becomes difficult to repudiate 'our' confrontationalists when the
same people may be 'our' defenders against whatever they provoke.
The times past when confrontationalism was seen as a menace become almost embarrassing. History is gradually refashioned as
'them' and 'us', except when some telling point against 'them' can
be made by suggesting otherwise. Potentially redeeming moments
can be reinterpreted as illustrations of the 'other's' lack of good
faith. Once they become debating points, they lose their reconciling possibilities. Benign intercommunal exchanges become inartic-
ulate. Once there is a real history of confrontation and reciprocal
violence between people, any intercommunal conversation about
the things that divide may look like and become a challenge. Fear
of giving offence becomes a barrier to any but symbolic or inarticu-
late displays of good will. Only antagonistic assertions are articulate
and simple. We are represented towards each other by rival self-
righteousness, and any awareness that the other has reason to fear
us is concealed from view. As such awareness can only grow into a
coherent and articulate thing through open exchange of thought
and feeling between 'us' and the 'other', it is in fact buried.

Let us therefore return to our introduction, and see what it is
that has ceased to be 'interesting' about the Famine and the events
surrounding it. What is lost when we look at the Famine either as
something which may have happened to Catholics but does not really concern unionists, or as the beginning of a British unionist
strategy to thin down the nationalist population in order better to
control it?

Before the potato blight of 1845-50, rural crisis was developing in large areas of the North from which the domestic weaving industry was retreating. A fairly restricted and disproportionately Protestant area of the inner North, proximate to spinning factories, had become a well-defined weaving centre.[9] The Famine destroyed crops (potato and oats), eradicating subsistence supplies of much of the rural population and undermining the livelihood of seasonal (migrant) harvest labour. But only in 1846-47 did food prices rise dramatically. In the inner North 1847 was the year of the Famine. While many areas with massive rural subdivision (especially those dependent on migrant harvest labour) were reduced to unmitigated destitution, weavers could (and had to) respond to high food prices or lower weaver incomes by intensifying their industry. Furthermore, after 1847 when the British government placed the burdens of relief upon the Poor Law Unions, dominant classes in localities with relatively limited distress could orchestrate ameliorative responses. Landlords still receiving rent, Poor Law Unions still receiving poor rate payments and Grand Juries still able to raise county rates, had a more manageable task than their counterparts in areas with extraordinary relief requirements and a disappearing tax or rent base from which to meet them. It is therefore true that areas of the inner North experienced the Famine in a different way from outer Ulster.

In some of the worst afflicted areas, Poor Law Unions tried to refuse repayment of government loans because they could not raise the local taxes, and charged the government with evading responsibilities which they said were its own (an incipiently nationalist approach to the crisis). If we look at the crisis in the North, it might be tempting to suggest that this explains the different legacies of the Famine today. At one level it may do. When the government in 1849 imposed a special rate ('Rate in Aid') on solvent Poor Law Unions to subsidise bankrupt ones, there were widespread protest meetings in the inner North, at some of which people talked of taxing the Protestant North to subsidise the Popish South. Actual differences between the experience of different areas must explain how platform orators who spoke about 'Northern prosperity' avoided being laughed at or thrown off their pedestals. But speeches about the Famine in the South being a divine punishment for Popery

(hence the exemption of the North) were rare, and became com-
moner decades later as a response to nationalist claims that only
Home Rule would remedy emigration. At one time things were
much more muddled. There were Orangemen joining the incipiently 'nationalist' protest against loan repayments in Cavan and
Fermanagh, while priests and Protestant clergy co-operated with
governmental schemes in other areas to raise voluntary subscrip-
tions to secure matching government grants. The short conclusion
is that at the time the Famine was experienced as a disaster, and that
even if its effects varied between different areas and (obviously) social classes within them, sectarian differences played a limited part
in interpreting what was going on at the time, except insofar as they
referred to actual visible differences. Later perspectives on the
Famine of the kind I outlined at the beginning have lost interest in
its shared aspects and the points of actual difference are implicitly
magnified; for example, the differential effects of the Famine may
be part of the reason why state institutions (and landlords) were less
discredited in the inner North than elsewhere; and contrasts between
the industry of 'Protestant' weavers and the total dehabilitation of
populations elsewhere have a foundation in fact. As the repeal
question in 1840 had already raised the question of power in Ireland
in terms of 'them' and 'us', it would have been very surprising if
some contemporary responses to the Famine had not been caught
in the same grid. But what is illuminating is that highly visible political interventions were made in this period that cut right across
the grid. And because they did so there are stories with reconciliatory
implications to tell.

On the eve of the Famine, O'Connell's repeal campaign col-
lapsed and from within his ranks the Young Irelanders criticized
him for the clericalism of his movement, for accommodating
British power to secure clerical advantage in the educational sphere
and public offices for repealers. For Catholics in the North, where
the Whig reforms in education and law and order were a very real
step toward equality and where public offices were very largely a
Protestant preserve, these criticisms seem to have miscarried. And
when the Young Irelanders came to Belfast in 1846, their meeting
was disrupted by local Repealers. Francis Meagher attempted to tell
the Protestants in his audience that they were right to oppose

O'Connellite repeal because it was tainted with Catholic ascendancy, and to stress that Young Ireland was a non-sectarian alternative. The *Newsletter,* pleased with this vindication of their opposition to O'Connell, paid Meagher and Young Ireland the back-handed compliment of recognizing their honesty and sincerity, while using the occasion to demonstrate that nonetheless the real repeal movement was 'essentially romanist'. All the same, a group of Protestant Repealers organized a meeting at which R.D. Ireland spoke the prevailing sentiment.

> The real danger to Protestant toleration consisted in the tardy concession of privileges and rights to Ireland ... as something to be taken from Protestants ... when England should be driven to her own shores (and Protestants) left to an overbearing and exasperated multitude who have been taught to look upon them as their enemies.

It is very likely that the reason why considerable numbers of Protestants were prepared to identify themselves with Young Ireland was precisely because it did not enjoy the sympathy of the only force that might have made it something to reckon with, namely the O'Connellite Repeal organisation. It was possible to speak pre-emptively in favour of Repeal as a possible non-sectarian compact because it was not being demanded by an 'overbearing and exasperated multitude'. The Whig government had reasons of its own, connected with suppressing Chartism in Britain, for magnifying the threat posed by the Young Ireland movement's progeny, the Irish confederacy. It permitted Orangeism in 1848 to reorganize itself as a counterweight to this virtually non-existent threat, indicating in the process that the Drummond system of centralized law and order might be abandoned when it suited English convenience. But in the aftermath, petitions were signed by Protestants and Orangemen in favour of clemency for William Smith O'Brien, the titular head of the rebellion. And at an Orange meeting in Garvagh the main subject was not the rebellion but the need to oppose government measures which it was thought would facilitate the ejection of tenants. In 1849-52 this tenant agitation blossomed into the League of the North and the South, involving Young Irelanders and the founders of the popular strand of Northern liberalism.[10] What they had in common was a view that the Famine was a common disaster, that emigration was a shared malignancy, that government was acting as a tool of landlordism. Differences about religious questions and about Repeal were clearly pronounced, but in the course of co-operating, efforts were made to explain to their respective followings how the experience of Protestants and Catholics differed. Halting and limited their efforts may have been, but efforts they were.

It is very easy to argue away the importance of the Tenant League. It can be shown that if the chips were down on the question of Repeal of the Union it would have been split asunder. It can be shown that it was defeated in the North by sectarian questions, although in fact there were other factors operating which made it substantially more difficult for the Northern Protestant tenant to organize against landlordism than his Southern counterpart, not least that landlords' social role had not been discredited by the famine experience. Let it therefore be said straight away that, for people today convinced of the uncomplicated righteousness of either unionism or nationalism, they will find nothing in the story of the Tenant League to shake their conviction. But for those who know they are trapped, they will find evidence of efforts made by such figures as James McKnight, editor of *The Banner of Ulster,* and Charles Gavan Duffy, the Young Ireland leader, to make a trans-sectarian class alliance work. This involved them in explaining to their own people what the world looked like to the other. In McKnight's case he had the task of persuading Northern Presbyterians that the infamous Ecclesiastical Titles bill – proposed by the Whigs and supported by all British political parties except the Peelites – was not a measure to defend Protestantism but an insult and offence to Catholics. He and Sharman Crawford, at a meeting in overwhelmingly Presbyterian Newtownards, spoke sympathetically of the plight of overwhelmingly Catholic South Armagh, where agrarian outrage broke out in 1851-52. While denouncing agrarian violence, they both denounced coercion acts, the 'violence of property' and the powers of eviction or 'extermination'. When addressing Orangemen, McKnight made his views on processions quite plain by speaking of the 'late lamented Thomas Drummond', reminding them that Drummond had pronounced the judgement, 'Property has its duties as well as its rights.' Gavan Duffy, at great

risk of discrediting himself amongst his own family and neighbours, went to a dinner in the hotel owned by the family of a particularly infamous Orangeman, Sam Gray, where a Tenant League
Branch was inaugurated. Accepting that all of these things have left
no visible mark on the history of antagonism, history can provide
the stories which make sense to reconciling purpose. It must simply
present the things which are now 'insignificant, unimportant', etc.,
without any shame or apology for doing so. The process that generates antagonized history works on all of us. We are all in different
ways magnetized toward antagonism and rivalry. Reconciling history
can only attempt to disintegrate the seeming coherence of the pattern by recalling the witness of those who, however 'ineffectively',
tried to do it.

If forgiveness is being open to a new relationship, concentrated
attention on the events which have become central to the antagonistic histories is unlikely to provide possibilities for a new relationship. The mainline histories which demonstrate the reasons for
antagonism, and which are remembered because identity depends
on the direction from which danger and humiliation emanate, only
help to the extent to which we learn each other's histories. This in-
duces empathy with the other and checks the self justifying logic of
our own. But this can only be a prelude to new relationships.
Empathy with the other and a distance from self justification are
not entirely new. What may be new – indeed what must be in a
new order – is that these past precedents, feeble though they may
have been, become interesting. Insofar as the national conflict in
Ireland is between groups denominated by 'religious' identity, it is a
question of searching for a history of ecumenism before the time
when anyone ever thought of using that word.

There are things we cannot expect from such history. First, it
will never prove the histories generated by antagonism 'wrong'. It
will at most demonstrate how pessimistic judgements about the
other, born of real experiences, turned into righteous causes.
Secondly, what counts as attempting to create a new world will depend upon the type of world the antagonism is generating. Such
history is therefore at a series of tangents to the antagonism and, as
story, makes no sense without it. Thirdly, it only makes any cumul-
ative sense because it is of service to reconciling purpose now.

Otherwise, from a purely academic point of view, it will look like meandering. The only freedom we have in looking at our past is to choose a different angle of vision, to look in the past for the things which we believe have healing power in the present.

Notes:

1. See Fred Singleton, *A Short History of the Yugoslav Peoples* (Cambridge: Cambridge University Press, 1985); Rebecca West, *Black Lamb and Grey Falcon* (London: Macmillan, 1982); Bruce Bigelow, 'Centralization and Decentralization in Inter War Yugoslavia', *South Eastern Europe* (1974), 157-72.
2. René Girard, *Violence and the Sacred* (Baltimore: John Hopkins University, 1977).
3. William Faulkner, *Intruder in the Dust* (Harmondsworth: Penguin, 1978), esp. 148-51,207-9.
4. West, *Black Lamb and Grey Falcon*, 83-8.
5. Martin Noth, quoted in Werner Keller, *The Bible as History* (London: Hodder & Stoughton, 1956), 357.
6. See Frank Wright, *Northern Ireland: A Comparative Analysis* (Dublin: Gill and Macmillan, 1987), chs 1, 2, 4, 5.
7. René Girard, *Violence and the Sacred*, 13-25.
8. See Wright, *Northern Ireland*, 11-20, 44-5.
9. Ibid., viii.
10. Charles Gavan Duffy, *The Legend of North and South* (Dublin, 1886). See also *Irish Peasants – Violence and Political Unrest, 1780-1914*, ed. Samuel Clark and James S. Donnelly, Jr. (Madison, 1983), esp. ch. 5, Paul Bew and Frank Wright, 'The Agrarian Opposition in Ulster Politics 1848-1887'.

History and Reconciliation: Frank Wright, Whitley Stokes, and the Vortex of Antagonism

Joseph Liechty

Can history have a reconciling role? Should historians be reconcilers? The late Frank Wright, political scientist and historian, wedded brilliant scholarship and commitment to reconciliation in his own work (and life), and he put a similar challenge to historians in 'Reconciling the Histories: Protestant and Catholic in Northern Ireland', an essay published in the first edition of *Reconciling Memories* in 1988. He called historians to aid the cause of reconciliation in Northern Ireland by attempting to reconcile the 'two opposed national histories' of Protestants and Catholics. This task will involve, he said, 'the uncovering of stories that are only important when they are of service to some pre-existing reconciling purpose'.[1] The work Wright proposed is unapologetically political and present-minded.

'National groups coexisting on the same soil tend to develop their nationalism in rivalry with each other,' said Wright, 'and the features of their histories that are most important to them are therefore the things that have clearest bearing on that antagonism.'[2] Once established, this tendency to base identity in rivalry and over against the other has tremendous powers of self-perpetuation. In the logic of national conflicts, 'the most significant in a vortex of antagonism are those who can both threaten violence and control the threat simultaneously',[3] a formula which gives key players on both sides an interest in maintaining antagonism through an intricate dance of violence and counter-violence, threat and restraint. Should the antagonism be resolved, their power would be dissolved. Even apart from considerations of power and interest, the dynamics of identity formed in rivalry tend naturally to create a spiral of deepening antagonism. In time, the memory that relationships were ever different, and the hope that they ever will be different, are all but lost.

Eventually memories of any less malignant inter-communal relationships are either belittled (shown to have merely concealed things that would blossom into malignancy), hijacked (to show how one community displayed a trust not reciprocated by the other), or forgotten (because ultimately they had an 'insignificant' effect on the present).[4]

What is more, using the example of Catholic and Protestant accusing each other of sectarianism, Wright demonstrated that plausible defences of both communities' positions can be developed 'without any serious distortion of historical fact. All that is required is that the standpoint of the observers reflect the direction from which threats of physical violence, humiliation and denigration are converging toward them.'[5] No wonder, then, that Wright believed 'reconciling moments of history are likely to look like tangents to a history of antagonism.'[6]

Given the potency and persistence of histories of antagonism, historians attempting to reconcile the histories of Protestants and Catholics in Ireland face fundamental difficulties. Even the task of finding sources will present uncommon problems. In historical epochs when the dynamics of antagonism were dominant, contemporaries often found 'countervailing tendencies' and unspoken strategies for coping too insignificant to merit much comment. However, the most important problem, said Wright, 'is that reconciling moments of past history are intrinsically uninteresting unless they serve some current reconciling purpose'[7] – unless the historian is predisposed to search for or recognize stories of reconciling significance, they are likely to appear as nothing more than insignificant, irrelevant sidetracks from the main story. If significance means visible effect on or relationship to the present, then historians must couch their work on reconciling moments in the unappealing language of insignificance.

Wright readily admitted the limits of history written to serve reconciling purposes. It will have no 'visible thread or continuity' apart from its tangential relationship to the history of antagonism. 'It will be partial, subjectively chosen and disconnected.' It must be prepared not only to accept the reproach of insignificance, but to embrace it – to 'announce the importance of the "insignificant", "unimportant", and "ineffective"'.[8]

Despite these limitations, Wright believed that 'the effort to reconcile histories' is not only desirable but necessary: that we may 'recover the simple truth that we are made different by experience and not by inherent qualities'.[9] In pursuit of reconciling history, we will find incidents and characters 'that demonstrate the difference between knowing national conflict is a malignancy and mistaking it for a righteous cause',[10] thereby learning how it is that 'pessimistic judgements about the other, born of real experiences, turned into righteous causes.'[11] Eventually we may even find that 'these past precedents, feeble though they may have been, become interesting.'[12]

Will Wright's appeal for present-minded and politically committed history writing alarm anyone today? Anxiety about such issues may seem positively quaint at a time when the concepts of neutrality, objectivity, and value-free history are thoroughly discredited, one of Ireland's leading revisionist historians concedes that 'the Irish political establishment after 1969' embraced revisionist interpretations of Irish history because these served best to bolster the political *status quo*,[13] revisionism's preeminent critic among historians proposes that historians should work within the tradition of 'the received version of Irish history' because it 'constitute[s] a beneficent legacy – its wrongness notwithstanding',[14] and one of our best literary critics brands history as 'inescapably a fiction' whose practitioners 'do not write about the past; they create the past in writing about it.'[15] In these conditions, which neatly match the currently fractious, splintered state of most academic disciplines in most places, making a case for reconciling history need not involve anything more than raising a flag and broadcasting a manifesto.

Even so, in 1994 the historian Paul Bew expressed the hope that 'now that there is a ... ceasefire on the streets, ... it may lead to ... some kind of ceasefire in the academy as well.'[16] This essay proceeds on the assumptions that maintaining or restoring some broad and loose professional unity among historians is an important endeavour and that the 'ceasefire' Bew prophesies is likely to take place. When it does, historians will recognize that whatever their differing political commitments, shared traditions of research, presentation, and debate create a useful common framework that should be respected and preserved, that present-mindedness and political commitment are often a danger to the integrity of historical scholarship, even if they are, in the strictest sense, always unavoidable, and that even if history is 'inescapably a fiction', the discipline's special relationship with facts and documents makes history qualitatively different from other fictions.

Fears about history written in 'service to some pre-existing ... purpose', whether reconciling or other, are entirely reasonable and deserve the fullest consideration. They will be best considered not in the abstract, but in light of a particular example of history written from a reconciliation perspective. Wright himself did not merely prescribe the reconciling of histories, he suggested how it might be done with a brief sketch of neglected dynamics and incidents in Ulster history between the 1830s and 1870s.[17] Rather than use his example, however, I want first to present from my own research a historical character who I believe has reconciling significance and then, in light of that example, to discuss the perils and possibilities of writing history for reconciling purposes.

* * *

The character is Whitley Stokes, and he expressed his ideas most fully in a 1799 pamphlet, *Projects for Re-establishing the Internal Peace and Tranquillity of Ireland,* which he wrote as a response to the rebellion of 1798. In 1799 Stokes was thirty-six years old, a fellow of Trinity College Dublin, a medical doctor, and an intensely religious member of the Church of Ireland. Like so many of his peers, he had been badly buffeted by the political turmoil of the 1790s, so sketching the course he steered through those years is essential for understanding the vision he presented at the end of the decade.[18]

Stokes's journey through the 1790s can be recounted as the story of three interlocking relationships: with Theobald Wolfe Tone; with the United Irish society; and with his nemesis, the lord chancellor, John Fitzgibbon (Lord Clare from 1795). Stokes and Tone knew each other from their days as Trinity students in the 1780s, and their relationship continued even after Tone left Ireland in 1795. Stokes was a fringe associate of the United Irish society from its beginning in 1791 and a friend of some of its key members until the rebellion. Fitzgibbon was an immensely powerful figure in Irish politics, a ferocious defender of Protestant ascendancy and opponent of Catholic relief, and for his pains a much feared and hated figure. Through his relentless pursuit of rebellious activities he came to suspect Stokes of treason.

Stokes's relationship with Tone first took a clearly political edge in 1791, when Tone started a political discussion club and invited Stokes to join. Although the club soon disbanded, it seems to have confirmed the friendship and mutual respect felt by the two men, who shared a passionate commitment to Catholic emancipation and parliamentary reform, the political goals of the early United Irishmen. In Tone's hierarchy of personal esteem, Thomas Addis Emmet and Thomas Russell occupied the first rank, while at the head of the second rank was Stokes, whose character Tone respected absolutely: 'In the full force of the phrase,' said Tone, 'I look upon Whitley Stokes as the very best man I have ever known.'[19] We know less about Stokes's opinion of Tone, because he never made direct comment, but the evidence makes it clear that he too valued their relationship. Despite their mutual regard, however, Stokes and Tone were not quite at ease with one another. They were quite different in public demeanour and religious conviction – Stokes reserved and devout, Tone boisterous and secular – but the essential difference was probably political. According to Tone, he and Stokes differed on 'many material points' of politics, but the sole example he gave was probably their primary disagreement: Stokes, he said, 'recoils from any measures to be attempted for . . . [Ireland's] emancipation which may terminate in blood'.[20] It was a difference basic enough to account for the edge of unease in their relationship.

When the Dublin Society of United Irishmen first met in the beginning of November 1791, one item of business was to elect into their society eighteen absent men, among them Tone, Russell, and Stokes. They were present at the next meeting on 9 November, at which a test of membership was introduced. The three newcomers objected to the test, but when it was passed by the group, Tone and Russell took it. Stokes did not.[21]

In fact Stokes never did join the United Irishmen, despite continuing invitations. His relationship with the organisation and with individual members remained strong enough, however, that a quite reliable government spy listed Stokes as a member.[22] In 1793, a

United Irish committee on parliamentary reform considered a variety of submissions, one of them from Stokes, the only non-member to contribute,[23] and a few months later he gave money for the relief of two United Irish leaders imprisoned for libel against the house of lords.[24] Later that same year, his United Irish connections brought Stokes before the house of lords secret committee for interrogation by Fitzgibbon,[25] who was implacable in his desire to identify and root out even the smallest hint of subversion. Relationships and correspondence with leading United Irishmen like Tone, Russell, William McCracken, and others, which continued almost to the eve of rebellion in 1798, were to cause Stokes great trouble.

On 16 September 1796, Stokes's correspondence with Russell, and through him with other Ulster United Irishmen and sympathizers, came to an abrupt halt when Russell and many of the other Ulster leaders were arrested, charged with treason, and jailed. In October 1796 the government supplemented their crackdown by calling up a yeomanry. Trinity immediately established a College Corps of four companies, one of them led by Stokes.[26] He later said that until then he had regarded himself as 'most perfectly a neutral man' in the contest between the United Irishmen and the establishment, but when he joined the College Corps he ceased to be neutral.[27] True enough, during the next year and a half he was active in preventing insurrection: by his role as a captain in the yeomanry, by persuading students to join the yeomanry and not the United Irishmen, and by urging Dublin Catholics, on the eve of a threatened French invasion, not to rise in their support. So Whitley Stokes, friend and fringe supporter of United Irishmen, had become Captain Stokes of the College Corps, and that would seem to be that.

Stokes did not, however, abandon his reforming convictions for an uncritical loyalism. Although with one possible exception he did nothing illegal or disloyal, several of his actions and acquaintances brought suspicion on him and finally left him within a hair's breadth of being expelled from his Trinity fellowship. In fact in 1797 Stokes's continuing connections with radicals brought him before Lord Clare and the secret committee on at least one more occasion, but Stokes was still not as intimidated as Clare would have liked. For example, in the autumn of 1797, Stokes learned

from a pupil of a military atrocity, the burning of a small village
and the murder of six residents. He communicated these 'strong
facts', as he called them, to a leading United Irishman, William
Sampson, who was active on a committee gathering information
for Lord Moira. Activities like this were entirely legal, but visits
with at least three United Irish leaders within the space of a few
months and in tense times left him wide open to suspicions of guilt
by association.[28] Even his position as a captain in the College Corps
did not always work in his favour. William Blacker, an Orangeman
and a student member of the College Corps, recalled that Stokes
had put himself 'in rather bad odour with his company' when on
some occasion of alarm he distributed, along with the munitions,
'an expression of hope that the lads would not use them against
their countrymen. From that time they placed little confidence in
him.'[29]

During these years Ireland's rising political tension was faithfully
mirrored within Trinity. By the beginning of 1798, at least four
groups of United Irishmen operated in Trinity, and many other
students flaunted their involvement with the Orangemen. Finally,
after the public distribution of a violently seditious pamphlet
claiming to speak for Trinity students, notices appeared requiring
all members of the college to come before a general visitation of the
college beginning on 19 April 1798.[30]

Visitation was the means by which severe disputes within the
college were settled. The visitors held sweeping powers, and their
word was law. In this case the visitors were two of the most abrasive
and hard-line supporters of Protestant ascendancy: Lord Clare, as
vice-chancellor of the University, and Patrick Duigenan, as a
deputy for the chancellor. Their mission was to extinguish United
Irish influences within the college, and their method was interrogation under oath.

The three-day visitation, which all students and fellows were required to attend, was dominated by a confrontation between Clare
and Stokes. Most of the students who might have provided intense
clashes with Clare simply refused to appear, but Stokes, so long as
he wished to have any chance of retaining his teaching position,
had no choice but to carry through to the end. Clare and Stokes
had met at least twice before in the secret committee, and Clare,

brimming with information gained there and from his position as lord chancellor, clearly entered this encounter with many suspicions and questions already formulated.

Their first exchange set the tone for what followed. College members were most curious to hear what Stokes would say for himself, for as one student recalled, 'the exceeding candour of Stokes and his known love of truth induced all to believe that he would at once declare whatever he knew, when asked, and many thought that he knew much.'[31] So when Stokes answered Clare's first question – did Stokes know the source of the pamphlet that this visitation? – with a firm 'no', Clare looked surprised and a murmur rose from the assembled college. Clare then asked if Stokes knew of illegal clubs or societies within the college, to which he replied, yes, he knew of societies of Orangemen who took illegal oaths.[32] At this, remembered the student, 'if the chancellor had been struck a violent blow, he could not have shown more surprise and indignation. He actually started on his seat at the audacious sincerity of this simple-minded man, and another murmur ran through the hall.'[33] Clare had not intended this visitation to tackle the Orangemen!

Of course Clare was too experience a hound to be thrown off the scent that easily. Stokes's interrogation, which was spread over several sessions, quickly took on something of a pattern. Clare did most of the questioning with Duigenan making an occasional interjection. They asked a few basic questions over and over again, with some variations and an occasional new one. At least nine questions were designed to determine Stokes's knowledge of United Irish activities within the college, and what he had done about it. Another set of questions was aimed at establishing the extent of his personal connections with United Irishmen. A third line of questioning has the feel of being based on popular rumour. Early in his questioning, Clare asked, 'have you not heard that one part of the system of [the] United Irishmen was a general massacre? [And] that you should have an opportunity of removing your family in due time?' But the simple unvarying question that Clare threw at Stokes over and over again, was, did you have any involvement with the United Irishmen since April 1797? For the most part Stokes handled these extremely difficult exchanges very well indeed. Nonetheless, he did suffer some tense moments, and twice he was worried enough to ask if Clare intended to deprive him of his fellowship.[34]

Of all that Stokes revealed, the incident in which he reported army atrocities to William Sampson seems to have been the most irritating and offensive to Clare and Duigenan. Stokes felt that communicating the story was a duty, but Clare found reprehensible a sense of duty that led Stokes to inform on the army but not to report either a 'direct act of treason although you twice took the oath of allegiance in my presence' or knowledge of a 'meditated insurrection'.[35] When Stokes admitted knowing of United Irish cruelties, Duigenan pressed him: 'do you not think it the duty of an honest man to give information of the outrages of rebels and traitors, as well as of the military?'[36] 'Yes, if they were equally unknown,' said Stokes, but as things stood, 'the lord lieutenant knows of one, not the other.'[37] In the end Clare was reduced to blustering, 'is it becoming a fellow of the college to hunt after Mr Sampson with accounts of military outrages? If you acquitted yourself as you ought, you would have had no time for such visits.'[38]

At the end of the visitation Clare and Duigenan handed down wide-ranging edicts and judgments. Nineteen students were expelled, and one fellow was severely reprimanded. Of Whitley Stokes, Clare said, 'if we were to go according to the strict line of our duty, I do not scruple to say, that we ought to remove him from amongst you.' But because they had heard much 'honourable testimony' on his behalf, and because he had proven that he did act against the 'enemies of his country', they would choose leniency. Their decision was that Stokes would be denied all pupils and prevented from taking a senior fellowship for three years. This sentence amounted to suspension without pay for three years, because while the senior fellows (to whose ranks Stokes would soon have been promoted) had a high income, the junior fellows' income was based solely on taking students. Then at the next ordinary triennial visitation, said Clare, 'we may see whether he has abjured all intercourse with the traitorous association, and wiped himself clean as a person countenancing a system of treason for the subversion of the established government of this country.'[39]

The visitation neither settled every issue it raised nor revealed every one of Stokes's political actions. But what it did very effectively was to put Stokes into a personal, professional, and political limbo. What Stokes made of his sentence would be a great test of character. The least lapse could have cost him his fellowship, so his likeliest response, and a very sensible and understandable one, would have been withdrawal into silence and inactivity. Or he might have become a loyalist's loyalist, to prove beyond all doubting the allegiance to established government that he claimed. Alternatively, if Clare had only succeeded in angering him, he might have been tempted to fulfil Clare's accusations by throwing his lot in with the United Irishmen.

Wolfe Tone, biding his time in France, was one who hoped for the latter option. Reading newspaper accounts of the visitation, Tone understood Stokes's dilemma: 'destroyed with one party', but not necessarily 'saved with the other'. It was a time for definite decisions, thought Tone. Stokes and those like him 'must be with the People, or against them, and that for the whole, or they must be content to go down without the satisfaction of serving or pleasing any party.' Tone's highest hope for Stokes was that 'this specimen of . . . [Clare's] moderation may give him a little of that political energy which he wants.' He had frequently heard from Stokes's own lips 'that nothing sharpened men's patriotism more than a reasonable quantity of insult and ill usage; he may now be a living instance, and justify his doctrine by his practice.'[40]

Ironically, Clare implicitly and Tone explicitly put much the same demand before Stokes: unequivocally declare yourself either a wholehearted loyalist or a revolutionary radical, or be condemned, in Tone's words, 'to go down without the satisfaction of serving or pleasing any party'. But Stokes refused to make the choice, or to withdraw. Instead he responded to them with his *Projects for Re-establishing the Internal Peace and Tranquillity of Ireland,* which developed another approach to Ireland's ills.

Stokes wrote *Projects* in 1799, while Ireland was still shuddering, at what had already passed in 1798 and in fearful anticipation of what might yet come. 'Ordinary virtue,' said Stokes, had been obliterated by civil war, giving propagandists endless inflammatory material. But those like Stokes, whose hope was peace, had a nearly impossible task: 'Describe the faults of either party, you inflame the other; arraign them in common, you make them despair of reconciliation.'[41] In that tense situation, he left aside discussion of the proposed union with Britain. Not that he lacked an opinion – like most of the Trinity fellows, he was strongly opposed – 'but,' he said, 'as I think, I can see measures more powerful with respect to the great object, the peace of the country.'[42] His proposals would be 'perfectly safe, and so completely unconnected with these political changes, that whatever becomes of them, or whatever arrangements may take place, these measures which I speak of deserve some attention.'[43] He set himself a daunting task.

Projects was in several ways a remarkable document. It was remarkable first of all for its content: at a time when most of those thinking about peace for Ireland were concentrating on combinations of security measures, education, legislation, and religion, Stokes used most of his pamphlet to advocate plans for relieving the economic distress of the Irish poor, with a particular focus on getting adequate land for them. His proposals were not the wishful thinking of a cloistered academic. In fact *Projects* was so well-argued and well-researched, including personal knowledge of the conditions of the poor, both urban and rural, that later economic historians have found him a helpful source. Projects was typical Stokes, offering a compelling union of idealism and practicality.

Projects was also noteworthy for its undergirding spirit of confidence in the poor of Ireland. One deep-rooted assumption of his age was that unequal distribution of wealth was not only necessary for society, it was at least in part the result of mental and moral deficiencies in the poor. But for Stokes the poor were simply not the problem. He was completely confident in their industriousness, and as for their character, he marvelled at the generosity of the poor. 'I have repeatedly known those, who had no rational assurance of food for twenty-four hours, take in the out-cast, with whom they had no connexion but fellowship in misery.'[44]

Although Stokes was fully alive to the dangers of his day, *Projects* was pervaded by a refreshing air of calm. According to Roy Foster, 'by 1798 every contemporary correspondence conveys a general mentality of fear',[45] and after reading the many 'state of Ireland' pamphlets produced between 1798 and 1800, one might reasonably describe them as variations on a theme of panic. Stokes, however, assured his readers, 'Depend upon it, this country is not so lost to

feeling, or virtue, but that you will soon find, that you have acquired confidence, and support'[46] as a result of compassionate and
just conduct. But this was precisely what many did fear, that
Ireland was lost to feeling and virtue. Even in the best of times,
Irish Protestants never quite escaped a fear of the Catholic, Irish
poor as an ignorant, sullen, and potentially vicious mass, a volcano
rumbling dangerously in the background. And 1799 was not the
best of times: the volcano had exploded, after shocks still lingered,
and confidence in what Stokes called the 'good-nature' of the poor
was a very scarce commodity among Protestants. He acknowledged
that some might find it strange that in a time of vast upheaval he
was discussing land prices, sanitation, and dung pits, but, he said,
'it is to be hoped that the time will at last come, when we shall cease
to destroy, or even to dread each other',[47] and then the people must
be employed and the land made productive. He was taking a longer
and calmer view than most of his peers could manage.

Near the end of his pamphlet, Stokes shifted his frame of reference. He had been addressing politicians in politicians' terms, but
now he wished to speak to Christians alone – 'I wish any man who
looks at these pages, who is conscious he is not included in that
number, to shut the book.'[48]

Stokes made two basic demands of Christians. One he addressed
to Protestant and Catholic alike, and it was peculiarly his own.
'Notwithstanding all the horrid crimes which the rebellion produced,' he insisted, 'I say after it, as I said before it, nothing but
mutual forgiveness can save Ireland.'[49] Quoting and paraphrasing
Jesus on Galilean rebels and Roman collaborators, Stokes insisted
that the Protestants burned at Scullabogue and the three thousand
Catholics slaughtered in New Ross were no more evil or guilty than
the rest of the Irish people, and unless Irish Christians changed
their ways, they might very well suffer the same fate.[50] 'So God
shall do to you, and more also, if you from your hearts forgive not,
every man his brother his trespasses.'[51] These, he said, were his 'sincere and unvaried sentiments', and although he did not say so, they
were also the moral logic behind *Projects*. It was characteristic of his
innate practicality that he did not leave his readers with a task of
forgiving by means of inner spiritual contortions, but gave them a
concrete programme to implement. It was also a mark of his will-

Catholic approval, although he did realize that Catholics might not acquiesce in his plans. This he was prepared to accept, because the goal of converting Catholics was subordinate to a simple desire for spreading religious knowledge, which he cared about 'incomparably more as a Christian than as a sectary'.[56] This increase in religious knowledge, he believed, must draw Protestants and Catholics closer together. Humbled by the biblical standard, they would find that 'the distinguishing mark of Christians is mutual love', and they would 'promise each other that they will never be led into [past errors] again'.[57]

In his plans for the conversion of Catholics, Stokes may justly be charged with naivete. He wanted every Catholic to be a Protestant, he expected some Catholic cooperation, and he desired that Catholics and Protestants should live together in mutual forbearance. But how these things could be fitted together outside his head he never developed – the contrast with the careful reasoning of his social planning is striking. His naïvete was widely shared, however. Protestants had few resources for comprehending the consequences of their proposals, because no serious, similar attempt had been made in their experience, and Catholic militancy was only in its infancy.

At the very end of *Projects*, Stokes developed two rationales, first political and then religious, for his various plans. His political defence was directed specifically to panicky Protestants, but it was just as effective as a rebuttal to Tone and other revolutionaries, with their certain convictions of what action the times demanded. He expected to be criticized for advocating reforms that were far too slow and unwieldy to deal adequately with a crisis that demanded – or so people thought – 'rapid and decisive measures, which may instantly put us in a state of safety'. But the desire for instant security was an impossible fantasy. 'Be calm, and attend,' said Stokes, 'human wisdom cannot devise any such measures.'[58] It was his conviction, which might have served as a motto for *Projects,* that while 'mischief might be done in a moment; good can scarcely arise but by a gradual process.'[59] All his schemes were designed to assist this slow advance of Ireland's welfare.

Stokes closed with an explicitly Christian rationale for his proposals, directed implicitly but unmistakably to Protestants. He

ingness to be judiciously silent when some expressions might
flame that he framed his challenges predominantly in the relati
acceptable language of 'mutual forgiveness', when the language
repentance – more self-critical and therefore more difficult – pe
haps better described what he asked of his fellow Protestants. Th
many reform proposals that made up the bulk of *Projects* were the
practical expression of what it would mean for Irish Protestants, as
land and power holders, to forgive the horrors of 1798, but even
more to repent for past injustice.

Stokes's other demand he put before Protestants alone, and in
this instance he only echoed a Protestant commonplace. He began
by addressing some questions to them:

> I ask, was not this the charge our Lord left to us all, 'Go and
> preach the Gospel to every creature;' and I ask, have we done it
> to our own countrymen? If we, possessed for an hundred years
> of all the means of civilisation, and religious instruction, unin-
> terrupted by war foreign or domestic, have left them in the state
> of nature, are we to wonder, that when all the world is gone
> mad, they turn on us like savages?[52]

By 1799 his questions could not be answered, they had become for
Irish Protestants an irrefutable indictment of their performance of
religious duty. Stokes was by his own account a zealous 'well-wisher
of the Catholics of Ireland',[53] but, he said, 'I hope my Catholic
brethren will not consider it as any deviation ... that I should wish
every one of them to be, what I would not on any account cease to
be, a Protestant.'[54] Here he stood with almost every devout
Protestant of the time who thought about the ills of Ireland and
their remedy: Protestants had failed in their basic missionary task,
and now they must finish what had been left undone, the conversion of Catholics. By 1800 Irish Protestants could avoid such a conclusion only by wilful neglect or latitudinarian indifference.

Stokes did not separate his two religious demands, forgiveness
and conversion, as he developed them, and the concern for forgiveness gave his plan for conversion some peculiar twists. It would be a
high-minded campaign. He would 'rely solely on the diffusion of
religious knowledge' without stooping to 'entice [Catholics] to my
belief by rewards, or terrify them from theirs by disabilities, or persecution'.[55] Furthermore, he seems almost to have expected

feared that Protestants complacently believed themselves 'the object of God's favour and protection'.[60] He asked them to consider instead that their safety thus far might well be more the result of God's long-suffering patience than his approval. 'It may be,' said Stokes, 'He chose to try by repeated, and encreasing dangers, whether you could be brought to effectual repentance, before he destroyed you utterly!'[61] Protestants must act quickly on the promptings of their consciences if they wished to gain God's favour. 'If you cannot do so, how can you hope, with such peculiar sources of danger, to escape the fate which seems to hang over Europe? ... If you cannot attain it, you are lost! If God be with us, who shall be against us!'[62]

Stokes lived another forty-six years, which he devoted to advocating this vision for reform and to living it out in an impressive variety of ways. If Stokes had like-minded companions or followers, however, they never coalesced into a group that was large, structured, or visible. Varieties of unionism and nationalism dominated politics, and although either might have taken up Stokes's proposals, neither did. Judged by the standard of visible influence on the future, Stokes was one of history's losers.

* * *

With the story of Whitley Stokes in hand, we may begin to assess Wright's proposal to use history for reconciling purposes. The first step must be to analyze the relationships between reconciling history, the mainstream of professional, academic history, and what Wright calls antagonistic history.

The most damning *prima facie* evidence against Wright's proposal is its apparent similarity of approach to the antagonistic history he criticizes. The problems of antagonistic history seem to stem from searching the historical quarry for chunks of evidence that can be used for contemporary political purposes. Wright's political purposes are reconciliatory, not tribal, but the process he proposes is the same: both reconciling history and antagonistic history involve commitment to pre-existing political purposes.

Despite this similarity, the difference between the two is much more basic than a mere contrast in the content of pre-existing purposes. Grasping the difference depends on understanding exactly why present-mindedness is a historical problem. Fundamental to understanding the past is a respect for the distance between past and present, resulting in an awareness that assumptions, values, and circumstances vary subtly over time, so that historians must constantly be wary of imposing modern presuppositions on the past. Because cultivating and implementing this respect is perhaps historians' most basic and hard-earned skill, and the one most alien to an untrained mind, historians must be forever diligent in stressing the divide between past and present. The gap is not absolute, however, and positions that overemphasize it run the risk not merely of antiquarianism, but of nullifying the entire historical quest for understanding. The same bridges between past and present that allow historians to seek understanding of the past will also carry a more limited traffic in meaning and even relevance.

The relevance traffic is more limited because understanding absolutely must precede any valid pursuit of relevance, and understanding, once established, will help to sort out the genuinely from the apparently relevant. The problem with antagonistic history is that the correct relationship between understanding and relevance is reversed, so that relevance precedes and determines understanding. When the needs of contemporary relevance are granted priority, the frequent result is distorted understandings of the enemy or simply ignoring the enemy. More troubling still, history is reinterpreted so that the real theme of history is the emergence of one's own community, and the modern shape of that community is imposed on the past. When the needs of relevance precede understanding, the results are a historiographical shambles.

In contrast, reconciling history as proposed by Wright, despite its equal commitment to pre-existing political purposes, is structurally safeguarded against the abuses characteristic of antagonistic history. The saving grace of reconciling history is the modesty of its self-understanding. It is built on the assumption that far from being the real dynamic of history, reconciliation is only present here and there, and then as a tangent to the vortex of antagonism. This emphasis on reconciliation as contingent is not simply a personal emphasis of Wright's or a happy scheme that he stumbled upon in a moment of inspiration, it is essential to reconciliation, which by its nature only exists in relationship to conflict.

Reconciling history, therefore, must seek a thorough understanding of the context which makes reconciliation necessary, or makes an action potentially reconciling, before it can begin to think about relevance – the proper relationship between historical understanding and relevance is intrinsic to reconciling history. In a similar manner, while reconciling history, like antagonistic history, might be said to have its own set of enemies, the demonizing of enemies, which is natural and useful to antagonistic history, invalidates the whole reconciliation enterprise. Understanding enemies as honestly and empathetically as possible is a fundamental necessity of reconciling history. To serve its own purposes, reconciling history must be accountable to all the standards of mainstream history save one: how significance is calculated.

In calling historians to pursue reconciling history, Wright does not comment on the relationship between mainstream history and antagonistic history. Near the end of his essay, he concludes, 'the process that generates antagonized history works on all of us. We are all in different ways magnetized toward antagonism and rivalry.'[63] However, the 'antagonised history' he has analyzed is not history as written by professional historians, it is history as remembered by divided communities. Are historians also 'magnetised toward antagonism and rivalry'? Certainly fundamental assumptions of the craft work against such magnetism. Antagonistic history depends on highlighting some evidence and ignoring other evidence; it is prone to simple explanations and indifferent to or contemptuous of balance. Professional history, on the other hand, requires attention to all the evidence and values complex explanations; if balanced judgment is not positively enjoined as a duty, balance is a natural, frequent, and even expected consequence of complexity.

If mainstream historians defy the full force of the magnetism toward antagonistic history, however, they do not avoid it entirely. No doubt traces of it can be discerned in the work of some historians. But this is insignificant in comparison to the way the whole canon of Irish history has been 'magnetised toward antagonism and rivalry'. By the logic of national conflicts, Wright argued, 'the most significant in a vortex of antagonism are those who can both threaten violence and control the threat simultaneously.'[64] If we were to judge the priorities and assumptions of historians of Ireland over the last fifty years by the proportion of words devoted to various subjects, we would surely conclude from the attention given to periods and incidents of conflict that the 'vortex of antagonism' is historians' chief interest and from the attention given to characters who can (or desire to) 'threaten violence and control the treat simultaneously' that historians accept the definition of significance characteristic of the vortex. Even an area of study like women's history, which has deliberately and effectively pursued the hidden, commonplace, and unheroic (even anti-heroic), does not entirely escape this magnetism, as evidence by the amount of attention given to revolutionary women. Mainstream history's working definition of significance is influenced by proximity to the vortex and its key players.

The vortex of antagonism is so prominent in Irish history that it deserves considerable attention. The relationships between the vortex, its dominant personalities, and many areas of Irish life will rightly be the subject of many historical studies – in fact, from the point of view of reconciling history, understanding these relationships is essential to its own work. Even if each of these studies was historiographically flawless in its own right, however, the net effect would almost inevitably be a lack of attention to action outside the vortex and especially to those who defined significance in different ways. An imbalance is left to be corrected.

The nature of this imbalance suggests a possible reciprocal relationship between mainstream history and reconciling history. Reciprocity will not mean equality, however, because mainstream history must rightly be the dominant partner. As suggested above, the primary and immense contribution of mainstream to reconciling history will be that mainstream history's fundamental quest for thoroughly contextual historical understanding is the necessary foundation for assessing the reconciling relevance of any historical episode or character. Beyond this, if mainstream history does not necessarily have any directly reconciling function, it does have a pre-reconciling, ground-clearing role by virtue of its commitment to complexity. Antagonistic history depends on fairly straightforward understandings of heroes and enemies and a clear line between right and wrong courses of action, but mainstream history offers little comfort to those seeking such clarity. If antagonistic history searches the quarry of Irish history for chunks suitable for lobbing at the enemy, mainstream history mines boulders of a weight and shape too unwieldy to serve as weapons. By doing its basic job, mainstream history performs an immense service for reconciling history.

From the vantage point of mainstream history, reconciling history's potential repayment on this debt may seem slight by comparison, but it is not insignificant. If the canon of Irish history is tilted to some degree toward the vortex of antagonism and its definition of insignificance, the concerns and perspectives of reconciling history offer a partial corrective. In this matter Wright underestimated the significance of reconciling history by describing it as 'the uncovering of stories that are only important when they are of service to some pre-existing reconciling purpose'.[65] In fact these same stories will also fill the mainstream purpose of making our account of the past as full and complex as possible. The case of Whitley Stokes is a good example. In 1998, as the 1798 industry is running at full throttle, the allure of the vortex of antagonism means that attention is centring on the United Irishmen and their establishment opponents. An important dynamic of the 1790s, however, was the way in which numerous United Irish supporters dropped out for various reasons at various points along the way, right up to the rebellion. To lose interest in them because they ceased to be United Irishmen is to concede too much to the logic of the vortex. Stokes is just one example of a phenomenon that deserves careful attention if the historiography of the 1790s is to be properly aligned. In the name of reconciliation, Wright called for attention to those outside the vortex and for a different calculation of significance. The same plea might be made in the name of restoring balance to a skewed historical canon.

The chief difference between mainstream history and reconciling history will be in calculations of significance. Mainstream history might employ a number of tests of significance, chief among them significance as understood by historical contemporaries and significance as measured by effect on the future; reconciling history will judge significance by the usefulness of an episode or character for modern reconciling purposes. The results are likely to be divergent if not diametrically opposed, and again Whitley Stokes illustrates the difference. There are sound reasons why mainstream history should take account of Stokes, but the final verdict is likely to be that Stokes was a bit player on the stage of history. By the standards of reconciling history, however, Stokes was a giant. These differing judgments need not be in conflict, they are simply the results of different tests of significance.

If historians may pursue reconciling history with integrity, they are certainly under no obligation to do so. Historians may in fact have specific reasons not to practice reconciling history. One might be a statement of priorities: with no hostility toward reconciliation or reconciling history, historians may judge that their time is better spent in other pursuits. Pragmatically, historians may calculate that one more analysis of some much-studied character or movement is more likely to bring professional advancement and public acclaim than an equally well done account of an obscure character of primarily reconciling significance – for career purposes, Charles Stuart Parnell is likely to trump Whitley Stokes every time. Politically, historians may dissent from the particular set of judgments that led Wright to advocate reconciliation in Northern Ireland. They may believe instead that the ascendancy of a particular political agenda – nationalist, unionist, or whatever – is a better goal than reconciliation, or a precondition of reconciliation.

In fact if historians could be said to have any obligations at all in relation to Northern Ireland, it might only be to ensure that any position they advocate is as carefully thought through as was Wright's. Assessing the prospects and conditions for peace was central to Wright's academic work, as furthering peace was central to his life. In 'Reconciling the Histories', Wright summarized his position as believing that reconciliation, while facing formidable and perhaps insurmountable barriers, is the best chance for peace. The alternatives would be victory or separation, and of these he says, 'victories would not be final and the intensified separation would not dispel the antagonism.'[66] The practical alternatives to reconciliation run from civil war at worst, to more of the low-grade but persistent violence that characterized most of the last thirty years, to a bare cessation of military operations that hardly deserves the name of peace. Historians who share Wright's analysis could contribute to the work of reconciliation.

* * *

To allow the possibility of pursuing reconciling relevance in history does not make it clear exactly what that relevance might be or how it can be appropriated. Pursuing the example of Whitley Stokes, we can in one sense identify a Stokes for everyone. The nationalist can point to Stokes's rejection of the union, desire for Irish independence, and passionately Irish identity, while the unionist can cite Stokes's position in the yeomanry and his rejection of republican violence; the evangelical can highlight Stokes's advocacy of a campaign to convert Catholics, while the ecumenist can embrace Stokes's tolerant spirit and insistence on avoiding doctrinal religious polemics. And on and on: there is a Stokes for the Irish language enthusiast, for the theologically heterodox, and even for the supporter of beleaguered Dublin Zoo – Stokes was the driving force behind its establishment in 1833. Wright said of 'potentially redeeming moments', 'once they become debating points, they lose their reconciling possibilities.'[67] The dynamics of potentially redeeming moments may be a little less fragile than Wright believed, but his point is essentially true, and it applies to Stokes.

In addition to the divisible Stokes, there is the Stokes who is inconvenient, even embarrassing, for modern reconciling purposes. For an obvious example, Stokes's zealous advocacy of converting Catholics does not fit the modern reconciliation agenda. By contextualizing his evangelistic hopes and pointing out their internal inconsistencies, I diminished or dismissed their relevance for today, which has the effect of making Stokes more palatable to modern tastes. Is this good history or a case of the distorting effect of 'preexisting reconciling purpose'? Another example. Stokes was generally an orthodox believer, but his christology was Arian, which could well have the effect of lessening his appeal to modern evangelicals who might otherwise be intrigued and challenged by Stokes. The absence of reference to his Arianism in this essay is due to pressure of space, not to any desire to conceal. But if I had explicated his theology, I would have put his Arianism in the context of his general orthodoxy; I would have emphasized the mildness of his Arianism, the absence of philosophical roots for it, the irony of its emergence from his firmly Protestant biblicism. And yet, however I might relativize and play down his Arianism, it may have been important enough to him that he needed to leave his

Trinity fellowship for reasons of conscience.[68] Would my approach be sound historical contextualizing or distortion for reconciling purposes? The root issue at stake is how to do full and simultaneous justice to the standards of professional history and the purposes of reconciling history. This tension will be the constant companion of anyone attempting reconciling history.

The problems represented by the divisible Stokes and the inconvenient Stokes will never be resolved by constant equations or foolproof techniques. While recognizing the priority of art over science in these matters, however, at least one principle can be articulated: if reconciling history's ultimate purposes are to be served, the mainstream, academic emphasis on respecting the gap between past and present can never be sacrificed for the apparent benefit of reconciling history's need for relevance. Applied to the divisible Stokes, this will mean that no simple transfer to the present of Stokes's programmes and positions can be considered. What may successfully cross the gap between past and present is Stokes's general approach rather than his particular programmes, the spirit behind his strategies rather than their specific content. With this principle in mind, it remains to suggest briefly some of the areas in which Stokes's example might be of use to modern reconciling purpose.

Wright gave only one specific example of what he anticipated the results of reconciling history might be: 'to find episodes that demonstrate the difference between knowing national conflict is a malignancy and mistaking it for a righteous cause'.[69] To read Stokes's *Projects for Re-establishing the Internal Peace and Tranquillity of Ireland* is to realize how deeply he felt and understood the malignancy of national conflict. It was this awareness that guided his course through the 1790s, his response to the rebellion of 1798, the reform programme he advocated in its aftermath, and the preoccupations of the remainder of his career. It was also the chief and stark difference between Stokes and Tone. If Tone understood the malignancy of national conflict at all, his course of action reveals his willingness to gamble that it was only a minor, surface tumour, a price well worth paying in pursuit of the righteous cause of breaking the English connection, and apparently with no significant lasting consequences once the righteous cause should be attained. Their differing judgments about the meaning and effects of national conflict were of vast consequence then, and they are scarcely less important now.

The typical mistake of those who recoil from revolution is to believe that the whole malignancy of national conflict lies in revolutionary violence, and consequently the counter-violence of the state becomes the solution to national conflict. Stokes is of reconciling significance because he knew that state violence had no such healing power. By his participation in the militia he clearly, if reluctantly, lived out a judgment that state violence was necessary to check revolutionary violence. His analysis in *Projects* demonstrates, however, that he knew state violence had only provided a temporary check to national conflict, not a cure. His projects were designed to reach the deep sources of malignancy, which remained intact. Today as then, state violence, whatever about its restraining function, has no power to touch the diseased core from which national conflict issues.

In the context of a twentieth-century crisis, W. B. Yeats wrote,
The best lack all conviction, while the worst
Are full of passionate intensity.[70]

In any crisis this contrast between the best and the worst results almost inevitably from the power of the vortex of antagonism to define who is significant: 'those who can both threaten violence and control the threat simultaneously'. Those we regard as the best may be powerful, significant people in placid times, but when the dynamics of conflict hold sway, they may well stand back from the vortex and its violence, thereby removing themselves from significance; the worst are more than willing to play the game of violence and threat, thereby acquiring the mantle of significance. For many of the best, torpor is the natural state when engulfed in a vortex of antagonism. Stokes was by the reckoning of his peers among the best, and he stepped outside the vortex and refused to act according to its definition of significance. Had he stopped there, slumping into passivity, his story would simply be poignant. In *Projects*, however, Stokes developed an implicit counter-definition of significance and an explicit programme for acting on it, which gives him exceptional significance for reconciliation purposes. *Projects* revealed one of the best full of passionate intensity in a time of crisis, a rare and worthy example for the best in every conflict situation.

Because Stokes, a patriotic man in a violent age, had so low an opinion of what violence could achieve, his patriotism took on a peculiar cast. We see in Stokes no high-flying rhetoric, no vigorous defence of his side's rights or privileges, no triumphal declaration of his side's superiority, no celebration of using and suffering violence for his side's cause. Instead we find a patriotism grounded in a desire to be of practical service to all the people of his nation, especially to those who have been on the opposite side of the recent conflagration; we find a man who, when he thinks about peace for his country, turns immediately to consider the welfare of the poorest in his society. Such an orientation is as rare and urgently needed now as it was then. Beside this kind of practical patriotism, any other looks shallow and shabby.

Because Stokes understood so clearly the malignancy of national conflict, he was willing to subordinate deeply felt political and religious goals to what he called 'the great object, the peace of the country'. Stokes was a strong supporter of Irish independence, yet he designed his programme for peace to be 'so completely unconnected with these political changes [union or independence], that whatever becomes of them, or whatever arrangements may take place, these measures which I speak of deserve some attention.'[71] Similarly, Stokes deeply desired the conversion of Catholics to Protestantism, and ironically it is here, where he is apparently most at odds with modern reconciling purpose, where he is perhaps most relevant. Because his Protestantism was centrally important to him, the conversion of Catholics was also important, and yet this was a goal he would pursue without a trace of coercion and with a ready willingness to settle for what he regarded as a secondary good – the diffusion of religious knowledge and harmony between Catholics and Protestants – should his primary goal prove unattainable. Northern Ireland has been bedeviled by unnegotiable political and religious goals. Should any substantial number of people take on a Stokes-like commitment to the peace of the country, accompanied by a similarly relativizing effect on ultimate goals, it would be an enormous asset for public life. It may even be a necessary condition of peace.

Stokes also points the way forward for reconciliation with his insistence that 'nothing but mutual forgiveness can save Ireland.'

Although forgiveness is ordinarily regarded as a peculiarly religious virtue, it is also essential to every society and all politics. The root biblical meaning of forgiveness is 'to let go', and without some mechanism for letting go of old grievances, every set of relationships, whether a marriage, a community, or a nation, will eventually collapse or explode. The Jewish philosopher Hannah Arendt has identified the political relevance of forgiveness, and her point applies equally to repentance: uniquely, these are reactions which retain something of the character of an initial action and therefore offer the possibility of injecting a fresh impulse into a situation characterised by automatic reaction.[72] Any hope for a genuine, lasting peace in Northern Ireland will probably demand some fresh, imaginative gestures, both small scale and large. The language of forgiveness and repentance need not be used – probably should not be used – but forgiveness and repentance it will be.

Much more might be added, but what has been said will suggest the general way in which Stokes might be relevant for reconciliation. As I write in 1998, we live in a moment not unlike the time when Stokes wrote his *Projects*. The violence has mostly stopped, but no one is guaranteeing that it is gone for good, and competing programmes for making a peace out of ceasefires abound. What Stokes offers in such circumstances is only an example, but it is a significant example: of one who refused to accept the logic of the vortex of antagonism, seized the opportunity of an end to violence to proclaim the things that make for peace, understood that the necessary changes would cut deep and take a long time, and subordinated – without abandoning – his preferred, specific political and religious outcomes to 'the great object, the peace of the country'. In this should be inspiration and courage for modern reconcilers. Reflecting on a story of possible reconciling significance, Wright admitted, 'for people today convinced of the uncomplicated righteousness of either unionism or nationalism, they will find nothing in the story ... to shake their conviction.'[73] The same is true of Whitley Stokes. Perhaps, however, the time has come when Stokes might be found interesting, even significant.

Notes:

1. Frank Wright, 'Reconciling the Histories: Protestant and Catholic in Northern Ireland', in Alan Falconer, ed.., *Reconciling Memories* (Dublin: Columba Press, 1988), 68.
2. Ibid., 69.
3. Ibid., 71.
4. Ibid., 70.
5. Ibid., 69.
6. Ibid., 68.
7. Ibid., 70.
8. Ibid., 71.
9. Ibid., 72.
10. Ibid., 71.
11. Ibid., 83.
12. Ibid.
13. Ronan Fanning, '"The Great Enchantment": Uses and Abuses of Modern Irish History', in Ciaran Brady, ed.., *Interpreting Irish History: The Debate on Historical Revisionism, 1938-1994* (Blackrock, Co. Dublin, 1994), 156-7; first published in James Dooge, ed., *Ireland and the Contemporary World: Essays in Honour of Garret Fitzgerald* (Dublin, 1988).
14. Brendan Bradshaw, 'Nationalism and Historical Scholarship in Modern Ireland', in Brady, ed., *Interpreting Irish History*, 212; first published in *Irish Historical Studies*, vol. 26 (1988-9).
15. Séamus Deane, 'Wherever Green is Read', in Máirín Ní Dhonnchadha and Theo Dorgan, eds., *Revising the Rising* (Derry, 1991), 101.
16. Paul Bew, 'Interview: "Ceasefire in the Academy"?', *History Ireland*, vol. 2, no. 4 (Winter 1994), 14.
17. Wright, 'Reconciling the Histories', 76-82.
18. For a much fuller account of Stokes in the 1790s, see Joseph Liechty, 'Irish Evangelicalism, Trinity College Dublin, and the Mission of the Church of Ireland at the End of the Eighteenth Century' (Ph.D. thesis, National University of Ireland, Maynooth, 1987), 390-469.
19. Theobald Wolfe Tone, *Life of Theobald Wolfe Tone*, ed. by William Theobald Wolfe Tone (2 vols, Washington, D. C., 1826), vol. 1, 41-2.
20. Ibid., 41.
21. William Drennan to Samuel McTier, [early Nov.] 1791 and [ca. 9 Nov. 1791], in D. A. Chart, ed., *The Drennan Letters* (Belfast, 1931), 62, 65-6.
22. Thomas Collins's lists of United Irish members, MSS 620/20/36, 620/54/12, 620/54/18, Rebellion Papers, State Paper Office of Ireland.
23. R. B. McDowell, ed., 'United Irish Plans of Parliamentary Reform, 1793', *Irish Historical Studies*, vol. 3, no. 9 (March 1942), 39-59.
24. Matthew Young, account of 1798 visitation, MS 1203, Trinity College Dublin Library, folio 40.
25. Ibid., folio 45.
26. John William Stubbs, *The History of the University of Dublin, From Its Foundation to the End of the Eighteenth Century* (Dublin, London, 1889), 295.

27. Thomas Prior, account of 1798 Trinity visitation, MS 3373, Trinity College Dublin Library.
28. Young, folios 47, 49, 44.
29. Blacker's journal, quoted in Constantia Maxwell, *A History of Trinity College Dublin, 1591-1892* (Dublin, 1946), 270.
30. Stubbs, *The University of Dublin,* 296-7; Young, folios 8-9.
31. John Edward Walsh, *Sketches of Ireland Sixty Years Ago* (Dublin, 1847), 164.
32. Prior, MS 3373; Young, folios 8-9, 30.
33. Walsh, *Sketches,* 164.
34. Prior, MSS 3373, 3363; Young, folios 9, 11, 39, 40, 42-7, 50.
35. Prior, MS 3363.
36. Young, folio 50.
37. Ibid.; Prior, MS 3363.
38. Young, folio 51.
39. Young, folios 77-8.
40. Tone, Life, vol. 2, 489.
41. Whitley Stokes, *Projects for Re-establishing the Internal Peace and Tranquillity of Ireland* (Dublin, 1799), 1.
42. Ibid., 2.
43. Ibid.
44. Ibid., 35.
45. Roy Foster, *Modern Ireland, 1600-1972* (London, 1988), 276.
46. Stokes, *Projects,* 50.
47. Ibid., 25.
48. Ibid., 43.
49. Ibid., 44.
50. 'There were present at that season some that told him of the Galilaeans, whose blood Pilate had mingled with their sacrifices. And Jesus answering said unto them, Suppose ye that these Galilaeans were sinners above all the Galilaeans, because they suffered such things? I tell you, Nay: but, except ye repent, ye shall all likewise perish. Or those eighteen, upon whom the tower in Siloam fell, and slew them, think ye that they were sinners above all men that dwelt in Jerusalem? I tell you, Nay: but, except ye repent, ye shall all likewise perish.' (Luke 13:1-5, King James Version)
51. Stokes, *Projects,* 44.
52. Ibid., 43.
53. Ibid.
54. Ibid., 44.
55. Ibid.
56. Ibid.
57. Ibid., 45.
58. Ibid., 48.
59. Ibid.
60. Ibid., 51.
61. Ibid.
62. Ibid.
63. Wright, 'Reconciling the Histories', 82.

64. Ibid., 71.
65. Ibid., 68.
66. Ibid., 72; for Wright's most detailed analysis of Northern Ireland, see Frank Wright, *Northern Ireland: A Comparative Analysis* (Dublin, 1987).
67. Wright, 'Reconciling the Histories', 79.
68. Unattributed legal opinion concerning whether Stokes can remain a lay fellow while not attending chapel, n. d., Mun P/1/1162, Trinity College Dublin Library.
69. Wright, 'Reconciling the Histories', 71.
70. W. B. Yeats, 'The Second Coming', *Yeats's Poems,* ed. A. Norman Jeffares (Dublin, 1989), 294.
71. Stokes, *Projects,* 2.
72. Hannah Arendt, *The Human Condition* (Chicago, 1958), 88.
73. Wright, 'Reconciling the Histories', 82.

The Reconciling Power of Forgiveness

Alan D. Falconer

How can I turn this wheel that turns my life
Create another hand to move this hand
Not moved by me, who am not the mover,
Nor, though I love and hate, the lover,
The hater? Loves and hates are thrust
Upon me by the acrimonious dead,
The buried thesis, long since rusted knife,
Revengeful dust.
…
Then how do I stand?
How can I here remake what there made me
And makes and remakes me still?
Set a new mark? Circumvent history?

This poem, 'The Wheel' by Edwin Muir, reflects a theme common among poets of his and of a previous generation.[1] W. B. Yeats, in his poem 'Vacillation', points to the way in which human beings are bound to their past and, above all, are unable to break out of the cycle of guilt at their own sins of omission and commission.[2] This same sense of impotence, conveyed by a cyclic sense of history, is central also to the writings of W. H. Auden and T. S. Eliot.[3] A similar frustration and anomie is experienced by members of the different communities in Ireland in the face of what Seamus Heaney has called the 'orphaned memories' of the different traditions. The different communities live memories without context which will always stay with them.[4]

The sense of impotence in the face of the past is matched by an equally powerful sense of impotence to fashion the future. In our contemporary societies, in the light of the seemingly intractable problems of famine in Africa and of economic underdevelopment

elsewhere, which are increasingly perceived as resulting from a lack
of will power by governments to tackle a problem which is capable
of solution, a strong feeling of powerlessness has arisen amongst
those working for a solution. A similar sense of impotence with
regard to the future is evident in the reactions to the nuclear question.
Citizens of European countries especially are asking whether
humankind must inevitably repeat the mistakes of previous generations. Edwin Muir's poem 'The Wheel' takes this sense of impotence
up when it speaks of 'Nothing can come of history but history.'

While 'powerlessness' is a constant theme of Edwin Muir's poetry,
the poet refuses to offer no more than a description of 'anomie' or
'angst'.[5] As in his other poems, Muir suggests in 'The Wheel' that
the cycle, the impotence, can be and has been broken. The poem
ends:

> Unless a grace
> Come of itself to wrap our souls in peace
> Between the turning leaves of history and make
> Ourselves ourselves, winnow the grudging grain,
> And take
> From that which made us that which will make us again.

In his other poems, this grace is evidently the activity of God in
Jesus Christ who frees humankind 'to make us each for each/And in
our spirit whole.'[6] Power to break the cycle, the impotence, is proclaimed to be the work of Jesus Christ, above all in making new and
in freeing humankind from the burden of the past and giving hope
for the future.

This perception of the poet of the importance of Jesus Christ is
echoed in the early writing of Hannah Arendt. She isolates two
major elements of the human condition as imprisoning people,
namely 'the predicament of irreversibility' and that of 'unpredictability'.[7] In this context, Arendt speaks of Jesus of Nazareth as the
'discoverer of the role of forgiveness', a discovery which, she asserts,
enables human beings to be freed from the predicament of irreversibility, from the constriction of past history and action, while
the category of 'promise' frees human beings to be able to act in the
future. For any disciple of Jesus of Nazareth, these two categories of
forgiveness and promise are essential, and are seen to belong to the
story of Jesus. For Edwin Muir and Hannah Arendt, out of their

analysis of the human condition as one of irreversibility and unpredictability, emerges what might best be called 'a proclamation' of the power of Christ, a power which is no less than the ability to change a situation or relationship. Poet and anthropologist indicate the importance of power and the paradigm of power in Jesus of Nazareth.

But Christians, while acknowledging in theory the significance of Jesus for understanding and exercising power, have often retreated into a cycle of inability. This contrast between theory and practice is stated succinctly by Monika Hellwig:

> We call Jesus Saviour of the world, and yet we constantly act on the assumption that the world as such (the world of human affairs, the 'real' world) cannot be saved but is doomed to perpetuate injustices and oppression, frustrating conditions of work, inauthentic and repressive interpersonal relations, dishonesty in the conduct of political and economic affairs, ruthless selfishness on the part of sovereign nations, conflicting expectations and destructive values. In our liturgies and our hymns, we hail Jesus as Prince of Peace, but in practice we seem to restrict the peace that we expect to find through him to peace of heart or peace of mind, while assuming that nations (including those that call themselves Christian) will continue to make war, to stockpile armaments and to kill for the national interest.[8]

Christians, as well as other members of the human family, have found themselves unable to embrace this power. Even at the level of reflection, theologians have either been reluctant to speak about power at all, or have spoken of 'power' only in negative terms, seeing power as antithetical to Christianity.

Among Protestant writers, there has been a tendency by some to equate the manifestation of power with sin, thereby suggesting that the Christian, if he is to be a follower of Christ, should renounce or eschew power. Rather strikingly, Emil Brunner does not treat the subject in his major works; neither does Otto Weber in his stimulating *Foundations of Dogmatics*.[10] Indeed as recently as the 1980 Melbourne meeting of the World Conference of Mission and Evangelism, a unit of the World Council of Churches, the churches were defining their task as that of renouncing power and becoming powerless.[11] While there have been notable exceptions, like Paul

Tillich and Karl Rahner,[12] the tendency in theological reflection has largely been to suggest that power is antithetical to Christianity, or at best a reality that has to be tolerated.

This tendency amongst theologians reinforces a cyclic view of history and gives the impression that change for human beings is not an option. Paul Tillich has perceptively noted, 'The confusion of the concepts (power and force or compulsion) has prevented a meaningful doctrine of power.'[13]

This confusion is perhaps understandable as a reaction to the concept of power adumbrated by some nineteenth century thinkers.

Nietzsche's answer to both the Enlightenment notion of progress and the sense of impotence of those who felt unable to be subjects of their own history was to stress the need for an intensified will to live, 'even to the extent of an unconditional will to power and to supremacy.'[14] Here power is seen to be a positive value as long as that power leads to 'my' supremacy. There is no analysis of the nature or modes of power. All that is emphasized is the importance of power in helping 'me' to grow or develop.

Nietzsche's colleague and friend, Jacob Burckhardt, reflecting on the results of the exercise of power in history, declared it evil:

And power is evil in itself, no matter who exercises it. It has no permanency but is a lust, and for that very reason insatiable, hence it is in itself unhappy and must accordingly lead to unhappy results ... Political authority takes it for granted that its primary task is to assert and increase itself, and power does not better man one whit.[15]

Here Burckhardt, in his analysis of events in history, is struck by the fact that power has been used in such a way that men and women have been subjected to the will of others. While a few people have exercized power, the many have been powerless. Yet once again no real analysis of the concept of power is offered by Burckhardt. Paul Tillich's charge that theologians have confused power and coercion applies equally well to these two important nineteenth century thinkers.

However, the fundamental meaning of the concept of power is 'to have the ability'. The New Testament word for power (dunamis) means 'to be able', 'to have the possibility to do', implying both capacity to do good and to do harm. Indeed the application of the term 'concept' to 'power' is misleading. Power is a word for actualization, as Paul Tillich noted:

> Power is real only in its actualisation, in the encounter with other bearers of power and in the ever changing balance of power which is the result of these encounters.[16]

Power is the capacity to initiate the new in relationship. Power can be creative, rather than destructive. Theologically, therefore, it is not adequate to speak of the renunciation of power, or of powerlessness. A closer examination of the uses of power is needed. The New York psychotherapist, Rollo May, in his book *Power and Innocence*, offers precisely this analysis.

Modes of Exercise of Power

An essential facet of a human being's nature is that he or she has the possibility to grow and develop – physically, mentally, and spiritually.[17] Human beings continually come to a knowledge of themselves. There is no point at which it is possible for anyone to give a comprehensive and final answer to the question, 'Who am I?' The individual is continually coming to self-knowledge through his or her contact with other persons. To be able to make his own self-affirmation in relation to others, however, requires strength or what Paul Tillich called 'the courage to be'.[18] This self-assertion is made in the context of the self-affirmation of others; it is in human relationships that we come to some sense of our own significance.

Rollo May, in his work *Power and Innocence*, relates this idea of self-significance to the exercise of power. These are so intertwined that he writes:

> A great deal of human life can be seen as the conflict between power on the one side (i.e., effective ways of influencing others, achieving in interpersonal relations the sense of the significance of one's self) and powerlessness on the other.[19]

May goes on to point five levels of power, present as potentialities in every human being's life:[20] (i) the power to be – the fact that an infant's actions elicit responses; (ii) self-affirmation; (iii) self-assertion – the assertion of our self-affirmation in situations of resistance; (iv) aggression – this arises when self-affirmation is blocked and manifests itself as the taking of someone else's territory for one-

self; and (v) violence – when aggression is ineffective. It is important to note that all these features, which are inherent in each of us if
we are to come to self-significance, are in fact terms of response to
relationships with others. Thus self-affirmation is seen within the
context of interpersonal relationships. The last three of May's
categories, however, are all responses to a situation of threat – i.e. to
a situation where the individual sees or senses that power is being
exercised against him or her so that they cannot affirm their own
being.

Rollo May continues his analysis by going on to point to those
uses of power which, when used by others, can either stifle or aid
the individual in the attempt to affirm the sense of self-worth. First,
those manifestations of the exercise of power which stifle the sense
of significance in other human beings and which, if they are constantly exercised, can elicit the response of aggression or violence.
Here May stresses three different modes of the exercise of power
equivalent to what Erich Fromm termed 'domination power',[21] viz.
exploitative, manipulative or competitive modes. By the use of any
or all of these, human beings in their desire to assert their own self-
significance, and the significance of their values, opinions, life-
styles and feelings, do so in such a way that the other person in the
encounter is diminished and demeaned. The other has to do what I
want him or her to do, and, to ensure this, I will manipulate a situation so that he or she can only act in a way which accords with my
needs. It is very important to emphasize that it does not in fact
make a lot of difference whether this sense of being made to feel less
than human is in fact based on a true perception of the situation or
not. The important point is that someone feels that they are being
made to feel less than human, i.e. that they are being denied the
opportunity to grow and develop in the way which they perceive to
be essential. If they feel that power is being used against them from
the same source continually, then they experience fear or anxiety in
relation to that source, whether it be an individual, group, bureau-
cracy or other states. Power, then, can be used to demean other
human beings. Power can be used in a destructive way. This form
of the encounter between human beings, individually or in groups,
might be described as 'destructive conflict'.

But power can also be used in a creative or constructive way.
Rollo May differentiates two different modes of this positive exer-

cise of power, equivalent to what Erich Fromm termed 'potent power',[22] viz. nutrient and integrative power. Nutrient power, May suggests, is power for the other person: power exercised on behalf of another, e.g. a normal parent's care for his or her children. Integrative power is power with the other person, i.e. standing alongside the other, helping him, her or them to assert their own sense of self-significance.[23]

Although the above analysis has been conducted largely in terms of the needs of the individual and of the way power may be exercized in relation to individuals, Rollo May emphasises that this analysis is applicable also to what might be termed 'corporate consciousness'. A group, society, state or region may feel that power is consciously being exercised against them, whether or not it is in fact. If this feeling persists, and if the source of the power loss is the same, then fear and anxiety emerge, and a variety of aggressive or violent responses become likely towards the source of the fear. But equally important is the fact that power can be used in such a way that groups, societies, states, or regions can be helped 'to be'.

May's analysis of the different modes of the exercise of power makes it difficult to adopt a rather too facile stance which points to the renunciation of power. All of us as individuals, groups and societies do exercise power. The question posed by that fact is rather, what mode of the exercise of power is to be employed? While all of us in fact exercise power in a destructive way and also in a creative way, how are we to determine a coherent way of acting?[24] Undoubtedly for some, the principle of coherence will be 'self interest,' as stressed in the Brandt Report on economic development even if that principle is to be modified to 'enlightened self interest'.[25] For the Christian churches, however, the principle of coherence must be related to the activity of God. What might theology have to say on reflecting on the analysis of power which we have undertaken?

Theological Reflection on the Exercise of Power

Power is capable of being exercised in both positive and negative ways. The portrayal of God's activity, especially in the Bible, tends towards an emphasis on the positive modes of exercise of power.

In creation, God acts in such a way that the creatures can respond freely to each other and to him. In a phrase made prominent by John Macquarrie, what is most typical of God is his 'letting-be', his conferring of being, his self-giving to the beings. This letting-be is both his creativity and his love.[26] Macquarrie goes on to emphasize that this 'letting-be' is not to be understood as a standing off from someone or something, but is a positive work of 'enabling to be'. He suggests that we are to understand 'letting' as 'empowering' and 'be' as 'enjoying the maximal range of being that is open to the particular being concerned'.[27] 'Letting be' therefore would be 'empowering for life in its fullness.'

This 'letting be' which is a positive exercise of power is described by Geddes MacGregor, the American theologian, as sacrificial love. The divine power is

> the power of sacrificial love. God does not control his creatures; he graciously lets them be ... Not only does God bring creatures into being to let them be; he creatively restores whatever seeks such restoration, so that the redeemed might indeed well be called a new creation, that is, a re-creation.[28]

While the activity of God as depicted throughout the Bible and Christian history may be characterised as a divine-human encounter in which God empowers human beings to be, such an activity is above all seen in Jesus Christ.

The Incarnation shows forth the being of God 'with us'. In emphasising the title 'Emmanuel' – God with us – in respect of Jesus, Matthew draws not only on an Isaiahaic expectation,[29] but also on an awareness of a God who travelled with the people, confronting them through specific conflicts.[30] Through these conflicts he widened their horizons so that they, the people, may have a fuller relationship with God and other people. Through this divine-human encounter, the people of God were reminded of their Covenant with God in which God empowered them to be. Through this divine-human encounter, the people of God were brought under judgement for exercising power in a way which tried to coerce, exploit or manipulate others. The prophets, for example, charge the people with this, precisely because it is destructive of relationships within and between communities, and does not reflect the way God has let them be, as is evident in the writings of Amos, Hosea, Ezekiel and Jeremiah, amongst others.

Above all, the Christian community saw this activity of God empowering people in Jesus Christ. The Letter to the Ephesians is a thoughtful articulation of the way in which the early church saw that Christ had enabled diverse individuals and groups 'to be', drawing them into a positive relationship with each other and with God. This is portrayed in the development of the concept 'peace' throughout the letter. The Ephesian letter is, however, no more than a reflection on the being of Jesus, as far as that can be discerned. In the gospels, Jesus empowers human beings, enabling them 'to be'. He frees people from their pasts so that they can enter positive relationships with each other, e.g. Zacchaeus. To take another example, the people in general, because their history inhibited any relationship of positive worth with the Samaritans, are freed 'to be' when a Samaritan is placed as the example of who is being most faithful to God in the Parable of 'The Good Samaritan'. By his use of 'integrative' power – standing alongside people empowering them – helping them 'to be' – Jesus provoked conflict. His very conduct acted as a judgement on those who sought to enter relationships by trying to control, manipulate or coerce people in such a way that the other is destroyed. Because of the way Jesus exercised power he was deemed to be a threat, and was therefore ridiculed, arraigned and eventually crucified.[31]

In this activity of liberating and empowering, the forgiveness of sins was a crucial factor. It was above all though forgiveness that Jesus of Nazareth seems to have liberated men and women from the burden of their pasts. I do not suggest that the past becomes unimportant, but that the past is no longer a burden. I shall explore this further in a later section. In telling the story of Jesus of Nazareth, a central place is given by the gospel writers to his activity in forgiving. From the very call of repentance by John the Baptist to the petition from the Cross, 'Father, forgive them', the forgiveness of sin appears as a leitmotif in the gospel, to such an extent that, as we have noted, Hannah Arendt attributes the discovery of the role of forgiveness in the realm of human affairs to Jesus of Nazareth. It is through this forgiveness that Jesus stands alongside men and women empowering them to be. Forgiveness is an act of 'integrative power' enabling the other to be, enabling the other to take responsibility for himself or herself.

In exploring the relationship between forgiveness and the modes of power, it is instructive to note those exercises of power which Jesus of Nazareth seems to have rejected. In his study, *The Forgiveness of Sins,* the English novelist, poet and theological writer, Charles Williams, points to the importance of the temptations of Jesus as the renunciation of 'destructive' uses of power.[32] God can only be loved and glorified by free people. Manipulation, coercion and competition constrain people to act and think what another demands that they act and think. If Jesus rejects the destructive modes of the exercise of power, then he equally rejects the 'nutrient' mode of the exercise of power. Jesus does not seem to take decisions for others, nor to think on behalf of others.

The very style of Jesus' teaching in parables requires the listener to respond, to think the matter through and act accordingly. Such a style of teaching is, of course, conflictual, jolting the listener out of concern with self and the maintenance of the *status quo*. The healing activity of Jesus also aims at empowering people to take responsibility for their lives in such a way that they are not bound by the infirmities of their pasts. The exercise of 'integrative power' is above all characterized by Jesus' activity in forgiveness. Through the forgiveness of sin the other is freed from the burden of the past and is empowered to take responsibility for his or her own actions. Hannah Arendt has written perceptively of this.

> Only through this constant release from what they do, can men (and women) remain free agents, only by constant willingness to change their minds and start again can they be trusted with so great a power as that to begin something new.[33]

This release which leads to freedom involves the subject embracing responsibility for past and future actions. The classic example of this in the gospels is the story of Zacchaeus who takes responsibility for his past by acts of restitution and who seems to embrace responsibility for his future thought and action, although this is in fact only implied by his encounter with Jesus. In this exercise of power Jesus enables Zacchaeus to become a free agent. This forgiveness is called 'a power, an energy'[34] by Charles Williams.

In exploring this understanding of the forgiveness of sin as an exercise of integrative power, it is important to expose the effect of sin. Sin basically denotes a broken relationship. By a hasty word, lack of consideration or sensitivity, we harm other people, even people whom we like or love. Often we exercise power over people, manipulating them so that they will think or do what we want them to think or do. At times we give people no option but to act according to our needs and expectations rather than their own. Through this we do not take the other seriously. The effect of this is that neither of us is able to be ourselves, to be free. The effect of this sin is that we carry round a certain burden of guilt with us. Every time we meet the other, there is an awareness of the way we parted at the last encounter. We are not free to develop the relationship. Either we avoid the person because we remember how things were between us on a previous occasion, or we feel free to develop the relationship only in the way it had been previously; thus we continue to try to manipulate. We are not free to let the relationship be one of mutuality.

This account of the effect of sin applies not only in the relationship between individuals, but also that between groups and also to relationship with God. The history of humankind's dealing with God, as seen in scripture and the history of the church, is riddled with the attempts by men, women and societies to manipulate God and tie God down to human caricatures and stereotypes. The history of the dealings of human communities with one another is no less destructive. Irish history throws up countless examples of the way in which one community tried to control the other communities by manipulation or coercion. Such an exercise of power was either condoned or at least not condemned by the respective Christian traditions. There was little 'empowering' in this spiral of alienation. Both the manipulator and the manipulated, the oppressor and the oppressed, have become imprisoned by the ensuing relationship, and carry the respective pain with them.

The forgiveness of sin, which is quite undeserved and unexpected, enables relationships to be freed from the burden of the past and to grow in a more wholesome way. As Hannah Arendt notes:

> Forgiving, in other words, is the only reaction which does not merely re-act but acts anew and unexpectedly, unconditioned by the act which provoked it and therefore freeing from its consequences both the one who forgives and the one who is forgiven.[35]

Forgiveness, then, is an exercise of power itself, which counteracts the destructive modes of the exercise of power and releases people to act anew. Such an exercise of power on the part of Jesus reflects his being-with-others.

It is this quality of Jesus' being-with-us which I think theological tradition has tried to characterise in 'kenotic christology'. While kenotic christology tended to imply that God gave up his Godness or divinity to act with human beings so that they might be empowered, it seems rather that this kenosis is in fact descriptive of the very being of God. I take it that this is precisely what John MacQuarrie, Geddes MacGregor and Paul Tillich are affirming with their starting points in the understanding of 'being', in trying to understand the nature of God as 'He Who Lets Be.' This is also what Jürgen Moltmann, with his starting point in the suffering of God, is trying to affirm.[36] Kenotic christology asserts that Jesus is 'He Who Lets us Be', empowering us so that we can enter relationships with each other and with God. Jesus acts with men and women in such a way that their response to him and others is free and in this activity of empowering others, he demonstrates his vulnerability. The life of Jesus is an affirmation of 'integrative power' – of being with men and women in the ambiguity of human life.

Towards the 'Reconciliation of Memories'

The implications of characterising forgiveness as 'integrative power' are enormous. The activity of forgiveness involves the partners of a relationship. Nobody can seek forgiveness on behalf of another. Nor can forgiveness be sought out of self-interest, as that would be another attempt at manipulating the relationship. Roger Schutz, prior of the Taizé Community, has written, 'You can never forgive out of self-interest, to change the other person. That would be a miserable calculation which has nothing to do with the free gift of love. You can only forgive because of Christ.'[37] The striking witness to the power of forgiveness which emerges so often from the pages of the diaries of so many Holocaust victims lies precisely in the fact that they enunciate forgiveness. No one can do it on their behalf. It is their relationships which have been fractured. They take responsibility for trying to create a new beginning.[38]

For those, then, who have perceived the unique importance of the forgiveness of sin offered by Jesus of Nazareth, and who stand in the event of Jesus Christ, they themselves need to become a community of the forgiveness of sin, as a sign or sacrament of that activity of Jesus of Nazareth. The Church is called to live the liberating memory of Jesus Christ.

Forgiveness and Memory

The importance of forgiveness for a proper celebration of the appropriation and reconciliation of memories has been emphasized by Dietrich Bonhoeffer. In his *Ethics* he wrote,

> If any man tries to escape guilt in responsibility, he detaches himself from the ultimate reality of human existence, and what is more he cuts himself off from the redeeming mystery of Christ's bearing guilt without sin and he has no share in the divine justification which lies upon this event.[39]

Forgiveness is to be a continuing process and activity. As John Patton notes, 'to have ongoing meaning any act of forgiveness cannot stand alone, but must be consistent with participation in an ongoing history.'[40] The process of forgiveness involves a number of stages. It involves an acknowledgement of the wrongdoing. Such an acknowledgement arises from listening to each other as we tell the story of the pain experienced by our communities, through which we stand with each other in solidarity and pain. Through the acknowledgement of the wrongdoing, responsibility is taken for creating and perpetuating the alienation of the communities. As responsibility is accepted, guilt is accepted. Such guilt is expressed through sorrow and through the commitment to change attitudes and behaviour, so that the destructive memories no longer determine contemporary attitudes and stances. The past itself cannot be changed. The acceptance of responsibility for perpetuating the memory of the past and allowing it to determine present relationships between communities creates a new situation. A new creation is born. But such a new creation requires the acceptance of a process of radical change.

One such example of this process at work is that undertaken by the United States Conference of Catholic Bishops in relation to the native American peoples. In 1992 they issued a statement on the occasion of the 500th anniversary of Christopher Columbus's arrival in America, entitled '1992: Time for Remembering, Reconciling and Committing Ourselves as a People'[41] in which they seek the forgiveness of the native American peoples for insensitivity to them, for the pain and violence inflicted, and the cultural dominance of the immigrants. They accepted the complicity of the church in this situation and took responsibility for phrasing anew the teaching of the history of these encounters. They also expressed their commitment to stand alongside the native American communities as they seek justice.

Costly reconciliation is the specific contribution of the churches to reconciliation in society. Reconciliation involves the process of forgiveness. It involves the self-critical reflection of the churches on their responsibility for the alienation of communities.

The churches, however, need to recover the importance of the process of forgiveness not only for their life in relation to community conflict, but also as they seek the unity of the church itself. The International Reformed-Roman Catholic Dialogue has sought to undertake a process of reconciling memories – through the hearing of the pain of the alienated communities and the acceptance of responsibility for creating communities-in-opposition. It has done so through the writing of the history of action, reaction and separation of the communities. It has articulated a common core confession of faith and seen different expressions of theology as different ways of trying to affirm the same theological insights. In this context it has then noted divisive issues which still need to be addressed. The Reformed-Mennonite International Commission went one step further, with an act of forgiveness at the battle sites at which the confrontation between the two communities took place. The importance of these dialogues lies in the common commitment to the search for the visible unity of the church as a direct contribution to the healing of communities, and challenges those who would seek to perpetuate divisions in church and society. Such dialogues make a direct contribution to the healing of divisions in society. The international dialogues, however, need to be seen as a spur for local churches to appropriate the insight and process of forgiveness.

We are called to a ministry of reconciliation – a ministry of self-emptying for the establishment of unity and *koinonia* as is evident in Jesus of Nazareth. Our calling is well phrased in the report of the

Fifth World Conference on Faith and Order in Santiago de Compostela:

> The dynamic process of *koinonia* involves the recognition of the complementarity of human beings. As individuals and communities, we are confronted by the others in their otherness, e.g. theologically, ethnically, culturally. *Koinonia* requires respect for the other and a willingness to listen to the other and to seek to understand them. In this process of dialogue, where each is changed in the encounter, there takes place the appropriation of the stories of action, reaction and separation whereby each has defined himself or herself in opposition to the other. The search for establishing *koinonia* involves appropriating the pain and hurt of the other and, through a process of individual and collective repentance, forgiveness and renewal, taking responsibility for that suffering. Confrontation with the other, individually and collectively, is always a painful process, challenging as it does our own lifestyle, convictions, piety and way of thinking. The encounter with the other in the search to establish the koinonia, grounded in God's gift, calls for a *kenosis* – a self-giving and a self-emptying. Such a *kenosis* arouses fear of loss of identity, and invites us to be vulnerable, yet such is no more than faithfulness to the ministry of vulnerability and death of Jesus as he sought to draw human beings into communion with God and each other. He is the pattern and patron of reconciliation which leads to *koinonia*. As individuals and communities, we are called to establish *koinonia* through a ministry of *kenosis*.[42]

Through a commitment to express *koinonia* in this costly way, I believe we will contribute to the healing of our divided societies and divided world. In so doing, we will be acting on a special insight of the Christian tradition, which has seen and experienced a power which alone can enable people to be, above all through the power of forgiveness, and which alone can herald the new. Thus the cycle of Edwin Muir's 'revengeful dust' is broken not by 'circumventing history', but by taking 'from that which made us that which will make us again'.

Notes:

A first draft of this paper was presented at the Oxford consultation of the Forgiveness and Politics project, associated with the British Council of Churches, July 1985.

1. Edwin Muir, *Collected Poems* (London: Faber, 1960), 105.
2. W.B. Yeats, 'Vacillation' in *The Poems,* ed. B. Finneran (Dublin: Gill and Macmillan, 1983), 251.
3. W.H. Auden, *For the Time Being* (London: Faber, 1945); T.S. Eliot, 'The Waste Land' in *Selected Poems* (London: Faber, 1954), 51ff. and 'East Coker' in his *Four Quartets* (London: Faber, 1959), 23ff. T.S. Eliot's 'Little Gidding', like Edwin Muir's poems, moves to a more theological affirmation as the way in which this cyclic pattern is broken.
4. Seamus Heaney, *Preoccupations: Selected Prose 1968-1978* (London: Faber, 1984), 21.
5. For 'anomie' see Max Scheler, *Resentiment* (New York: Schocken Books, 1972), 69f; for 'angst' see Soren Kierkegaard's writings.
6. Edwin Muir, 'The Annunciation', in *Collected Poems,* 117. The preoccupation of Muir with the theme of Journey, The Way, The Road, is also evidence of the possibility, for him, of change, movement, and power.
   A rather too brief acquaintance with Irish poetry suggests to me that this sense of the ability to move, or change, is largely absent. As far as I can see only the early sagas, and the writings of Patrick Kavanagh and Seamus Heaney, offer any vision of the ability to break with the past and shape the future. The cyclic constriction appears as the main theme of Brian Friel's play *Translations* (London: Faber, 1981).
7. Hannah Arendt, *The Human Condition* (Chicago: Chicago University Press, 1958), 236-47.
8. Monika Hellwig, 'Christology and Attitudes toward Social Structures' in *Above Every Name: The Lordship of Christ and Social Systems,* ed. Thomas E. Clarke (New York: Paulist, 1980), 13f.
9. Paul Tillich blames the Ritschlian school of theology for this as they contrasted the love of God with his power in such a way that power disappeared and God became identified with love in its ethical meaning. See his *Love, Power and Justice* (New York: Oxford University Press, 1954), llf.
10. Otto Weber, *Foundations of Dogmatics,* trans. Darrell Goder, 2 vols (Grand Rapids: Eerdmans, 1981).
11. Commission on World Mission and Evangelism, *Your Kingdom Come: Mission Perspectives* (Geneva: World Council of Churches, 1980).
12. Tillich, *Love, Power and Justice;* Karl Rahner, *Theology of Power* (Baltimore: 1966).
13. Tillich, *Love, Power and Justice,* 45.
14. Friedrich Nietzsche, *Werke III,* 468. The same motif is central to his *Thus Spoke Zarathustra* (Harmondsworth: Penguin, 1961).
15. Jacob Burckhardt, *Welgeschichtliche Betrachtungen,* 131, quoted and trans. by Jan Lochman in an unpublished lecture, 'Thine is the Power: The Power of God and the God of Power', 1.

16. Tillich, *Love, Power and Justice,* 41.

17. Cf. the work of Jean Piaget.

18. Paul Tillich, *The Courage To Be* (Glasgow: Collins Fontana, 1962).

19. Rollo May, *Power and Innocence* (Glasgow: Collins Fontana, 1976), 20f. The author is a psychotherapist in New York. At the 1982 Conference of the Catholic Theological Society of America, John Coleman, in a keynote address, gave a similar analysis of power, drawing also on the work of Rollo May. He defined power as the capacity to sustain a relationship – influencing and being influenced; giving and receiving, etc. *CTSA Proceedings* (1982), 1-14.

20. May, *Power and Innocence,* 40-45.

21. Erich Fromm, *The Fear of Freedom* (London: Routledge, Kegan Paul, 1960), 139; for a more delineated examination of aggressiveness see Erich Fromm, *The Anatomy of Human Destructiveness* (London: Jonathan Cape, 1974), 185-218 and the Epilogue.

22. Fromm, *The Fear of Freedom,* 139.

23. May, *Power and Innocence,* 105-110. Even with this positive category of nutrient power, however, it is possible that a destructive effect may occur. The exercise of nutrient power could lead to dependence or to paternalism – factors which Rollo May seems to leave out of account.

24. This ambivalence in the use of power also applies to Christians and the churches, as we take part in what Gregory Baum terms 'the ambiguity of Christianity', and what David Jenkins calls *The Contradiction of Christianity* (London: SCM, 1976).

25. See Willy Brandt (Chairman), *North-South: A Programme for Survival* (London: Pan Books, 1980), especially the chapter on 'Mutual Interests', 64-77a. Bill MacSweeney argues this as the principle of coherence for a nation's foreign policy; see 'Morality and Foreign Policy' in D. Keogh, ed., *Central America: Human Rights and U.S. Foreign Policy* (Cork: Cork University Press, 1985).

26. John MacQuarrie, *Principles of Christian Theology,* 2nd ed. (London: SCM, 1977), 209, 225.

27. Ibid., 348.

28. Geddes MacGregor, *He Who Lets Us Be: A Theology of Love* (New York: Seabury Press, 1975), 15.

29. Matthew 1:23. Isaiah 8:8, 10.

30. See my elaboration of this theme in 'Theological Reflection on Human Rights', *Understanding Human Rights: An Interdisciplinary and Interfaith Study,* ed. Alan D. Falconer (Dublin: The Irish School of Ecumenics, 1980).

31. In trying to enunciate the fact that Jesus seems to exercise integrative power, it is tempting to overlook those incidents in the gospels where Jesus is portrayed as using force. I do not feel that I have managed yet to integrate these conflicting ideas. In making the attempt to do so, however, I have found Paul Tillich's analysis of power and force in *Love, Power, and Justice* (45ff) to be helpful. Tillich notes that that which is forced must preserve its own identity, otherwise it is not so much forced as destroyed. Power, he asserts, may need compulsion but only to act as a stimulus for being. It seems to me that on

those occasions where Jesus is portrayed as exercising compulsion, it is to initiate a change so that the other might be freed from his or her own past in such a way that they can take responsibility for their own lives in the present.

32. Charles Williams, *The Forgiveness of Sin* (Grand Rapids: Eerdmans, 1984), 52ff. The same direction of thought is evident also in Eduard Schweizer, *The Good News According to Matthew* (Atlanta: John Knox Press, 1975), in his commentary on Mt 4:1-11.

33. Hannah Arendt, *The Human Condition* (Chicago, 1958), 240.

34. Williams, *The Forgiveness of Sin,* 50f.

35. Arendt, *The Human Condition,* 241. The importance of the 'unexpected' response to such exercises of power has been highlighted as an essential measure in breaking the ties to the past and enabling people to be free by René Girard in his writings. See especially his *Violence and the Sacred,* trans. Patrick Gregory (Baltimore: John Hopkins University Press, 1979).

36. Jürgen Moltmann, *The Trinity and the Kingdom of God,* trans. Margaret Kohl (London: SCM, 1981). See also Lucien Richard, *A Kenotic Christology: In the Humanity of Jesus the Christ, the Compassion of Our God* (New York: University Press of America, 1982); and Roy S. Anderson, *Historical Transcendence and the Reality of God* (Grand Rapids: Eerdmans, 1975), 179.

37. Roger Schutz. Cf. Leo Tolstoy, *Resurrection* (New York: New America Library, 1961).

38. See the powerful expressions of forgiveness in Etty Hillesum, *A Diary* (London: Triad Granada, 1985).

39. Dietrich Bonhoeffer, *Ethics* (London: SCM, 1971), 185.

40. John Patton, *Is Human Forgiveness Possible?* (Nashville: Abingdon Press, 1985).

41. Text in *Origins* 21:31 – 9 January 1992.

42. Thomas F. Best and Günther Gassmann, eds., *On the Way to Fuller Koinonia. Official Report of the Fifth World Conference on Faith and Order, Santiago de Compostela 1993,* Faith and Order Paper no. 166 (Geneva: World Council of Churches Publications, 1994), 232-3 (section I, para. 20).

Forgiveness and Community

Gabriel Daly

Recent interest in the theme of politics and forgiveness raises certain basic questions both about the concept of forgiveness itself and about how groups can practise it. This paper is an attempt to examine both questions. My title is therefore initially disjunctive. I am making no assumptions about the possibility and character of communitarian (including political) forgiveness. Instead I shall concentrate on the nature and scope of forgiveness in itself with a view to asking subsequently whether and how a community as such can forgive. I have found myself both drawn to the idea of political forgiveness and puzzled by its semantic implications. Can a community be said to forgive in the way that one individual forgives another? I shall argue that the most fruitful approach to this question is through analogy; but even with this in mind we are left with the further question of whence one derives the dominant or control model. I shall in fact derive it from individual interpersonal relationship, and I do so in full awareness of the severe critique of liberal individualism made by political theologians.

I agree with the main lines of this critique, including its summons to exchange the privacies of pietistic and existentialist subjectivism for the objective realities of social and political concern. Nevertheless I cannot help concluding that in our necessary attempts to give a social and political reference to the language of traditional Christian theology we run the twofold risk of (a) excessive reaction against personalism and (b) equivocation in the use of certain traditional terms, especially those employed in soteriology. The word 'forgiveness', in my submission, provides a relevant instance of both risks.

First there is the tendency to take 'forgiveness' as a functional synonym for 'reconciliation' and 'atonement', whereas it is a more specific word than either. Alienation or estrangement can occur for

reasons which do not necessarily include a specific offence or specific offences for which forgiveness needs to be sought or granted,
even implicitly. 'Reconciliation' is arguably the most generic term
in the vocabulary of soteriology. It correlates antithetically with
'alienation', which in the modern world is a word with both
Marxian and Freudian associations. Theologians in their perfectly
defensible quest for cultural relevance will almost inevitably wish to
admit resonances from either or both into their thinking. In both
cases, however, they must reckon with a rejection of transcendence
which makes Marxian and Freudian thought not merely circum-
stantially but radically reductionist. Both Marx and Freud put forward a secularist soteriology in which there is no place for forgiveness.
Christian soteriologies which admit Marxian or Freudian resonances
have therefore to take this absence of the concept of forgiveness under
conscious consideration and control.

Forgiveness and Analogy

F. W. Dillistone in his classic study, *The Christian Understanding
of Atonement,* warns against investing any single word, especially
one from the vocabulary of soteriology, with the authority to embody an immediately agreed meaning or to evoke a standard response.

> The reconciliation about which I speak may not be an answer to
> the precise problem of estrangement with which my neighbour
> is concerned.[1]

We need, says Professor Dillistone, to examine 'the general framework within which the language of estrangement and reconciliation gains meaning'. Most of the major soteriological terms are analogical models linguistically signalised by metaphors. While the
ability to create metaphor is one of the glories of the human
imagination, we should not underestimate the equally human and
perverse capacity for driving metaphors too hard and too far in the
direction of univocacy, with consequent destruction of their original
power to suggest what Paul Ricoeur has called a 'surplus of meaning'.[2]

Univocation occurred early in Christian theology when the
Fathers, for example, took the text, 'The Son of Man came not to
be served but to serve and to give his life as a ransom for many' (Mk

10:45) and asked the semantically fatal question, 'To whom was the ransom paid?' It was a question which drove a fine and evocative metaphor on to the rocks of deficient sensibility. It was also a question which alerts us to the role of the imagination in the business of theological interpretation. There is what might be called an impressionistic ambiguity about some metaphors which even 'the loving inquisitiveness of the Schools' should leave undissected.

If classical Christian theology occasionally strayed in the direction of univocation in its theological language, post-Enlightenment theology has tended in the opposite direction, namely, towards equivocation. It continues to use classical terminology, but it risks using it in a manner and with a reference which evacuates the sense and reference of the original usage. Soteriology is especially vulnerable to this semantic drift. Dietrich Weiderkehr has remarked, 'Many of the traditional designations are to all appearances verbally retained and command the same respect as before, but they are really the vocabulary of psychology and the social sciences.' He goes on to ask provocatively, 'Can the Christian proclamation of salvation introduce its traditional revelation of sin and its promise of eternal healing into these new mediated experiences without adapting to an ephemeral vogue and yet without talking about something totally different and alien?'[3] I would wish to answer that question affirmatively, but only under the proviso of a carefully controlled methodology rooted in awareness of the analogical character of what is going on. Metaphors die if they are not given fresh reference; and if they die, they lapse into a pseudo-literalness which often distorts the original insight.

Analogy, however, is a wider concept than metaphor. Redemption, for example, is a soteriological model clearly signalized by a compressed metaphor. 'Reconciliation' and 'forgiveness' are not so obviously metaphorical, unless one is prepared to dig deep into their etymology. But the contextual reference of reconciliation and forgiveness is no less analogical than any of the other soteriological terms. Both receive their definitive meaning from the circumstances which bring them into play. Those circumstances can range from the trivial, e.g., forgetting a birthday or anniversary, to the cosmic horror of the Holocaust. One rarely speaks of forgiveness without some degree of ambiguity, if only because offence and culpability are not inseparable. We need 'forgiveness' also for our non-culpable offences against others, just as we need healing for the wounds which we incur simply by being human. Recognition of the analogical character of forgiveness becomes particularly important when divine and human forgiveness are related to each other and are invoked in the same context. With an uneasy glance towards the shade of Karl Barth, I would wish to argue that we know something about divine forgiveness from our experience of human forgiveness, its possibilities, and its limitations.

Forgiveness as Transcendental

Can forgiveness be a purely secular reality quite devoid of transcendent reference or significance? The question will be important in any enquiry we may wish to make into communitarian or political forgiveness. I am not asking whether unbelievers can practise forgiveness. Obviously they can. But I would wish to argue that in doing so they give unwilling and perhaps unwitting testimony to the divine spark within them. An act of forgiveness may take place in a totally secular context and have no explicit or intended reference to God, but the believer is not thereby prohibited from seeing it as an objective testimony to divine presence and action. It is not implausible to argue that the idea of forgiveness spontaneously suggests a religious context; and this fact may paradoxically militate against a recognition of its social and political implications. The introduction of forgiveness as an ideal into a political context may actually appear to rob that context of its secular autonomy, which in turn may lead the politically minded theologian to play down its transcendent reference. Forgiveness is not, in point of fact, a prominent feature in much political theology, presumably because it can seem to act as a brake upon revolutionary ardour. It is extremely difficult for a politician to speak of forgiveness, and sometimes even of reconciliation, without sounding like a preacher. There is, in short, something inescapably 'religious' about forgiveness and atonement. I should like to explore this contention with the help of a scene from Iris Murdoch's novel, *Bruno's Dream*.

Bruno's Dream

Bruno is nearly ninety. At several points in the novel we share in

his confused musings on his past life, especially on his marriage to
Janie. We learn of his single infidelity to her for which she had re-
proached him for the remainder of her life. Janie having discovered
his affair, continues to live in the same house as Bruno but resolutely
refuses to forgive him. She frequently commands him to her room
there to berate him. One day Bruno hears the sound of her stick on
the floor summoning him to her room for what he intuitively
knows will be the last time. He does not go, because he cannot bear
to hear her condemn him with her dying breath. The terrible decision has haunted him ever since. Bruno, it should be noted, is not
religiously inclined. Very early in the story we are told that he 'had
never bothered with religion, he had left that to the women, and his
vision of goodness was connected not with God but with his mother'.[4]
As the novel ends we find him, aware of his own imminent death,
reflecting on his desperate desire for Janie's forgiveness and on his
dread of being cursed instead. With the absolute clarity afforded by
the prospect of his own death, Bruno reflects that 'if there is something that matters now at the end it must be the only thing that
matters.'[5]

"If only it could work backwards, but it can't."
Some people believed that too. That life could be redeemed.
But it couldn't be, and that was what was so terrible. He had
loved only a few people and loved them so badly, so selfishly. He
had made a muddle of everything. Was it only in the presence of
death that one could see so clearly what love ought to be like? If
only the knowledge which he had now, this absolutely nothing–else–matters, could somehow go backwards and purify the
little selfish loves and straighten out the muddles. But it could
not.
Had Janie known this at the end? For the first time Bruno saw it
with absolute certainty. Janie must have known. It would be impossible in this presence not to know. She had not wanted to
curse him, she had wanted to forgive him. And he had not given
her the chance.
"Janie, I am so sorry," murmured Bruno. His tears flowed. But
he was glad that he knew, at last.[6]

Bruno's dying reflections raise two questions which belong to eschatology and therefore to the transcendent dimension of history.

First there is the clarity and truth made uniquely possible by the existential awareness of imminent death. Then there is the matter of how forgiveness can 'work backwards'. The prospect of death not merely concentrates the mind by removing most of the motives for duplicity, but in Bruno's case produces the insight that what matters at the end is the only thing that matters. He has of course to assume, on the basis of his own experience, that his wife Janie must have felt the same. For the dying Bruno this insight into the scope of forgiveness has the character of universality. As it is with him now, so it must have been with Janie. If one questions this universality, Bruno's conclusion can seem no more than wishful thinking.

It is, however, the implication that forgiveness must collapse the structure of timespace that most challenges us here. Forgiveness has indeed to 'work backwards' if it is to have universal value and purpose. If it is to mean anything, it needs to share somehow in the quality of eternity as Boethius understood eternity. It has to embrace the offence, the offender, and the offended in an act of 'total, complete, simultaneous possession'. Forgiveness, in short, is both a symbolic mediation of God and a transcendental experience arising out of human limitation. It both makes God present and, to the extent that even the most perfect expression of human forgiveness falls infinitely short of what it promises, stirs up a further longing for what is divinely possible. Bruno's phrase, 'working backwards', is a homely equivalent of what Helmut Peukert calls 'anamnestic solidarity' in his attempt to delineate a communications theory which is applicable to the entire human race, past as well as future. Historically the past is closed; eschatologically it remains open.[7]

Ambiguity

There is in real forgiveness a divine-human ambiguity which makes it difficult to distinguish what is of God from what is of man. Forgiveness is an instance – perhaps the most challenging instance – of love, and as such it shares in the mystical ambiguity of the Johannine proclamation that 'God is love.' Whenever and wherever there is forgiveness, even of a totally 'secular' kind, there is God. This contention could offend not only unbelievers but also a certain type of Protestant and a certain type of Catholic sensibility. Protestants who are anxious to affirm the total sinfulness of men

and women and their inability to contribute anything of their own
to the salvific process will not wish to accept any blurring of the
boundaries between divine and human action in matters to do with
salvation. In the Roman Catholic tradition there has been a similar
disposition to interpret grace (actual grace) as a sort of divinely im-
parted moral shove against the grain and in the direction of true
Christian behaviour. A juridical attitude to forgiveness, such as that
which has characterized much Neo-scholastic Catholicism, reserves
the transcendent dimension of forgiveness to the divine remission
of sin normally mediated by divinely sanctioned ecclesial authority.
Inter-human forgiveness is here seen merely as a moral act devoid
of immanent, not to speak of numinous, significance. When forgiveness is treated sacramentally, and thus inserted into a formal
ecclesiastical structure, it is also juridicized; the minister acts *in per-
sona Christi* but, from the standpoint of sacramental efficacy, with
the impersonality and impassivity of a high court judge.

Ecclesiastical mediation of forgiveness has the almost inevitable
effect of removing the spontaneity and intensity of God's offer of
forgiveness as portrayed by Jesus. Much of the immediacy of the
gospel paradigms is lost in circumstances which introduce an almost
inevitable note of calculation common to all ecclesiastical mediation, from medieval penitentials to later confessional practice. The
analogical relationship between human and divine forgiveness is
easily obscured by socio-liturgical procedures, much as these aim to
provide a social and ecclesial setting and reference. The Sermon on
the Mount makes it abundantly and uncomfortably clear that
inter-human forgiveness is a moral imperative with universal application. The gospel roots this universal imperative in the comprehensive generosity of divine forgiveness. What we have freely received
must be freely, if analogously, distributed. Human forgiveness is an
analogical mimesis of divine forgiveness; and love of enemies is its
paradigmatic test. Many stratagems have been thought up for dealing with the angularities and attitudinal discomforts of the Sermon
on the Mount. Such stratagems include the medieval distinction
between the precepts and the counsels, the Lutheran doctrine of
the Two Kingdoms, Schweitzer's idea of the interim ethic, and so
on. It would be cynical to see in these stratagems only devices for
attenuating the demands of the gospel. They are all genuine at-

tempts to make the gospel relevant to life as it has to be lived in the world at any given moment. The New Testament, however, is not concerned, on the whole, to enter casuistically into circumstances by asking 'What if ...?' It is concerned with a forgiving disposition which is to be always on call.

When Brendan Behan suggested that the first item on the agenda of any meeting of Irishmen was a split, he was being unduly nationalistic. A potential split ought to be taken as read on any human agenda. This is no more than a realistic recognition of what our theological ancestors were trying to say when they coined the term 'original sin'. It is both politically and theologically realistic to act on the assumption that there will be a split, and therefore to plan from the outset the means of damage control and subsequent bridge-building. This ought perhaps to be the Christian's most characteristic contribution to all social gatherings ranging from parochial committees to large-scale political enterprises. There is an unillusioned directness about the Letter to the Colossians: 'Be forbearing with one another, and forgiving, where any of you has cause for complaint: you must forgive as the Lord forgave you.' (Col 3:13)

A community of forgiveness is here envisaged as a community comprising individuals who accept forgiveness as an ideal to be practised in the ordinary and sometimes frictional exchanges of human relationships. The problem for political theology (of the sort which is concerned about forgiveness) is how to give this network of interpersonal exchanges the impact of a block vote, and it raises once again the question of whether and how a community, as an entity, can be said to forgive in any sense which retains some measure of univocation. Is there a collective consciousness which can be said to be the subject of an act of forgiveness? We are faced here with all sorts of questions about how a group achieves solidarity of sentiment, especially of a sentiment like forgiveness which reaches into the depths of moral, psychological, and religious experience.

Forgiveness has a psychological dimension which is indispensable to its deepest meaning. By saying that I leave myself open to the charge of psychologism, i.e., of reducing forgiveness to its psychological element and of overlooking other no less important elements. Nevertheless this difficulty must be faced. It is for psychologists to indicate the possibility and character of group consciousness and to determine how that consciousness relates to the consciousness of the individuals who comprise the group. We are today reacting against the individualism and personalism of the romantic era; but such reaction is not a charter to abandon the inescapably individual and personal characteristics of a phenomenon such as forgiveness. Let us look, then, more closely at some of these characteristics, notably that of sacrifice.

Sacrifice

A reflection from Dag Hammarskjöld's journal offers a clue to the sacrificial character of forgiveness in its deeper reaches.

> Forgiveness breaks the chain of causality because he who 'forgives' you – out of love – takes upon himself the consequences of what you have done. Forgiveness, therefore, always entails a sacrifice.[8]

In many cases such taking of consequences upon oneself calls for some kind of imaginative substitution, i.e., a placing of oneself in the offender's shoes. Take for example the case of parents of a child who has been killed by a drunken driver. Let us suppose that the offender has been courageous enough to face the parents and express his shame and contrition (having first ascertained the readiness of the parents to meet him). Let us further suppose that either or both of the parents feel that more is being asked of them than a dignified and brief encounter and an absence of overt recrimination. The sort of forgiveness which would be appropriate – though heroically so – to this situation would stem from their ability and willingness to override their own emotions sufficiently to imagine what it must be like to be a drunken driver who has killed a child and must now live with the consequences. Such imaginative substitution would rest partly on sheer human solidarity and partly on recognizing that the roles could be reversed without any serious straining of plausibility. The 'sacrifice' of which Hammarskjöld speaks would here consist not merely in conquering anger, disgust, loathing and all other rebarbative emotions natural in the circumstances, it would involve abandoning the psychological solace offered by the indulgence of these emotions. It would no longer be possible to think of the driver as an unforgivable lout. Instead he would be invested with a 'redeemed' humanity which would make hatred of him impossible.

The example of the drunken driver may look like a case of special pleading in that it lends itself to imaginative transposition. If one were to choose instead an offence involving sheer malice, say, an act of deliberate slander, one would be forced to concede that the forgiving imagination would find it harder to function, even with the best of wills, simply because the would-be forgiver might not be able to make the imaginative leap into the subjectivity of the offender. Some kind of imaginative exchange of subjectivities, however, would seem to be necessary if politically estranged communities are to be reconciled. Their members have in some way to experience the implications of a common humanity. This will almost certainly mean reckoning not merely with the right of the other community but also with the lived experience of its members. Yet I have heard such imaginative exchange of subjectivities described as a kind of treason. When communities have been long estranged there has to be a shriving of memories (which enables the process to 'work backwards') and a shriving of dreams (which will come from the recognition that one community's dream may be the other's nightmare).

Does forgiveness, however, necessarily imply some kind of understanding of the offence? The question is important for at least two reasons. First there is, as I have suggested, the danger of a psychologism whereby one reduces the objective ontological character of sin to its purely psychological dimensions. Second, there is the danger of moral determinism. This could work on the principle *tout comprendre, c'est tout pardonner.* Commenting on this slogan of deterministic behaviourism, Isaiah Berlin showed its derivation to lie not merely in moral determinism but actually in the whole western philosophical tradition from Plato onwards, and specifically in its conviction 'that reality is wholly knowable, and that knowledge and only knowledge liberates, and absolute knowledge liberates absolutely'.[9] In short that 'to explain is to understand and to understand is to justify'. Once again we are alerted to the analogical character of forgiveness. God's forgiveness of sin stems not from his omniscience but from his love. There is something objective to be forgiven, and no degree of psychological insight or moral empathy can remove that fact. Forgiveness is not synonymous with understanding, for either God or man, though there are instances where human forgiveness may depend on a willingness to understand as far as possible through the medium of the imagination; while in every instance it is only God who sees the heart.

The concept of forgiveness as a universal imperative has to face a far sterner test than that of avoiding psychological reductionism. Are there instances of crime so awesome in magnitude that they render the prospect of forgiveness both irrelevant and morally intolerable? The Holocaust puts the universal scope of forgiveness implicit in Christianity to its severest test. In the words of J. B. Metz one can no longer do theology with one's back to Auschwitz. Can one, however, face Auschwitz at a remove and yet with authenticity? What is abundantly clear is that those not directly involved must use the greatest circumspection in their invocation of forgiveness in this context. Perhaps the only sure course is to listen with painful humility to those who were directly affected.

The Holocaust

Ulrich Simon is such a one, and he puts the case against forgiveness in the context of the Holocaust with deeply-felt conviction. He believes that 'our moral feelings tend to be outraged even by talk of forgiveness in this connection'.[10]

> There is a sin against Man and Spirit which Christ declared to be unforgivable, and Auschwitz is this sin against Man and Spirit. It is the supreme act of blasphemy, and the men and tools who caused it neither desire nor can receive the forgiveness of their sin.[11]

Although Professor Simon refuses to discuss Auschwitz in terms of forgiveness, he is ready to discuss it in terms of ultimate meaning. Where Richard Rubenstein was moved by the thought of Auschwitz to write that

> few ideas in Jewish religious thought have been more decisively mistaken, in spite of their deep psychological roots, than the terrible belief that God acts meaningfully in history.[12]

Ulrich Simon is able to sanction the possibility of a theology of Auschwitz as long as 'it's findings issue in prayer, for we can face the horror only by coming to terms with it liturgically'.[13] Professor Simon's invocation of prayer in respect of Auschwitz suggests that such cosmic manifestations of evil have to be approached religiously or not at all, but that not even a religious approach permits one to speak of forgiveness in the case of such huge crimes against humanity. We are here dealing with events which lay bare the raw nerve ends of all that is ultimate in human concern. The problems posed for theodicy by the fact of Auschwitz are shattering, but our attention is directed here less to theodicy than to its implications for human forgiveness. Only those who were victims have the right to speak of forgiveness. For the rest of us it would be a gross impertinence. We are, however, entitled to enquire with reverence whether there were victims who did in fact forgive.

There is a prayer which comes not from Auschwitz but from Ravensbruck where 92,000 women and children died. This prayer is one of the miracles of religious history – almost as awesome as the conditions which produced it were numbing. Although it is now widely known and celebrated, I make no apology for citing it yet again.

> O Lord, remember not only the men and women of good will, but also those of ill will. But do not remember all the suffering they have inflicted on us; remember the fruits we have bought, thanks to this suffering – our comradeship, our loyalty, our humility, our courage, our generosity, the greatness of heart which has grown out of all this, and when they come to the judgement let all the fruits that we have borne be their forgiveness.[14]

In the light of that glorious prayer, offered by a nameless woman and placed beside the dead body of a nameless child, I would with respectful hesitancy question Professor Simon's claim that 'none of the victims at Auschwitz wrought atonement'.[15] Christians believe that there is only one mediator between God and man and that by his blood alone are we redeemed; but may one not speak of a mystical unity between Calvary and Ravensbruck when a victim of the latter reproduces so perfectly what the former was intended to effect? Pascal's remark that 'Jesus will be in torment until the end of time' gives us warrant to speak analogically of atonement in these circumstances. All that Jesus achieved on Calvary was present in the heart of that nameless woman in Ravensbruck, whether or not she was a Christian. Her prayer manifests the kingdom of God in all its splendour. In a sense it bridges the infinite distance between God and man. It is a manifestation of divinity which gives flesh and blood to the daring patristic conviction that God became man that man might become God. On Calvary man's inhumanity to man became in a unique way man's inhumanity to God, who responded not by annihilating his failed creation, but by giving back to men and women the result of their sin transformed now into a sign of forgiveness and hope.

To see the figure on the cross as a symbol of forgiveness and reconciliation calls for an act of interpretation which can easily go unnoticed – precisely as interpretation – by believers, principally because tradition has already, as it were, made the interpretation for them. Even unbelievers share to some extent in the cultural implications of this socio-religious interpretation. The cross is inescapably associated with Christian culture, and that culture survives in considerable part into a secularist age. All of which makes it difficult for Christians to see the secular horror and degradation of Calvary and therefore to appreciate the demand it makes on the interpretative imagination. Without this act of Faith-inspired interpretation it is impossible to relate Calvary to Auschwitz or to any other manifestation of man's inhumanity to man. Among the many horrors inherent in the memory of Auschwitz is the fact that the persecutors were the lethal product of the long disease (much of it latent) of a Christian anti-semitism which was a denial of everything that Calvary represented. Repentance for Auschwitz implies repentance for every Christian manifestation of anti-semitism. This is yet a further reminder of the radically eschatological character of repentance and atonement.

We are surrounded in the world by the symbols of alienation and human offence. The Christian is sent into the world to proclaim and live the values of the divine reign which Jesus proclaimed and incarnated. That proclamation has at its heart the assurance of God's forgiveness and the injunction to mediate in a human manner that divine forgiveness. In the risen Christ God gives humanity not merely a future it had no right to expect but a redeemed future, a future with hope, which it had still less right to expect. It was the crucified Christ who was raised in a divine act which transformed shame into glory. That forgiveness works not only backwards but forwards into both the historical and absolute future. It frees the forgiven for action on behalf of others. But it lays a radical obliga-

tion upon those who have responded in faith to the Father's raising
of his murdered Son to new life: to be thus forgiven is to be both
empowered and enjoined to forgive each other. Forgiveness is
therefore at the heart of Christian community, however analogously
it has to be practised. The Christian community is by definition
and charter a community of forgiveness precisely because it is a forgiven community. How is this to be expressed in all the diverse circumstances in which Christians find themselves in the world? The
remainder of this paper will be taken up with reflection on the
communitarian character and implications of forgiveness.

Summary
Let me first, however, summarize some of my previous con-
tentions. Forgiveness is neither an univocal nor an equivocal concept.
It has to be approached with an analogical imagination capable of
interpreting the facts of any situation which calls for reconciliation
and the healing of wounds which have been inflicted by specific offences. It begins as a residual disposition which may be actualized at
any moment and brought to bear on the ambiguities of the many
situations which call it into play. These ambiguities include such
considerations as culpability (e.g. diminished responsibility) and
group solidarity (e.g. a community suffering guilt by association
with its delinquent members). Forgiveness is analogical in that
while its paradigmatic instance occurs in one-to-one relationships,
it is the community which supplies the language for its identification and specification, and it is in the community that it has to be
practised. Forgiveness is one of the principal signals of transcendence – a contention which seems to be borne out by the difficulty
of giving it an exclusively empirical and non-religious reference.
Forgiveness is therefore eschatological in that it is a mark of the in-
breaking kingdom of God. When true forgiveness occurs, there is
God. This divine presence is ontological and symbolic and not
merely juridical or psychological. For the Christian the reality of
forgiveness is ultimately tested by the paradigmatic instance of love
of one's enemies, which is psychologically impossible in many cases
if one is not prepared to undertake some kind of imaginative substitution. This imaginative substitution becomes particularly important in the case of alienated communities. Finally, one has to ask

whether some offences are so enormous that they cannot be forgiven because they destroy the language which invests forgiveness with meaning and reference. This question may be answered in the negative as long as one does so with extreme sensitivity to what is involved.

The Forgiving Community

To call the Christian Church a community of forgiveness is arguably to veer towards the equivocal element in analogical predication. Is one speaking empirically, eschatologically, ontologically, or juridically? Is one describing the local community or the *catholica*? Is one speaking of divine or human forgiveness? The ambiguities inherent in the phrase 'community of forgiveness' strain analogy to its limits. Yet one is hardly free to despair of discovering a univocal element. Without a firm if limited element of univocation, analogical interpretation would be impossible and therefore rational discourse about forgiveness would be impossible. There is, however, the lexical reference of the word from which we can at least make some sort of provisionally univocal start. 'To cease to resent', 'to pardon', 'to remit' are dictionary synonyms. They at least provide a context in ordinary universal and non-theological experience. The challenge to Christian theology is how to relate this human experience to God's self-disclosure and action in the world. I have already intimated my own preference for an ontological and symbolic centre of reference: where there is forgiveness, there is God. It does not matter where or between whom this forgiveness occurs. When it does occur, the divine element in men and women is activated. How one relates this to the work of Christ is a christological problem of daunting complexity. Karl Rahner's concept of the 'anonymous Christian' is a brave but unsatisfactory attempt to link the universality of divine grace with the specific limitations of a particular historical faith. The universal scope of forgiveness has often been severely attenuated in Christian history by a rigid doctrine of predestination or by a rigid application of the dictum *extra ecclesiam nulla salus*, both of which appear to negate the universality of divine forgiveness and to sever the link between divine and human forgiveness. In both instances the community of forgiveness becomes a segregated, tightly-knit association of believers no longer interested in the universal character of forgiveness.

Rosemary Haughton in her book, *The Transformation of Man: A Study of Conversion and Community*, examines two communitarian responses to the divine offer of salvation in Christian history. She calls them respectively 'the community of the transformed' and 'the formation community'. The transformed community is well exemplified in the seventeenth century groups of radical Protestants who found themselves unable to live and worship according to their consciences under the Stuarts. Many of these Separatists set up communities abroad. They afford a clear example of how a group of Christians, conscious of being called out of a sinful world by a conversion experience, organized their daily lives in autonomous communities. Mrs Haughton praises their fervour, devotion, and charismatic gifts but regrets their rigidity, smugness, and occasional hypocrisy.

The second type of response to the offer of salvation is the 'formation community', of which Mrs Haughton takes the Benedictines as being a typical example. Here salvation has been traditionally seen as lying in the future. It has to be striven for. The virtues of this type of community are humility, respect for authority and for the material things that make life and worship together. Its defects are that its members 'are wide open to minimalism and tepidity, to evasion of personal responsibility and flight from decision.'[16]

Mrs Haughton convicts both types of community of confusing the sacred and the secular. 'One way imposes behaviour proper to contact with the sacred as the norm of secular life, the other treats secular life as if it were sacred.'[17] She believes that true Christian community would keep sacred and secular 'distinct and related'. In terms of forgiveness it might be said that the transformed community had the better theology: the Christian ideal is to set out to forgive one another because we have been forgiven by God. There is however the problem of post-conversion sin which troubled the early Church, as it must trouble any community which lives in the light of an unrepeatable conversion experience. The formation community did not have this problem, since it acted on the assumption that salvation has to be worked for under grace across a lifetime marked by some success and much failure. The formation community expected failure and planned accordingly. Before the change of consciousness brought about in the Roman Catholic

Church by the Second Vatican Council, the formation community, living under rule and vows, set out to live a 'more perfect life' by practising the evangelical 'counsels' which were not deemed to bind the wider Christian community.[18] The formation community promoted constant renewal of effort and conversion, but conversion did not feature prominently in its vocabulary and was rarely if ever thought of as a decisive unrepeatable moment. Recent reforms have not changed this attitude. Although conversion has today a much more prominent role in Roman Catholic spirituality, it is normally understood as a continuing process and not as an unrepeatable event. The formation community is typically Catholic in that it tends to sacralise power, to display theocratic pretensions, and to attach disproportionate significance to the mediation of God's mind and will through church authority. It allows generously for human weakness, but it does so by appearing to regulate divine forgiveness, rather in the spirit of the parent who takes the gift box of chocolates away from the child with the purpose of doling out the contents under conditions of prudent control. The transformed community, on the other hand, aims at a spirituality of all-encompassing and non-calculating intensity. It protests at the intrusive character of Catholic ecclesial mediation. It allows the child to keep the chocolates, but on the understanding that the child will behave like an adult. If the child does not behave like an adult, the system breaks down and even logic itself may be infringed by attempts to demonstrate that the signs of salvation are present. (This illustration has literal reference when we remember that the Separatists sometimes beat their children to make them look more saved. St Benedict beat his 'in order that they may be cured'.[19] The children, of course, found both eschatologies equally painful.)

Roman Catholicism places heavy emphasis on the sacramental manifestation of divine forgiveness with consequent ecclesiastical control over its mediation. Protestantism removes the mediation with consequent privatisation of the whole process. Neither appears to affirm the ontological, if analogical, unity of divine and human forgiveness. Without this unity it is difficult to create a realistic community of forgiveness, that is, a community which lives out divine forgiveness by expressing it analogically in interpersonal and social relationships and in a network of symbols designed to

manifest the inner aspiration to forgiveness and to evoke it by out-
ward sign.

There is a christological implication in all this. 'Who can forgive sins but God alone?' (Mk 2:7) was the theological objection
brought by the authorities against Jesus's offer of forgiveness to the
paralysed man. Some Christian apologists, by an extrinsic coupling
of the forgiveness with the subsequent miraculous healing, utilised
this text as proof of Jesus's divinity. They were, however, unwilling
to accept that the divine forgiveness was rooted in the human compassion which Jesus felt for sinners. They thus neglectcd the gospel
evidence that both the healing and the forgiveness were motivated
by human compassion. Monophysites and Nestorians, each in their
different ways, accepted the premise of Jesus's accusers, the former
deriving the forgiveness from a single, divine, nature in Christ, the
latter affirming two natures but attributing forgiveness only to the
divine. The consequence of Chalcedonian doctrine has been the
depreciation of the human element in divine forgiveness, making
human forgiveness less an extension of, than a heteronomous ad-
junct to, divine forgiveness.

In Roman Catholic Neo-scholastic theology and spirituality, the
radical distinction made between nature and supernature promoted
the heteronomy. Love of neighbour was undertaken *propter Deum,*
and this could subtly turn the neighbour into the raw material for
one's acts of charity. (I am not suggesting that only Neo-scholastics
practised this spiritual pragmatism, merely that their doctrine of
nature and supernature gave it a theoretical underpinning.) The
words of Jesus about care for those in need, as described in the 25th
chapter of Matthew's gospel, were frequently interpreted: 'As long
as you did it to one of these, I took it as though you were doing it to
me.' Eduard Schweizer's defiant anti-mysticism puts him curiously
close to the old Neo-scholastic supernaturalists:

> We are therefore dealing neither with mysticism, in which the
> line between God and man is blurred, nor with Stoic identifica-
> tion of God with all mankind, but with an act of charity to a par-
> ticular individual who may not be appealing or sympathetic.[20]

Against both supernaturalism and moralism, I wish to argue for
the immanent, if imperfect, presence and manifestation of divine
forgiveness in human forgiveness. The recognition that Jesus's acts

of forgiveness were divine acts in a human mode and were inspired by human compassion can be made the christological basis of communitarian forgiveness (assuming, of course, that one accepts some form of incarnational christology). Karl Barth, redoubtable opponent of *analogia entis* that he was, could nevertheless write:

> It is when we look at Jesus Christ that we know decisively that God's deity does not exclude, but includes his *humanity*.[21]

What are the political implications of all this for Christians? Since politics is about how society sets up communicative structures and organizes itself for government, the political process almost inevitably entails the giving of offence. A split on the agenda is implicit in all political process. The Christian who engages in this process can scarcely claim that the hard facts of political life dispense him or her from any attempt to practise forgiveness in the political arena. Politicians are not dispensed by the exigencies of a public life from the demands of interpersonal morality. What, however, about the social and political embodiment of forgiveness? Is it, or can it be, something more than the sum of the individual attitudes of its members?

Though political action can certainly create symbols of forgiveness, it cannot compel individual citizens to participate internally in these symbols and in the reality to which they point. Internal participation is nevertheless a necessary feature of forgiveness in its deepest and characteristically Christian sense. Laws and administrative procedures can indeed reduce the occasions for offence and can penalise external manifestations of prejudice and hatred; but they cannot produce the inner disposition which is the heart of unfeigned forgiveness. The will to forgiveness in a group depends on the disposition which each of its members brings to the group. This fact makes forgiveness different from most other kinds of reforming social action. Social and political reforms can be brought about without any inner disposition towards forgiveness or reconciliation on the part of those affected by the reforms.

To question the spiritual limitations of politics does not imply the view that politics is an essentially sinful activity, or at least more sinful than other human activities. It simply means recognizing the danger of political reductionism and serves as a further reminder that there are limits to the scope of analogy in applying the concept of forgiveness. Forgiveness, more than anything else, demonstrates both the need and the limitations of political action. Bringing in legislation which will serve to reduce the occasions of community hostility is altogether desirable and laudable; but it is not forgiveness. It may indeed help to create an atmosphere favourable to forgiveness, but law and public administration are concerned with external actions not, directly at least, with interior dispositions. This is not to disparage the benefits of political initiative in matters of social antagonism. It is merely to recognize the transcendental character of forgiveness. As Aristotle pointed out in a different context, the virtues of the good citizen are not necessarily those of the good man.

However much we politicize our theology, there always remains an area of religious concern which finally escapes the influence of politics; and forgiveness in its gospel sense belongs to this area. Lest this remark be taken to imply acquiescence in false consciousness, I must emphasize that I am presupposing preliminary political action which does what it can in the public arena before going on to reflect on the interior deficiencies inherent in that arena.

Charles Davis has remarked with admirable clear-sightedness that just as mysticism without politics is false consciousness, so politics without mysticism is 'mere business'.[22] It is 'only when Christians as Christians engage in politics that they experience the transcendent reality of God as limiting the political.'[23] The politics of reconciliation is particularly open to transcendental experience precisely because, if entered into from a genuine concern for peace and justice, it poses questions about human nature and its God-directed dynamism which politics is incompetent to answer. It is when this 'limit situation' is reached that forgiveness in its Christian sense becomes possible. The will to reconciliation may begin as a vague desire to end hostilities or make the neighbourhood safer, and as such it is enormously important and beneficial. The task of the Christian, however, is to extend the process inwards into the hearts of men and women where it ceases to be 'mere business' and becomes an exercise in bringing about the kingdom of God.

Notes:

This paper was also delivered to the joint meeting of the Irish Theological Association and the Society for the Study of Theology in Belfast, April 1986.

1. F.W. Dillistone, *The Christian Understanding of Atonement* (Welwyn, 1968), 12.
2. Paul Ricoeur, *Interpretation Theory: Discourse and the Surplus of Meaning* (Fort Worth, 1976), passim.
3. Dietrich Weiderkehr, *Belief in Redemption: Concepts of Salvation from the New Testament to the Present Time* (London, 1979), 48.
4. Iris Murdoch, *Bruno's Dream* (London, Penguin Books, 1970), 13.
5. Ibid., 266.
6. Ibid., 267.
7. Helmut Peukert, *Science, Action and Fundamental Theology: Towards a Theology of Communicative Action* (Cambridge, Mass., 1984).
8. Dag Hammarskjöld, *Markings* (London: 1966), 163.
9. Isaiah Berlin, *Historical Inevitability* (London, 1954), 41-2.
10. Ulrich Simon, *A Theology of Auschwitz* (London, 1978), 66.
11. Ibid., 71.
12. D. Callahan, ed., *The Secular City Debate* (London, 1966), 142.
13. Simon, *A Theology of Auschwitz*, 47.
14. Cited in M. Craig, 'Take Up Your Cross', *The Way*, vol. 13 (Jan. 1973), 30.
15. Simon, *A Theology of Auschwitz*, 90.
16. Rosemary Haughton, *The Transformation of Man: A Study of Conversion and Community* (London, 1967), 240.
17. Ibid., 241.
18. T. Matura, *Gospel Radicalism: The Hard Sayings of Jesus* (Dublin, 1984), provides a convincing rebuttal of this view once widely accepted in Roman Catholic spirituality.
19. *Rule*, ch. 30.
20. Eduard Schweizer, *The Good News According to St Matthew* (London, 1975), 477-8.
21. Karl Barth, *The Humanity of God* (London, 1967), 46, original italics.
22. Charles Davis, *Theology and Political Society* (Cambridge, 1980), 181.
25. Ibid., 68.

A Struggle for Justice and Reconciliation: Forgiveness in the Politics of the American Black Civil Rights Movement, 1955-68

Donald W. Shriver, Jr

At home in the churches' confessional and 'cure of souls', forgiveness sounds in the ears of moderns as a transaction between an offended party, perhaps God, and a single offender. The word has acquired heavy individualistic overtones.

In that ancient context of penance, however, one social feature of forgiveness stands out: the term refers at once to a judgment against wrong and a restoration of the wrongdoer to a community broken by the wrong. Forgiveness is a complex act that asserts moral offence while holding out hope that the offender can both repent of the offence and enter again the community.

Both in concept and practice, modern theologies and ideologies have shown little interest in transfers of this combination into large-scale political struggle. Theologians from Luther to Reinhold Niebuhr have split 'love' and 'justice' into paradoxical or tension-suffused relation; liberal and socialist theories have paid attention to the interests of vulnerable individuals or exploited groups; but in general all such theorists treat justice as a priority in time, strategy, and concept over against secondary concerns for renewed community between the victims and the agents of injustice.

A serious attempt to interpret forgiveness as a term appropriate for political ethics and political strategy must break with this pattern.

Examples of the difficulty of such a break are legion in the history of every country. The thesis of this essay is that in much of the Black American Civil Rights movement of the 1950s and 1960s, the world had a rare example of a combination of a political struggle for justice with a simultaneous struggle for reconciliation between the antagonists in the struggle. My aim here is to summarize some of the strategic resources which the black leaders of the Civil Rights movement brought to or learned in the movement. By 'resources' I mean a diverse set of leverages for change or latent powers which the culture and society of American black people brought to this struggle.

The temper of what follows is empirical. The theory – that it is possible to combine a sustained social effort for justice with an equally sustained intention of a new community inclusive of all parties – I see spelled out in certain practices of the Civil Rights movement. I am more interested in recording these practices than in pretending to understand them in a comprehensive theological, ethical, or political theory. My inclination away from the systematic fits my particular biographical relation to the movement: as a white person, born in Virginia and inheritor of a racially segregated national society, I was *an object of* the protest marches of the movement before I came to be an occasional subject in the marches and other related events. Certainly the movement happened to some of us white Southerners before we did anything to help make it happen. It helped us more profoundly than we helped it. When we, with our white faces, write about it, therefore, we do well to defer to its eventfulness rather than to our propensity for understanding and explaining the events. The best understanding and explanation of the Civil Rights movement will be written by its black participants. White writers may make their best interpretative contribution if they abide by the limits of their observer-status in much of this history.[1]

The Central Paradox: The Black Slave American

Preliminary understanding of the Civil Rights movement of twentieth century America requires an observation of a phenomenon so difficult to understand as to verge on paradox: the inclination of the vast majority of black people in the history of the United States to aspire to full citizenship in the country that enslaved them. Amazement at this phenomenon is more appropriate than most white Americans have ever believed. A beclouded racist mentality enables them to take for granted the desire of newly freed slaves to become American citizens. Vincent Harding (whom Martin Luther King, Jr encouraged to become the 'committed historian of the movement'), underscores his own amazement here in his account of one of the earliest 'civil rights rallies' in the post-Civil-War history of black people in the United States – The Coloured People's Convention in Charleston, South Carolina, in November of 1865. Attended by over two thousand freed slaves, the Convention ended with an 'Address to the White Inhabitants of the State of South Carolina'. In the Address were these paragraphs:

> We are American by birth, and we assure you that we are Americans in feeling; and in spite of all the wrongs which we have so long and silently endured in this country, we can yet exclaim, with a full heart, 'O America, with all thy faults we love thee still.'
>
> … We would address you – not as Rebels and enemies, but as friends and fellow-countrymen, who desire to dwell among you in peace, and whose destinies are interwoven and linked with those of the whole American people, and hence must be fulfilled in this country.

Comments Harding: 'One can easily imagine the inner struggles which the black delegates had to wage in order to approve a document calling their former masters 'friends and fellow-countrymen'. And again: 'What manner of men and women were these? Refusing to flinch in the face of the past, attacking the criminal system that had bound them, they extended the "right hand of fellowship" – a distinctly Christian phrasing – to the former criminals, offering to build together a new society.'

> It was a fearful dialectic, especially as the emerging Afro-Americans realized that if their vision prevailed they must ultimately do the work of rebuilding in concert with the people who had been their legal owners, who had been the despoilers of their women, breakers of their men, exploiters of their labour, murderers of their children, or a host of guilty bystanders. Still, at great inner cost they were calling for a new beginning – not forgetting the past, never forgetting it, but seeking to overcome it, to transform its meaning through the creation of a new future.[2]

The latter words are a functional definition of forgiveness in politics, the definition I will assume below. It is a very apt definition, for it matches both the traditional complexity of the concept of forgiveness in Western religious history, and it provides some analytical touchstones for identifying a political transaction as implicitly forgiving: is the past remembered and condemned as wrong? Is there movement towards 'overcoming it', changing the relationships that still bear the weight of past wrong? Is there rejection of mere revenge and some empathy proffered the wrongdoers? And does the overcoming take the form of a 'new future', especially a new community between the wronged and the wrongdoers?

Among Americans dead and living, no group has exhibited positive answers to such questions in national political dialogue so actively as have black Americans. To discerning eyes, their resources for such answers were visible in the Charleston Coloured People's Convention. But the Civil Rights movement of a century later heightened that visibility for many more white Americans than had eyes to see in 1865. Below I try to summarize the resources.

Resources for Forgiveness in Politics: the Civil Rights Movement

The best-known leader of the Civil Rights movement, Martin Luther King, Jr, consistently appealed to two strands of tradition in his public statements about the aims of the movement: the American Constitution and the Bible. Finally cleansed, through a Civil War and three amendments, of its anti-democratic tolerance of slavery in its 1789 version, the Constitution could have been a formidable legal lever against political racism in the United States, especially after 1865. Restating the great Jeffersonian liberal democratic dream, Lincoln spoke of 'a new nation, conceived in liberty and dedicated to the proposition that all men are created equal'.[3] But the translation of such rhetoric into substantive justice, into equal enjoyment of civil rights by all citizens, has always required in the American political system combinations of police protection and court decisions, which after 1865 were regularly subverted by racist elements in official and popular American culture. The segregation laws of the 1890s, for example, promulgated by all southern States, acquired the official blessing of the Supreme Court in its 1896 decision to permit 'separate but equal' public schools for white and black people. Only when that court reversed itself, declaring public school segregation illegal in 1954, did the Supreme Court and Constitution together begin to look, to many black leaders, as powerful levers for changing the institutions of racial discrimination in American society generally. Not by coincidence is the Civil Rights movement's beginning usually dated from 1955.

But the legal, constitutional side of the resources for change had, at most, ambiguous relation to the other side of Martin King's normative claims upon the political processes of this country – the religion of the Bible. Only from this side did the word 'forgiveness' enter his rhetoric and that of his followers. If we ask what distinctive elements of political strategy and power entered the movement and furnished groundwork for its expressions of forgiveness in its politics, we have to take note of the following.

The Churches, Social Sustainers of Memory

The Charleston Convention met in a Presbyterian Church. Its 'Address' spoke of the 'silent' endurance of injustice by many black slaves, and the Convention itself was a significant breaking of that silence. Inside the black churches of the antebellum South, however, such silence had already been broken. Largely self-organized, often illegal, and usually furtive, these black slave congregations were the only social structures really controlled by their members; and this condition persisted right into the twentieth century. Some of these churches (the African Methodist Episcopal Church, for example) owed their origins to public breaks with church racial segregation as early as the eighteenth century. The majority of them came literally 'out of the woods' in the post-1865 era.

Even in 1989, the black churches of the United States remain the clearest and most abundant examples of institutions built and controlled by their black members. Without the experience of organized church life, one could hardly account for an event, six months after the end of the Civil War, that brought together two thousand blacks in Charleston; and this event was a precedent for many to come. The laws and practices of the old slave system aimed, among other goals, at depriving black people of their ability to function as a culture, community, and social power apart from the system. The illegal black church – organized around the religion and language of the enslaver – provided a social counterpoint to the injustice of the system. It kept alive memories of Africa, discerned in the democratic rhetoric of white Americans its inconsistency with slavery, nourished silent protest, counselled its members on the arts of surviving in the face of the enemy, protected them from the enemy when it could, and reinforced with religious vision a polity in which freedom and equality were realized in the relations of black members to each other. Remarkable in the history of Christianity is this adaptation of the religion of enslavers to serve the liberation of the slaves.

The very organization of the black church in the centuries before 1955, in short, laid some foundations of the Civil Rights movement. Activating black church people for public protest and political struggle was a second step, not always taken easily by many of these people. But the church had kept the memory of black history alive, and it had provided experience of black initiative and control of an organisation. It thus provided two ingredients of a viable formula for the injection of forgiveness into politics: an accurate memory of what needed to be forgiven and an experience of social solidarity by which to measure the humanity of other solidarities.

A Will to Convert the Enemy

A commitment to continue living in some civil-political relation with one's enemies is qualitatively different from a commitment to destroying them. Implicit in the Address of the Charleston Convention was the knowledge that white society would require vast institutional and personal converting before it 'interwove and linked' the lives of black people with the whole of the society. On the contrary, white-dominated society continued to signal to black people its latent and active capacity for destroying them.

'Conversion' here means the same two-sided change that inheres in the concept of forgiveness: a wrong must be recognized as wrong and a new relation, minus the wrong, will be envisioned if not achieved. On the side of the wrongdoers, too, this means a willingness to live in that new relation; and for many white Americans, that has come down to an unwillingness to have their sins forgiven or to live in the new relation with its overtones of concession from the once-offended side. I can be personal on this point: the polity of the black Christian churches has been segregated in practice but seldom if ever segregationist in principle. The proof of this over many decades has been the openness of black church congregations to white visitors, an openness never assumed at the height of the 'Jim Crow' system in white churches. White congregations endured crisis regularly in the 1950s and 1960s over whether they

would seat black visitors and even accept black members. By contrast, never in my life have I felt unwelcome in a black church, so
routine is the non-segregationist assumption in that church's life.
Late in the 1960s, as the 'Black Power' movement took hold of
some segments of the Civil Rights movement, segregated political
strategies began to surface publicly; but so long as integration and
equal access to public services were the aim of the movement, a
church open to white and black people remained blacks' fundamental old analogue to the new open society.

Deeper than tolerance of whites, in this church culture, was the
hope that any person or group from the white community, willing
to sit as equals in church pews, was a candidate for membership in a
desegregated civil society. Some 'converts' to the Civil Rights movement (including this author) underwent their conversion in integrated church settings prior to the fifties. Common to every such experience, on the white Christian side, was the embarrassing new
double-awareness that (a) Christian principle was always on the
side of integrated church and (b) the experience of actual equalitar-
ian relation between Christians, e.g. around a communion table,
might make the principle real for the first time in one's life.

Perhaps the most radical idea of Martin King and his church
associates was that, in analogy to a church open to all people, a society similarly open could be constructed *and the enemies of such a society converted to membership in it.* Such a hope meant the rejection of principled and practical dualisms between human relations
in the religious and the civil communities – a dualism like that of
classical Lutheranism, for example. It also meant a confidence in
change of institutional rules and personal feelings sufficient to sustain an ongoing conversion from the old ways of 'separate and unequal'. Central to this vision, again, was the intention of black people, unjustly treated from time immemorial, to live in civil company with the architects of that injustice and their descendants. The
requisite reciprocity, implicit in the intention, met resistance in the
great majority of white people in American society; and as resisters,
they were the enemies of the movement. The radical hope was that
their resistance could change to consent, at least grudging, and
eventually to acclamation.

The Practical Political Power of Non-Violence

Assessments of Gandhi's non-violent strategy for inducing the British to quit India have frequently pointed out that in relation to another kind of enemy, e.g. Nazis, the strategy might have failed miserably. What if, in face of enemies you are unwilling to destroy, they are only too willing to destroy you? The case is similar, others say, in modern South Africa: its government will destroy any number of black lives to maintain its apartheid-based system.

One need not invoke some elusive high virtue slumbering in the depths of British and white American culture, however, to justify the non-violent strategy for opposing their violence-backed social systems. Nor need one be a consistent pacifist politically. Non-violence as a strategy for change may indeed appeal to a love of justice in some enemies' hearts, but the more ordinary appeal is to the enemies interests in paying the costs of just change in preference to the costs of maintaining injustice. Overwhelmingly, in Gandhi's India and Martin King's USA, the leaders of the movement tried to put the known interests of enemies to the service of their own interests. The interests included both the 'ideal' and 'material' interests of Max Weber, sometimes in dense interconnection.[4] For example, the final settlement for change in Birmingham, Alabama, in the spring of 1963 – after images of police dogs and fire hoses had gone their way around the world via television – came largely at the behest of a coalition of local white business people who knew the danger of Birmingham's reputation for violence to their own economic interests. Informal networks of new black-white leader relations got built from such pressures, sometimes at white initiative.[5] In hundreds of places around the South, the sit-ins and demonstrations of the movement played knowingly at the strategy: 'appeal to their pocketbooks'. More subtle, on the margin between material and cultural interests, was an appeal to local politicians to solve their own problems of interracial conflict without resort to either State or Federal officialdom. In Birmingham, to continue with that example, blacks had good reason to fear the State police as more dangerous and racist than the local police. They intentionally let it be known that 'we want the city police, whom we respect, to take charge'.[6]

In every community of the United States, the sense that 'we can solve our own problems' was strong, and recourse to the intervention of federal law enforcement officials was commonly perceived as a drastic local failure. Such local failures were many, leading in 1957 to national guard troopers around Central High School in Little Rock, Arkansas, and federal marshals escorting black children to school in New Orleans in 1960. No local white leaders relished the thought that this could happen in their own communities. Leaders of the Civil Rights movement knew this, and they regularly held over the heads of their political antagonists the threat of 'calling in the (US) Justice Department'. Such a threat as a final resort underscored something essential about the struggle: the intention of movement leaders to live side by side with their local antagonists in a new kind of political, economic, and social relationship. They sought local solutions as a key to locally sustainable new relations of justice. They thus had their own local version of the language use by Oliver Tambo (exiled leader of the African National Congress) in 1985 about the future of his country. 'We see a South Africa … that in spite of our history has become integrated … We all belong to South Africa and South Africa belongs to us all.' The crucial terms here are the first person plurals: a new level of inclusiveness that brings some people into political community for the first time without excluding the former opponents of such a community.

Non-violence has the power, in these circumstances, of *anticipating* this new relationship in the very forms of conflict preceding it. The new integrated society was not, in the movement's view, to be one in which violence to enforce justice substituted for violence enforcing injustice. All revolutions presuppose the desirability of such a substitution; but they thus carry in themselves the seeds of instability, since political change cannot be stable if reduced to the question of who has the power now to coerce whom.[8] Consent is an ingredient of real political power, and interest fosters consent. Eventually all social reformers will seek a combination of interests and consents to stabilize their reform. The wisdom of many leaders of the Civil Rights movement consisted in their determination and skill at mobilizing some of the needed interests and consents prior to the legal changes. They offered time and opportunity for this mobilizing by adopting the non-violent strategy as an invitation to the new relationships. As a black businessman in Birmingham, Ed Gardner, put it as he recollected the tensions of 1963:

(The segregationists) were armed to the teeth. They were prepared for violence and they could handle violence. But we
caught 'em off guard with non-violence. They didn't know what
to do with non-violence.[9]

Forgiveness Within the Movement

Early in the Montgomery bus boycott of 1955-56, an elderly
black woman said to Bayard Rustin: 'I've been around a long time.
These Negroes in Montgomery are never going to stick together.
They're going to run downtown and tell the white folks everything
we're doing.'[10] She was identifying what Martin Luther King, Jr
was to call 'the cancerous disease of disunity'[11] among American
blacks, beginning with their local communities.

Builders of political movements know from experience that the
relative internal solidarity needed for public impact requires many
a compromise between parties in the movement; and a neglected
aspect of democratic compromise is its empirical kinship with forgiveness. If the parliamentary system depends on the forgiveness of
sins – on willingness to leave old animosity behind in the name of
new collective achievements – then so does any political movement. Signs direct and indirect illustrated this principle at every
turn of the Civil Rights movement in the years 1955-68.[12]

The questions at stake in these internal struggles were no different from those of intragroup politics of all sorts: is there an over-
riding cause for whose sake the compromise of lesser interests is
worthwhile? Will interpersonal hostilities control choices of leadership and strategy or take second place to the conflict with the real,
external enemy? While disagreement reigns on the very definitions
of what 'sins' have been committed, will that argument continue in
the undergirding assumption that, whatever the diversity of sins,
these sinners intend to stick together? And do they thereby prepare
each other experientially for an eventual day of reconciliation even
with the enemy?

It seems clear that a political movement which practises no forgiveness internally will find its unity in constant jeopardy and itself ill-pre-
pared to extend forgiveness one day to the enemy. One of the unique
powers of the Civil Rights movement was here, with its source in the
culture of the black Church. Harding describes an incident in the jail at
Albany, Georgia, in 1961-62, that portrays this culture at work.

The invidious class distinctions that had plagued Albany and so many other similar black communities were momentarily forgotten as people from every level of life and experience were jammed into cells. One woman, Norma Anderson, the wife of the osteopath who led the movement, told me that she had never known an experience of communion in a church which equalled the deep unity she felt one night as she and eight other tired, thirsty, frightened, but courageous women in a cell built for two persons, passed around an old canning jar of water, sharing so much more than the lukewarm liquid that they drank.[13]

Forgiveness After the Achievement of New Power

A common experience among many white southerners, in the period following their defeat in the Civil War, was enormous fear of outbreaks of violence among newly freed black slaves. While the Charleston Convention was going on, many whites in South Carolina believed the rumour that 'the negroes have organised military forces in all sections of the State, and are almost certain to rise and massacre the whites about Christmas time'.[14] The psychology of this fear is an old story in the history of repression: the repressors attribute to their victims a capacity for revenge-in-kind once they come to power. Such an expectation is tangible in the utterances of many a white South African today.

Of any reformers or revolutionaries it will be fair to ask if they will manage to avoid repeating the crimes of their enemies once they come to power. In one respect, at least, the behaviour of American blacks in the Civil Rights movement is no fair analogy to South Africa: 'black power' in the United States for the predictable future will remain minority power. Hence the arts of survival against a still-dominant opposition may include the prudent restraints of minority politics generally. But this truth must not obscure a more remarkable truth about the behaviour of black leaders once they acquired new influence in American politics in the post-1968 era: they used this power to change the quality of many a white-black political relationship. There is no more dramatic illustration of this than the apparent impact of the Civil Rights movement upon the behaviour of one of the most notorious racist politicians of the fifties, Governor George Wallace of Alabama. As the Voting Rights Act of 1965 was about to be passed by the US Congress, several leaders of the Selma Movement – where voting was the chief issue – stood in the Governor's office in Montgomery and talked with him as he had seldom if ever been talked with before by black people.

> We met with him for ninety minutes, at which time I was spokesperson. We really challenged the Governor that day on a moral basis. I wouldn't let him get into the political arena. I said to him that 'I am speaking to you as a Methodist preacher to a Methodist layman', which he is, and I said, 'God has given you great gifts, of leadership, powers of persuasion, and he will call you to account for how you use them.'
>
> And he said, 'Well, I don't advocate violence.' I said, 'You don't in so many words, but you do … You are responsible for dividing us, and you are responsible for the violence.'
>
> … He probably for the first time got to see face to face how the black community felt about him and his leadership. And we weren't bitter, we didn't attack him in any vicious manner, but I did try to impress him with the moral responsibility that was his.[15]

At this point in his career, George Wallace began to moderate his appeals to racial prejudice among his white constituents; and by 1980, in one of the ironic political turnabouts in the history of American politics, recently enfranchised black Alabama voters could take partial credit for re-electing Wallace to yet another term as governor of that State. There was some forgiveness in that black support.

In fact, even in those counties of the South where blacks came to compose a voting majority, the transition to many new black faces in elective office occurred with few publicized traces of retaliation or even public rehearsals of the sins of the past. Even so militant a participant in the Mississippi Movement of the sixties as Hartman Turnbow, whom Martin King never convinced to adopt a theory of nonviolence, stated in the mid-seventies that he considered Mississippi now as the best place to live in the whole country. He was at peace in his retirement here now, he said, for here,

> You can just enjoy yourself better. It's just a better living. A better way of life. And I'm gon' finish it right here … I'm saying for a poor person, it's just gettin' right.

As Howell Raines comments on this remark,

> The Turnbows' story, repeated thousands of time, is what trans-
> formed the South from a region of despair to the new heartland
> of American optimism.[16]

Anticipation of revenge is the despair of entrenched power as it
foresees the access of new power to the previously powerless. The
willingness of the latter to remember the past only to be sure it is
not repeated in the new power-relations is the hope of political
change. And one name for that hope is forgiveness.

The Unique Power of Black Religion: A Conclusion

This is hardly a full summary of how black participants in the
Civil Rights movement of the fifties and sixties injected forgiveness
into the dynamics of their politics; but the pervasive source of this
forgiveness – not easily analysed into elements – is the taproot of
black Christian religion.

In the late seventies, Vincent Harding assessed the enduring
political impact of the Civil Rights movement upon American politics, in a symposium sponsored by the University of Mississippi, as
follows.

> Now, largely as a result of the movement King represented …
> the old America has been cracked, wedged open, cannot be the
> same again. Now, the forces which were absent from the first of-
> ficial beginning of America, in the days following July 4, 1776 –
> the blacks, the women, the Native Americans, the Chicanos, the
> students, and many more – all who were then pressed aside are
> now present … King helped create the possibility that all of us
> might break beyond our own individual and group interests and
> catch a vision of a new America, create a vision of a new com-
> mon good in a new future which will serve us all. He saw that
> our needs were economic *and* spiritual, political *and* moral, social
> *and* personal, and as the end, the beginning approached, he was
> groping his way towards a new integration … Let America be
> born again.[17]

In the modern world no final 'integration' of diverse interests and
cultures seems likely for any country calling itself democratic. A
'new integration' seems always called for as the boundaries between
justice and injustice rove and shift in political society. As all these

new groups reach for power in the United States of the future, black people themselves may find new scope for their own moral-political history; and, indeed, they may experience the new forces, which the Civil Rights movement helped admit to this society, as competitors. Further, the Christian base of a large part of the Civil Rights movement may suffer erosion within the black community itself. Religious kinship cannot be presupposed between it and all the other 'communities' of American political life.

Nonetheless, if the central claim of this essay is true, then the black religious heritage has already made a contribution to the always-threatened political unity of the United States by proving, from three and a half centuries of presence, that great social crime can be endured, resisted and overcome without the utter destruction of community between the sufferers and agents of the crime. That is the final test of the presence of forgiveness in a political event.

The taproot of that presence in black history has been religion. To black religion, in the final analysis, we owe the peculiar power and integrity of the claim, in American history, that there is a political form of the forgiveness of sins.

White observers of the Civil Rights movement, like myself, were reared to be sceptical of the transfer of the 'tender' sides of religious belief to the rough-and-tumble of secular politics. To our experience of and in the Civil Rights movement we owe the chastening of this scepticism in ourselves. We saw religion at work politically as we had not seen it before.[18]

Dramatic testimony to this has come in recent years from the eminent American child psychiatrist, Robert Coles. As a psychiatric medical resident in New Orleans in 1960, he observed the massive hostility of white parents to the Federal Court-ordered desegregation of that city's public schools; and, in particular, his interest gravitated to the several black children who went to two elementary schools boycotted solidly by white parents. One of the children, six-year-old Ruby Bridges, attended her school alone, was escorted for weeks by federal marshals past angry white mobs, and sat in a classroom all day with her one teacher. In great detail and considerable awe, Coles has narrated Ruby's story to dozens of audiences in the United States. In her, apparently, he sees something like Harding's 'reborn America'. And the heart of what he saw in Ruby came in an incident that occurred one morning as she walked into school. Her teacher reported to Coles that Ruby's lips were moving as she passed the white hecklers on the sidewalk. Pressed to tell him what she was saying out there, Ruby replied:

'I was saying a prayer for them.'

'Ruby, you pray for the people there?'

'Oh yes.'

'Why do you do that?'

'Because they need praying for.'

'Why you especially?'

'Because if you're going through what they're doing to you, you're the one who should be praying for them.'

And then she quoted to me what she had heard in church. The minister said that Jesus went through a lot of trouble, and he said about the people who were causing the trouble, 'Forgive them, because they don't know what they're doing.' And now little Ruby was saying this in the 1960s, about the people in the streets of New Orleans. How is someone like me supposed to account for that, psychologically or any other way?[19]

Neither social science nor white American culture, reflects Coles, 'accounts' for anything in terms of mystery. But this may be as near to an account as any reporter, psychiatrist, or theologian is likely to come. Forgiveness is a political possibility for many American black Christians because for them God is real.

Notes:

1. This essay depends heavily on longer, historically richer, and more detailed accounts of the Civil Rights Movement in a case study, 'Forgiveness and Politics: The Case of the American Civil Rights Movement', by the author, published as a part of the Forgiveness and Politics Project.

2. Vincent Harding, *There is a River: The Black Struggle for Freedom in America* (New York: Random House, Vintage Books, 1983), 327-8.

3. The Gettysburg Address, 1863.

4. I use these terms loosely, not finding in this conventional Weberian dualism, based on that of Kant, an accurate divider of political motives, especially in the Civil Rights Movement.

5. Vincent Harding, 'A Beginning in Birmingham', *The Reporter Magazine*, vol. 28, no. 12 (June 6, 1963), 15.

6. Ibid., p18.
7. *The New York Times,* week of September 1, 1985.
8. Cf. Hannah Arendt, *On Violence* (New York: Harcourt, Brace, and World, 1969).
9. Howell Raines, *My Soul is Rested: Movement Days in the Deep South Remembered* (New York: B.P. Putnam and Sons, 1977), 141.
10. Ibid., 56.
11. Ibid., 93.
12. Ibid., 434, 447.
13. Harding, 'So Much History, So Much Future: Martin Luther King, Jr and the Second Coming of America', in *Have We Overcome? Race Relations Since Brown,* ed. Michael V. Namerato (Jackson, Miss: University of Mississippi, 1979), 52.
14. Harding, *There is a River,* 323.
15. Raines, *My Soul is Rested,* 223. The spokesperson was Rev Joseph Lowery, future President of the Southern Christian leadership Conference.
16. Ibid., 20.
17. Harding, 'So Much History', 75-76.
18. Pat Watters, *Down to Now: Reflections on the Southern Civil Rights Movement* (New York: Random House, 1971), 16-17.
19. Robert Coles, 'The Inexplicable Prayers of Ruby Bridges', *Christianity Today,* vol. 29, no. 11 (August 9, 1985), 19-20.

On Shame and Hurt in the Life of Nations:
A German Perspective*

Geiko Müller-Fahrenholz

I

In his book *Menschen und Mächte,* the former West German chancellor Helmut Schmidt recalls a small, yet influential incident.
When Brezhnev came to Bonn in 1972 (it was the first visit of leading representatives from the then USSR to the Federal Republic),
he and some other members of his government spent one evening
in Willy Brandt's home. All of a sudden Brezhnev began to talk
about the atrocities of the German Army in his home country.
Apparently overwhelmed by these memories, he poured out more
and more terrible stories. When he had ended Helmut Schmidt
began to talk about his experiences as a young soldier in that very
army in Russia, about his bad conscience, his worries and that he
had meant to do nothing but his duty. And then he states:
'Probably it was this *exchange of bitter war memories* that signifi-
cantly contributed to the *mutual respect* which has characterized
our relationship between 1972 and up to his death ...'[1]

In the confidential atmosphere of Willy Brandt's home – a
trusted friend of both – these two statesmen take the courage to
travel back on the road of their memories to the tormenting past of
World War II in which Nazi Germany aimed at the destruction of
the Slavic peoples. It takes great strength to honestly face the sorrow, anger and bitterness which shape these memories. It is a moment of unconditional and disarming openness, an entry into deep
grief when the heart is allowed to speak its truth. The two men,
who had once been relentless enemies, met each other at the most
vulnerable point from which their 'bitter' memories originated.
Their exchange transformed them into trusting and respectful partners,
without of course removing their substantial political differences.

* Since this chapter was written, Dr Müller-Fahrenholz has continued his work on
this subject. See, for example, his *The Art of Forgiveness* (Geneva: WCC, 1997).

They met each other at the root cause of their bitter memories but they got there by different roads. That is to say, the memories of the Russian are different from those of the German. The Russian speaks of humiliation and degradation, of unjust and unimaginable sufferings. (More than 20 million people in the Soviet Republics lost their lives.) And if one keeps in mind the favourable and trusting image of the Germans in centuries of Russian life, culture and politics, the murderous onslaught of World War II becomes all the more stupendous and hurtful. Brezhnev's bitterness is that of a victim, filled with the experiences of subjugation and near-annihilation.

The bitterness of the German consists of experiences of massive guilt mixed with helplessness and misguided patriotism. There is the shame of having been part of a murderous army, of having been misused, and of not having found the way or the courage to openly resist.

The point that I wish to make is this: it is possible and necessary to distinguish between memories of shame and memories of hurt. While Schmidt is wrestling with his shame *(Scham)* Brezhnev has to come to terms with his hurt *(Kränkung)*. Obviously, the emotions surrounding shame are different from those accompanying hurt. Without going into detail here, we might say that shame tends to provoke self-accusation and self-justification, reproach and spite, whereas hurt tends to produce distrust, resentment and exaggerated security needs.[2]

The precious thing which happened to these two politicians was that in their exchange of memories they caught a glimpse of the other's hurt and shame. In making the other's memories their own, they freed each other from the bitterness of their past and, without fully knowing what they were doing, cleared the way for trust and respect.

II

A few years ago, a middle-aged German travelled to Stalingrad. The Russian lady interpreter in Moscow asked him, 'Why do you want to go to Volgograd?' And feeling that this was not a formal but a sympathetic question he responded, 'Because my father died there.' On his return to Moscow, the interpreter came to him and wanted to know what he experienced in Stalingrad. He told her, 'I was there! I have put my hands in the waters of the Volga river. I have felt the earth of Stalingrad in my hands. I was close to my father.' Then she said with tears, 'My father also died during the war.' And there was a great closeness between the two, members of the generation of daughters and sons, as they wept together: common mourning and an indescribable joy.[3]

I consider this a revealing story because it shows also that the members of the next generation, the daughters and sons, need to travel back to the memories of the great war which continues to have such a bitter impact on their lives. In the case of these two persons it is the loss of their fathers. 'Stalingrad' is the symbol of the horror which casts a long shadow over the life of the post-war generation, both in the Soviet Union and in Germany. It is not only a symbol of shame and hurt, but also of loss and immense sadness.

The two persons recognise in each other that they are both victims. The feeling of loss and fatherlessness is deeper than the knowledge that their fathers were bitter enemies. And it is in recognizing that loss that they are able to weep together. They suffer together as they share each other's hidden grief. The great joy that rises up in them comes from the discovery that a daughter and a son of the war-generation can heal each other's sorrows.

Here, too, the honesty of facing the bitter memories releases reconciling and liberating joy. It confirms the truth of the Hasidic saying that 'remembering is the secret of reconciliation'.[4]

III

As a member of the first post-World-War-II generation, I would like to emphasize the massive psychic impact of the Nazi period. Some say, 'Enough is enough.' After fifty years, we should stop groping around in our Nazi past and burying our heads in shame. But this is bad advice. It is an established psychological fact that parents cannot but implant in their children the social and emotional catastrophes which they have experienced. The children of the war – and post-war years – have not only imbibed the horrors of burning cities, of flights and refugee camps and of massacres. They have also absorbed the psychic numbing of their parents in concentration camps or extreme war situations, the massive cataclysm of faith of those German women and men who had put all their trust in Adolf Hitler and who, in 1945, found themselves utterly and completely betrayed, their 'sacrifices' misused. It has taken four decades to realise the ongoing damage of the war on us.

By 'us' I do not only refer to the Germans – and, to a similar degree, the Austrians – who need to come to terms with their history of shame. I also refer to the generation of sons and daughters in the European countries involved in the war. In my encounters with women and men from Holland, Denmark, Norway, Finland, Poland and the Soviet Union, I have had to realize with sadness that they have to deal with a history of hurt, too. This is much more obvious among the children of the survivors of the Shoah (I prefer this term to the more widely used term 'Holocaust'), as can be seen very clearly in Helen Epstein's *Children of the Holocaust*.[5]

It needs many years to gain enough distance in order to be able to see the various impacts of this war. Thus far too little attention has been given to the question of how memories of hurt can be overcome. Memories of humiliation and degradation will not lose their painful sting by re-emphasizing the guilt of the other. In psychoanalytical terms, that would be a projection which serves to conceal rather than to heal one's own hurt. John Patton has shown that reconciliation cannot take place unless there is repentance on the side of the guilty and a giving up of 'righteousness' on the side that has been hurt.[6] In other words, there has to be a sense of compassion that begins to understand the other side, that begins to grieve about both the shame and the hurt. Compassion bears the pain of the past. It no longer tries to accuse, to suppress, to condemn, to refuse. It allows the memories to uncover the origins of shame and hurt. Such memories will bring deep sorrow. But it is through such sorrow and grief that we set each other free from the chains of past wrongs so that we may freely move towards a new future together.

I have tried to elaborate what happened in the two stories mentioned above. I think they are stories of forgiveness. They show that forgiveness is a process that involves both sides. It is mutual. It is not always clear how it begins. Perhaps it needs a third party that provides some trust and protection (e.g. the private home of Willy Brandt). It will not happen unless the guilty party indicates its desire to be forgiven. But it can only be the victim that forgives. It is

the side that has been made passive that regains its activity in the
act of forgiving. Through it, persons who had been made objects
and sub-human become again masters of their destiny.

IV

Forgiveness is widely regarded as a religious term. Does it follow
then that only religious people can experience forgiveness?
Obviously not. The philosopher Hannah Arendt has pointed out
that forgiveness is an every day event among human beings.[7] It is
the process by which we liberate each other from the irreversibilities
of the past. If we did not have this possibility, we would always be
chained to past acts, and our actions would always be guided by retaliation and revenge. Forgiving is the act in which this chain is
broken. Although provoked by a past act, it is not conditioned by
it. Thus forgiving liberates both the one who is being forgiven and
the one who is forgiving from the consequences of the past.

Arendt thinks that Jesus was the first person in history to discover what forgiveness can achieve in the realm of human affairs.
She underlines this with interesting references to the New
Testament, not least to the well known petition of the Lord's
Prayer: 'Forgive us our trespasses as we forgive those who trespass
against us.' Surely, however, human beings before Jesus and outside
the range of his teachings have experienced and practised the art of
forgiving. If this were not so, one could not speak of forgiving as a
normal human potentiality.

But the reference to Jesus elucidates a point to which Arendt has
not given sufficient attention. Jesus was able to break through the
irreversibilities of the past because he lived by the strength of God,
whom he was the first to call 'Father'. This observation shows that
there is a third factor in the process of forgiveness, namely that
specific element of strength, faith or trust which makes us sufficiently free from the feelings of guilt, shame and anger, to act independently and to make the forgiving and reconciling move.

This 'third factor' may be characterized as the transcending and
contingent element in the relationship of persons, a spark of
courage to open up, that moment of daring and trusting which
causes the heart to jump over the fence. It is this surprising energy
which lays down the dividing walls between us. (cf. Eph 2:14)

I would maintain, therefore, that forgiveness does not happen between only two parties but is of a triadic nature. This is very clearly visible in an event which was recalled by the Russian Metropolitan Pitirim. When the first delegation of (West) German church leaders came to Moscow to begin a theological dialogue with representatives of the Russian Orthodox Church they took part in a service of worship. During that event they expressed their shame about the horrors which the Germans had brought to the peoples of the Soviet Union and asked to be forgiven. In the great worshipping crowd, many had tears in their eyes as they remembered the cruelties and losses of that time. Then they said, 'God may forgive you.' And they moved to the German church leaders, asked to be blessed and kissed their crosses as they are used to doing with their own priests and bishops.[8]

The Russian worshippers are saying, '*God* may forgive you.' But in saying that they kiss the crosses of the former enemies, and ask for their blessings. This signifies that they are prepared to treat them as if they were their own bishops. They are acting in a forgiving way but not without invoking God to provide them with the liberating strength to overcome their hurtful memories.

In religious contexts, this third or transcending element will often be associated with God. But this does not mean that such a transcending element could not occur outside religious or ecclesial settings.

What happened between Brezhnev and Helmut Schmidt may well have been facilitated by the privacy of Willy Brandt's home. Perhaps this was the factor which transcended the boundaries of polite small talk. Call it God, or Holy Spirit, or friendship, or compassion, or faith in our common humanity – there are many ways to trigger off the process of forgiveness.

V

Hannah Arendt deplores that the every day phenomenon of forgiveness has not yet been taken seriously in political life. Therefore politics has tended to be of the reactionary kind, following the pattern of rebuke, reprisal, and retaliation. But why is it that forgiveness has not been accepted as a political possibility? Arendt maintains that this idea has remained enclosed in its religious context and that forgiveness has become associated with the high claims of divine love so that the fact has not been realised that forgiveness is a human possibility.

I have difficulty with this argument. If forgiveness was indeed a normal, human capacity it would also have had an impact on politics. After all, politics is a human activity, and it is only too obvious that politicians are as much guided by their very personal preferences, fears and values as by rational analyses and/or national interests. Perhaps the following two considerations may help us to come closer to the point.

a) It is difficult to transpose personal categories such as forgiveness – and that applies equally well to everything that I have said about shame and hurt – into the realm of politics. Is it adequate to use concepts and ideas which are based on personal and psychological phenomena to describe societal processes and the behaviour of nations?

We know that there is only a very limited truth in talking about the 'character' of peoples. It is equally hazardous to employ religious and psychological terms to 'analyse' historical processes and emotional situations of peoples. It must be clear from the outset that we may only use such categories with the utmost caution.

But having said this, there are such things as collective memories, for instance, of great victories, or traumatic defeats. Although they may have a different impact on individuals, they are exerting considerable influence on public consciousness and life. Such memories are reflected in myths and sagas, in stories, songs and dances. They find expression in public symbols and cultural traditions. Moreover, it is these memories which can be used in all kinds of propaganda, and on which public and political life is relying more or less consciously.

There is an intricate relationship between the history of wars and defeats, domination and oppression, on the one side, and layers of arrogance and fear, disappointment and anger, on the other. On this basis, politics is defined as the defence and propagation of national interests over against those of others. The type of thinking that is based on the fear of the worst possible event has its origins in this dilemma. This also applies to national stereotypes and enemy images.

b) However, as long as politics is performed on this antagonistic basis, there is little chance for forgiveness because there is little room for the 'third factor', the transcending element, to play its role.

Here it is important to look for persons, groups, peoples and organisations which are able to serve as facilitating agents. We may point to such persons as Olaf Palme or Willy Brandt who gained – and generated – trust beyond their own countries. We can also point to neutral countries which are able to serve as trust-building agents, e.g. Finland in the Helsinki Agreements. Most of all the United Nations and their agencies help to bring about new perspectives which are able to transform antagonistic structures between nations.

In this context one must also ask, 'Is there a special role for religions?' Surely one would expect that the Christian churches should have learned from Jesus the art of forgiving? And as they move into a worldwide ecumenical fellowship, should they not be prepared to serve as a transcending power between the peoples to whom they belong? This is indeed happening here and there.

To give an example, again from my own background: in 1965 the Council of the Protestant Churches in Germany issued the so-called *Ost-Denkschrift*. In it they argued that all claims to the Eastern parts of the German Reich ought to be abandoned and the new boundaries be accepted as a consequence of World War II. This memorandum created a wide and bitter debate in the Federal Republic. But it broke the chain of past irreversibilities and paved the way for the famous and successful 'Ostpolitik' of the Brandt government in the early seventies.

This and other examples indicate that the churches can indeed exercise an ecumenical ministry of forgiveness and reconciliation. But this ministry is still rather weak and will remain weak as long as the churches do not find ways to overcome their own histories of condemnation and separation. As long as they find it impossible to invite each other to their eucharist they will have little credibility in calling their nations to engage in a politics of forgiveness.

VI

With this last reflection I am returning briefly to the two stories

which I mentioned in my first point. They tell of encounters between persons. In their close interactions these persons were able to
help each other in their shame and hurt and to recognize each other
in unexpected ways of respect and joy. My final question is, 'Can
there be public symbolic acts in which something similar takes
place?' A telling incident comes to mind here. Many will recall that
strange moment during Willy Brandt's visit to Warsaw. As he visited
the memorial of the uprising of the Jews in the Warsaw Ghetto, he
knelt down, all of a sudden, apparently overwhelmed by the memories of that horrible part of the Nazi past. It was a spontaneous act
and surprised all who saw it. But its meaning was understood almost instinctively. It was the symbolic expression of shame and a
plea for forgiveness which expressed the feelings of many Germans
and which was valued very highly by non-Germans, notably the
Polish people. They understood the sincerity of that gesture which
was all the more acceptable and even disarming since it came from
a German who had himself been a resistance fighter against Hitler.

But there were also many in Germany who criticized this symbolic act. They felt that Brandt had shown too much weakness and
that he had made himself exploitable. Obviously it is not easy at
first to see that this type of weakness in reality reveals a rare kind of
strength. There can be no doubt that Brandt's unexpected gesture
made it easier for Polish people to overcome their deep hurt and to
become his political partners.

I think we ought to search for public symbolic acts which un-
derline the uniting and reconciling elements in the histories of our
nations. We have enough memorials of heroes of all kinds, but who
and where are the heroes of 'the integrative power of forgiveness'
(Alan Falconer)?

The war that Nazi Germany waged against the Soviet Union
brought death to more than 20 million people. To this day no
representative of my government has had the heart to publicly recognize this terrible fact. Is it not reasonable to hope that such a declaration may make it easier for the Russian peoples to address whatever shame they feel with regard to their (Stalinist) past?

I think we need to set in motion processes in which the bitter
memories of our peoples are brought out into the open and healed.
We need to trust that in such weakness lies our strength; for unless
we risk losing face we will surely ruin the face of the earth.

Notes:

1. *Menschen und Mächte* (Siedler Verlag, 1987), 18f, italics mine.
2. Cf. John Patton, *Is Human Forgiveness Possible?* (Nashville: Abingdon Press, 1985).
3. This account of Hermann Roth can be found in E. Raiser, ed., *Brücker der Verständigung,* (Gutersloher Verlagshaus, 1986), 15.
4. This word is found in the Memorial of Yad Vashem in Jerusalem. In full it says: 'Forgetting prolongs captivity. Remembering is the secret of reconciliation.'
5. New York: G. P. Putnam Sons, 1979.
6. Cf. Patton, *Is Human Forgiveness Possible?,* ch. 4, 'Defending Against Shame with Righteousness', 93-116.
7. In *The Human Condition* (Chicago: University of Chicago Press, 1958), esp. 33.
8. Cf. epd-Documentation 5/88, 73.

Silence that Leads to Peace

Carol J. Birkland

There is a season for everything, a time for every occupation under heaven ... a time for keeping silent, a time for speaking. (Ecclesiastes 3:1,7).

Writing anything 'timely' about the Israeli/Palestinian conflict is always a risk. No sooner has the final period been affixed to the final sentence than circumstances once again prove how difficult it is to make definitive judgments about a conflict that has defied the efforts of peacemakers for over thirty years.

However, recent events give some indication that both parties may soon be willing to embark on a process which might demonstrate that they have begun to understand what most of the rest of the world has known for some time: that for the benefit of both Israelis and Palestinians, the land of Israel/Palestine must be shared rather than claimed as the exclusive property of either party.

For the past twelve years I have known individuals on both sides of this conflict. At times I have been awed by their ability to empathize with their enemy's suffering; at other times I have been appalled by their unwillingness to look beyond anti-Israeli and anti-Palestinian stereotypes which provide irrefutable evidence proving that indeed their enemies are less than human.

Specifically I also learned something about myself as I have tried to play the role of mediator and peace-maker. What I learned has to do with reconciliation – a word we Christians often use and one which, out of ignorance, we sometimes rather carelessly apply to conflict situations.

Dietrich Bonhoeffer wrote about 'cheap' and 'costly' grace. What I will attempt to write about here is 'cheap' and 'costly' reconciliation as it relates to the Israeli/Palestinian conflict. Perhaps the lessons I have learned about when to be silent and when to speak might be of assistance to those who in other situations struggle to be faithful to the Christian vocation of peace-making.

Faced with conflict situations, it might not be too much of a generalization to state that we post-Enlightenment Christians almost always prefer talking to silence. We put great faith in our ability to 'talk things out'. Reasonable people, we believe, have the intellectual and communicative gifts to resolve their differences, and as a result we do not quite know what to do with the above piece of wisdom from Ecclesiastes which seems to advocate the positive aspect of keeping silent.

In the summer of 1986 I was travelling in Israel, the Occupied West Bank and Gaza, gathering material for what was to become a book of interviews entitled *Unified in Hope: Arabs and Jews Talk about Peace* (Geneva: World Council of Churches, 1987). I spent about a month interviewing a number of Israelis and Palestinians who had distinguished themselves by their willingness to talk to persons on the other side of the conflict.

Both my motives and those of the people I interviewed were, without doubt, good. My objective was to allow these 'reasonable' people to speak for themselves so that negative stereotypes might be destroyed and the innate humanity of both Israelis and Palestinians made evident to all who read the book.

Cheap Reconciliation

One day in Tel Aviv I met an Israeli named Willy Gafni, a director of a public policy organization called The International Center for Peace in the Middle East. Gafni, an ex-Israeli military officer, told me a story which now, after a year and a half of the Palestinian Uprising, makes much more sense than it did at first hearing.

A few months after the 1967 War which marked the beginning of Israeli occupation of the West Bank and Gaza, Gafni, through a Palestinian friend, arranged to meet the former vice-mayor of Ramallah whom the Israeli military government had expelled from that city to the town of Jericho. This would be Gafni's first meeting with a Palestinian leader, and he was anxious to make a personal contact and begin an exploratory dialogue.

According to Gafni the first half-hour of the encounter was a disaster: 'He was citing his slogans, I was citing mine. We couldn't find any beginning of communication between us.' Finally, in frustration, Gafni said, 'Look, can't we talk like equals?' 'But we are not equals', came the vice-mayor's reply. 'I am lying on the floor and you are standing with your foot on my neck and telling me, from the height of one and three quarter metres, that we should talk like equals. We are not equals. You are the conqueror and I am the conquered.'

Twenty years were to pass between the time of Gafni's conversation in Jericho and the beginning of the Palestinian Uprising in December, 1988. During much of that time the Palestinian community acted the part assigned to it by the Israelis: that of a defeated, humiliated people. For twenty years the Palestinians proceeded to blame a host of others for their problems. The Israelis were blamed for the Zionist enterprise, Europe was blamed for having created the situation making Zionism a political necessity, and the United States was blamed for its unquestioning support of Israeli policy. Indeed while the blame had its basis in fact, the Palestinians, consumed by an attitude of defeatism, invested what little energy they had in assigning blame rather than in taking responsibility for their community. It was not until two years before the Uprising that one began to hear young Palestinians say openly that it was about time Palestinians took their fate into their own hands. If Palestinians were to achieve their goal of political self-determination, these young Palestinians said, they and they alone had to be responsible for the achievement. Nobody was going to grant their goals as a free gift. Many of these same young people also were not interested in speaking with Israelis, no matter how liberal their politics or how involved in the Israeli peace movement.

Certainly some dialogue did take place, but in retrospect it was a 'cheap' dialogue – lacking substance on both sides. On the Israeli side one sensed enormous good will, but an inability to understand honestly the reality of Palestinian life under occupation. At a deeper level, there was also an unwillingness to deal honestly with a history regarded as glorious, but one that was directly responsible for incredible Palestinian suffering.

On the Palestinian side – at least in relation to those Palestinians who were willing to talk – there was the nagging problem of the humiliated conquered speaking with the conquerors. Even among those Palestinians who routinely met with Israelis on a professional and personal level, one sensed their inability to relate to their Israeli counterparts as equals. Not a lot had changed since Gafni's encounter with the vice-mayor twenty years earlier.

It is not without pause that I describe many of the efforts towards reconciliation emerging from this kind of dialogue as 'cheap' since it was, in reality, not costly for either Palestinians or Israelis. Israelis did not have to face the kinds of difficult political and social questions which were more comfortably ignored, and Palestinians did not have to face the fact that not only were they a defeated, humiliated people, but worse, they had achieved precious little in the previous twenty years to make their situation better.

Costly Reconciliation

Everything changed when in December, 1988, the people of the Gaza Strip decided that they had enough of the occupation. They picked up stones and began to throw them at the Israeli army. It was in the picking up and throwing of the stones that the Palestinians were able to cast off their humiliation and move towards a point where they now seem able to engage in the kind of 'costly' dialogue with Israelis which may bring true and lasting reconciliation.

From a Christian perspective one wishes that this Palestinian transformation might have occurred through non-violent methods and no loss of life. However, that was not to be the case, and one can only be thankful that the level of violence and the loss of life have not been greater.

Almost one year ago Mubarak Awad, the director of the Palestinian Centre for the Study of Non-Violence, told a group of Palestinians meeting at the Lutheran Church of the Redeemer in East Jerusalem that, 'If we want our freedom, we must be ready to personally suffer for it.' Less than a month later, Awad was arrested by the Israeli police and, after a legal battle waged by both Israeli and Palestinian lawyers, he was deported from Israel.

It was clear from what Awad said that day that Palestinian self-respect had been forged by the Israeli use of collective punishment in response to the stone throwing. He never departed from his personal commitment to the non-violent struggle, stressing again and again his wish that the struggle be carried on in a non-violent manner, but he spoke for the entire Palestinian community when he said, 'As a result of the Palestinian Uprising, I can meet any Israeli, I can look him in the eye, and shake his hand not as his inferior, not as his superior, but as his equal.'

True reconciliation occurs between equals. The two parties need not be politically equal. If that were the case, the Palestinians would have little hope of challenging the Israeli military and political system. In order to begin a dialogue for peace, however, it is critically important that the politically oppressed party view itself as equal to its oppressor. This is not the kind of equality that comes only through violent acts, rather it is the kind of equality that comes from a community's hard won self-respect. It is the notion of equality which must exist in the minds of those seeking their political rights.

In the case of the Palestinian community it was not until they chose silence rather than the talk which had previously masqueraded for 'costly' reconciliation that they began to view themselves as legitimate partners for peace talks with Israel. Palestinians are no longer afraid of Israelis. They have abandoned their collective inferiority complex, and because of that they are ready to make peace with the Israelis.

As this process has been a costly one for Palestinians, so has it been costly for Israelis: they can no longer ignore Palestinian political demands. Sooner or later, they must sit down with Palestinian representatives to grapple, not rhetorically, but realistically, with the hard political issues which must be solved before a just and lasting peace is achieved.

While the Palestinians are no longer afraid of Israelis, Israelis continue, despite their massive military power, to be afraid of Palestinians. There are legitimate historical reasons for this fear, but it is fear linked to a specific historical situation that no longer exists. Nonetheless it is a fear which must be assuaged before peace can come, and difficult as it may be for Palestinians to accept, it is a fact that only Palestinians can rid Israelis of this fear.

Generosity Based on Strength

One of the Palestinians interviewed in the summer of 1986 was Raja Shehadeh, an attorney from Ramallah and one of the co-founders of Al-Haq, the West Bank human rights organisation associated with the International Commission of Jurists in Geneva.

During the interview Shehadeh talked at length about the difficulties of trying to protect people's rights in a place where they have no rights. He talked about a situation where the Israeli authorities had appointed a number of Palestinians to serve in an official capacity as part of the military administration in the West Bank. Their position now gave them authority over their fellow Palestinians, and Shehadeh lamented the fact that they were abusing their authority by dealing harshly with the same people he was trying to protect legally.

Shehadeh said that listening to these Palestinians (today they would be called collaborators) made him realize that

> it is only the weak (who) seem to get at the weak. To be magnanimous and generous you have to be strong ... I realized how Christ had completely turned the tables, and showed how the weak could be strong and generous by forgiving. The act of forgiveness carries a lot of power. It is an assertion of one's dignity to have the means and ability to forgive ... It may be difficult to understand, but idealistically speaking, I think that if there is to be peace here, there has to be forgiveness ... We have to forgive them (the Israelis) for what they did to us.

An Israeli general has said of the Palestinian Uprising: 'The Palestinians have discovered the strength in their weakness and the weakness in our strength.' The Uprising has not only given Palestinians their dignity, it has given them the strength to forgive Israelis, and herein lies the answer to Israeli fears.

There is a time to speak and there is a time to keep silent. When Palestinians stopped talking and picked up stones, they gave credence to the wisdom of Ecclesiastes. If that silence had only been replaced by more silence, there would be no wisdom in it. However, with their newly discovered dignity and strength for forgiveness, the Palestinians will speak after their silence, and in so speaking honestly and empathically with Israelis will, I think, make the step toward peace which has been far too long in coming.

Northern Ireland and the British-Irish Relationship

Frank Wright

This article is about the importance of British-Irish governmental co-operation to the settlement of the Northern Ireland conflict. Britain and Ireland have been allies to opposing national communities in Northern Ireland. If they allowed these groups to dictate their agenda, they would be drawn into deep conflict with each other. Northern Ireland is the frontier zone in which all that is conflictual in British-Irish relations has been concentrated. The main thing that makes it different from the much more violent situations in Lebanon and Cyprus is that the external parties to the Northern Ireland conflict – Britain and the Irish Republic – will not go to war over it. Nor in all probability, will they be drawn in, each to support their own nationals in a confrontation, as happened to Greece and Turkey in Cyprus in 1963-5. This means that the forces of panic and fear, which often rapidly partition or repartition such places, are not likely to be let loose here. The British and Irish governments have two other possibilities. One is to co-operate to create a new relationship with each other, each accepting the other as the guarantor of its national community within Northern Ireland. The second is to agree that they cannot do this, but that they will loosen their relationships with the communities within Northern Ireland in order to avoid any escalation of conflict between themselves. In both cases the two governments will be distrusted and opposed by at least some of their own side. In the first case they live with the expectation that the trust they develop between themselves will make wider trust possible within Northern Ireland. In the second they respond to that distrust by reducing their responsibilities. They will then accept the intensity of conflict as an unchangeable fact.

It is necessary then to point out that the lack of control the British and Irish governments have over the different communities may have a positive aspect. In Cyprus the external governments were looked upon as reliable allies by the internal groups; but their control was almost directly proportional to their own willingness for confrontation with each other. If the British and Irish governments are to create a framework which reduces to a minimum the chances that any internal confrontation can set off a real panic, they will not only have to cooperate, but to create the clear expectation in Northern Ireland that they will cooperate. Having been allies of the internal groups in Northern Ireland when these were in confrontation, the two governments cannot expect the switch in their own relationship to be easy. Cooperation is valuable when it gives as clear a picture as possible of a future for Northern Ireland, and when it creates the expectation that any groups hoping to force the two governments into collision with each other will encounter their co-ordinated opposition.

Some of the criticisms of politicians for not engaging in talks about devolution, and the debates about whether to suspend the Anglo-Irish Agreement or not in order to make this possible, may be overlooking a major issue. No one could have expected the unionists to like the Anglo-Irish Agreement initially. They will be unable to show their followers any possible advantage from it unless they can see British-Irish government cooperation yielding gains in security and acceptance by nationalists of the continued existence of Northern Ireland. Therefore to become preoccupied with getting the unionists to the negotiating table – and either failing to achieve this or doing it at the price of letting the Anglo-Irish Agreement go – may let the governments slide out of the necessity of developing their own co-operation. For better or worse, the way unionists and nationalists relate to each other in Northern Ireland is very much affected by the relationship between the wider nations to which they belong.

The antagonistic relationship, as in other situations of national conflict, is primarily about the relationship of both communities to State power. In the first part of this article I will show that what distinguishes the two communities is opposing expectations of the British State and of each other. These expectations regenerate themselves through generations. Probably the only way to shift this negative cycle is by a determination on the part of both governments to create an explicitly bi-national system of government within Northern Ireland.

In the second part I will draw attention to the consequences of the conditionality of the British claim to sovereignty over Northern Ireland, and suggest that, while it has been an advantage to have softened the clash of sovereignty claims that existed between the UK and the Irish Republic before the signing of the Anglo-Irish Agreement in 1985, the creation of a bi-national context requires much greater clarity.

In the third part I will show that such change cannot be brought about unless what is happening is clearly spelled out. It may be that the governments have very good reason to fear that such change is impossible. But to create symmetry in the relationship between the two communities in the North, the expectations of both towards the State must change qualitatively. It is not only necessary that unionists should no longer be able to determine the terms of the union between Britain and Northern Ireland; it is also necessary that nationalists come to be part of Northern Ireland and know that they are coming into the same relationship to State power as the unionists. The paradox of the Anglo-Irish Agreement is that to avoid annoying unionists too much, it could not or did not go far enough to make nationalists (of any kind) feel their position in the North entrenched. Unless that happens, nationalist leaders can hardly take responsibility for the North and provide unionists with the security that communal equality needs to promise and eventually bring them.

The Circle of Pessimistic Expectations

In national conflicts, law, order and justice are not just some of the issues that happen to arise from other causes. National conflicts, once they are fully developed, revolve around these matters. It is from these that differences, which are too painful to talk about, arise and then remain as walls between peoples. Such peace as Northern Ireland has enjoyed has not been like the peace most Europeans experience; it has been more like a mutual deterrence relationship. Unionist historical experience has been that nationalists must be deterred from making trouble. They have found it possible and sometimes necessary to defy British governments to show them that British rule depends upon unionist compliance. Nationalist experience has been that they have been treated as alien; Britain, whatever the vague wishes of particular governments, will always do in the end what unionists dictate. People remember the parts of their history that have some kind of echo in their present relationships.

The precariousness of Northern Irish society is that the two communities relate to each other in rather the same way as two potentially hostile countries might, but without the advantage of distance between them which allows the relationship to be conducted by diplomats. In most societies nearly everyone takes the effective operation of the judicial system for granted. Criminalizing offenders lets the rest of society (often very hypocritically) believe that it is always possible to establish guilt by finding out who struck the first blow. People do not even have to be very interested in what the reasons were why a blow was struck. There are no socially accepted reasons for private violence, and each time the law acts, it cancels ongoing pretexts for violence (e.g. vengeance). In such a society, free from the expectation of violence of anything more than an isolated criminal kind, people more or less routinely trust each other, whereas the same trust displayed in a situation of communal deterrence requires a measure of faith or risk.

In Northern Ireland people are often physically attacked for who they are and what group they belong to, not for anything they have done themselves. Violence can spread from one incident in a chain reaction, or fester as an ongoing feud. For this process to work it is not necessary for people to agree with the violence done by their own community. They only have to understand what is happening and to be frightened by it. Then, however much they dislike the violence done by their own people to others, the other side's violence is seen to be more dangerous. This process can develop until communities end up accepting the protection of violent people in their own group, even if they know that these same people played a big part in starting it.

From around the 1830s British governments sometimes tried to stop sectarian conflict in the North of Ireland. Local people often saw this as intervening in an arbitrary way in something that had been going on for years. If the government tried to criminalize (isolate) someone involved in violence or provocation, many people either agreed with what that person did or at least thought they had been provoked. Few people of the same religion as the offender would consider what the law did was just, because they 'knew' it was only bad luck that that person was the particular link in the chain of violence that the law tried to remove. They could always point to provocations that came from the other side and went unpunished. When the British government was having difficulty keeping control of the South of Ireland, it was much easier to take the side of Protestants in the North, so that at least someone supported British law. The stronger nationalism became in the South, the more closely was Britain linked to unionism in the North.

In the long run this meant that Catholics in the North came to expect that in any sectarian conflict the law would end up against them or at best neutral, and Catholics who opposed British law with violence were never seen as ordinary criminals. Thus there were very few Fenians in the North in the 1860s but Catholic support for the Fenian amnesty movement was general. The ambiguous feeling of Catholics about Fenians and their successors proved to Protestants that they could not be trusted. The suspicion is the reason and (or) excuse for all the vigilante practices of unionist society and these can rarely be criminalized, because they seem understandable to many unionists who personally disapprove of them. Thus the circular aspect of deterrence relationships is that they always generate justifications for their existence.

Once a dominant community knows it is deterring those it has defeated, it is also distrustful. Protestants got used to the idea that if they thought the British were taking the side of the Catholics, they could defy the government, which could not in the long run govern without unionist support. Although this relationship was already well established, the setting up of the devolved government of Northern Ireland in the 1920s exacerbated it. The partition of Ireland left Irish nationalists in the North with the hope that somehow the Irish Free State would be their support, even though they were separated from it. That same possibility was an eternal threat to Ulster unionists. It is inconceivable that new relationships can develop, if one community still has the sense that it is in control and taking precautions against the other, and if the other has the sense that in the last analysis they will be governed against. The question is whether there is any possible institutional arrangement that the two governments, each acting as guarantors for their community, can now work out which would both change the expectations and the reality. If they cannot do this themselves, it is quite unrealistic to suppose anyone else can.

The Need for a Transcendence of Bi-nationality

So long as there is conflict between Britain and Ireland about the North, some internal groups will always behave as though they can rely upon the external support of one of the governments to strengthen them against their opponents within Northern Ireland. More militant groups know they have to create confrontation if they want to draw their own guarantor into conflict on their side. In contrast to most other experiences of social peace, fear is everywhere. Peace is always about capping a potential conflict. People can fear that the law either will not protect them or it will in some way even tolerate or help their enemy. They can fear that violent people on their own side might stir the other side up to attack them. And they can be afraid that criticism of those who support violence will lead to them being branded as traitors. Fear does not just divide people, it also unites them.

It is often said that people get on very well with each other, so long as they are not stirred up by trouble makers. But in fact good community relationships usually consist of politely avoiding all subjects which touch upon communal differences and about which everyone fears there can be no purpose in talking. The result of this kind of good feeling is that very little is learned about what the other side experiences and feels. Even with friends of the other side, people often do not know how far they share the opinions or feelings of hostility they have heard from their spokespersons. It is easy to see all those in the other community united together against one's own group. Good feeling can be plagued by anxiety about stumbling upon unbridgeable differences and accidentally giving offence, so many things remain unspoken. The feared end of such discussions, which friends avoid having, is that this land is our land and yours – if you accept our terms. Expressions of a hostile kind, by contrast, are not inhibited in this way. Everyone is in danger of being represented towards the other community by the worst things that come from their own group. In the same way they often

judge the other group on the basis of the worst political statements
made by their leaders, when these pass without contradiction. The
two communities have been trapped in a mutual threat relationship, which is what the national antagonism is primarily about.
Without a clear undertaking from the two governments that they
will work together to make this land belong equally to both communities, there can be no transcendence, no point upon which
people can come together.

Guarantor Relationships and Sovereignty Claims

Today we are apt to think that the Ulster Protestants' Britishness
is an anachronism, because it does not have much of an echo in
mainland Britain. Almost certainly the real reason for this lack of
concern is hidden from view. When a settlement of disputed
Germanic areas was imposed in the 1919 peace treaties, leaving mil-
lions of Germans under Polish or Czech rule, people in Germany
and Austria suddenly became very concerned. The well known
Sudeten Germans were a 20 per cent minority in Czechoslovakia
and many people thought it quite in order that Hitler set out to
bring them into Germany. If Britain had been defeated in the First
World War and obliged to accept a united Ireland imposed by the
Germans, it is very possible that the Ulster British minority would
have become a British Sudetenland. But because Britain kept
Northern Ireland, British people forgot about Ulster. It takes people of our own nation to be taken from us before we even think
about them. For example, it took an Argentinian invasion of the
Falkland islands to let most UK citizens even know they existed, let
alone that they were British and indeed important enough to fight
for. Nations do not have any clear transcendental principles about
how to deal with disputed national zones, so they are in danger of
being first drawn into rivalry and afterwards finding the reasons for
the fight. People desire very much whatever others have shown
them is desirable by taking it away from them. The Republic has
desired Northern Ireland very much, because Britain took it. Now
that the Republic is beginning to be given some influence over the
North, we are beginning to see clearer signs that many of the people in the Republic really do not want it.

Since at least the late 1960s, people in Britain have seen Ulster as
a slightly British place with a lot of religious bigotry. This has led to

a sense of distance which has had a two-edged effect. It meant both that there was no mainland British disagreement about the need for Stormont to be made to introduce civil rights reforms, but also that Westminster was reluctant to take direct responsibility for imposing them. To have done this would have entailed asserting Northern Ireland's place in the UK far more firmly. Leaving the initiative with Stormont meant that Britain eventually got stuck in its historically 'normal' position in relation to the two communities when the honeymoon ended in 1969-70 after the initial military intervention. The formula that Northern Ireland is British so long as the majority wishes is a diplomatic way of softening the clash of sovereignty claims with the Irish Republic and of reducing Northern Ireland's significance for British-Irish relations. It is a way of making sure that commitments are not entered into that would permit Northern Ireland to be 'Falklandised'. But it has also encouraged two beliefs, firstly that the unionists will eventually be persuaded to leave the UK, and secondly that their wish to remain part of it is somehow abnormal, rather than simply arising from the fact that they are British.

These latter implications are dangerous. They make it easy to represent any British move to accept the guarantor role of the Republic in relation to the northern nationalists as a prelude to abandonment of Northern Ireland and not as a move toward communal equality. It is not possible to tell unionists that from now on Northern Ireland will be bi-national, that the British unionist community will be equal with the Irish nationalist community in the North, and that both will be upheld by their respective British and Irish guarantors, if in fact the British guarantorship towards unionists is being allowed to crumble. Because the loyalists have been rejecting Britain as a guarantor since the Anglo-Irish Agreement, Britain itself may well be despairing of its guarantor relationship to unionists. Yet the only possibility of laying the foundations of a bi-national structure depends upon both external governments being able to act as guarantors for their national community in Northern Ireland. And if they accept that this is impossible, it is very likely in reality to become impossible. This may please some loyalists and some advocates of British withdrawal for a while, but the actual result will be to reduce even further any British efforts to do anything

other than to take the line of least resistance in its dealings with
Northern Ireland.

Problems of Intergovernment Co-operation

In making the Anglo-Irish Agreement each government probably hoped to get some of the benefits of joint-sovereignty without
actually committing themselves to it in a clear and definitive way.
The British looked for more Irish responsibility for their security
efforts, while the Irish looked for power to deal with nationalist
grievances about law, order and justice. But they almost certainly
hoped that they would not have to develop joint-sovereignty
arrangements too far themselves. The clause in the Agreement
facilitating devolution provides that a devolved power-sharing administration may take charge of some areas of government, and
that these matters will then no longer be the concern of the Anglo-
Irish Conference. It may even be that the two governments expected
the Anglo-Irish Conference would only exist, after a while, as a
reserve device to discourage the unionist majority from breaking
off power-sharing with nationalists, as happened after the Ulster
Workers Council strike in 1974.

Let us first consider how the fear of proclaiming any move towards joint-sovereignty shaped the development of the Anglo-Irish
Agreement. One of the requirements of communal equality –
needed to break the circle of pessimistic expectations – is that the
British-unionist and the Irish-nationalist relationships become relatively symmetrical. Therefore one of the biggest difficulties in any
move away from the pre-1985 situation was to re-establish Britain's
relationship to the unionists as their guarantor, in spite of their
hostile reaction to the Anglo-Irish Agreement. One of the greatest
perceived weaknesses of the Agreement, even if the behaviour of
unionists helps to make it self-fulfilling, is that the nationalists are
represented by the Dublin government in a way that the unionists
are not represented by the British.

Those responsible for the Agreement felt obliged to show that
they had made no drastic changes in their own positions. The actual
words of the Agreement suggest a quite limited change.
Nationalists had reason to fear that the consultative powers of the
Republic would be very limited; but unionists were easily convinced that it was a conspiracy against them because unionist lead-

ers had not been consulted about it. The British government gave the impression that it was taken by surprise by the scale of unionist opposition and set out to persuade them that not very much had changed. In its dealings with the Republic's government, for whatever reasons, the Agreement has become an arrangement within which well established postures have not changed very much. At all events the Irish government seems to have little more influence than before and has shown little sign of being asked or being able to take more responsibility for the North. The row over the Stalker Report, and the crisis over the Gibraltar incident and its aftermath, followed well established paths. The SAS-IRA confrontation set the agenda of Anglo-Irish relations and, worse still, of the tension within Northern Ireland. Identities defined by the position of groups in relation to threats of force were exacerbated anew. Once again the distinction between nationalists who support the IRA and many who do not was blurred in a common opposition to the behaviour of the SAS and the power that authorized it. Unionists were presented with a spectacle that suggested nationalists were no closer to accepting the existence of Northern Ireland than before the Agreement. The Ryan extradition affair drew out, in as sharp a relief as possible, opposed experiences and expectations of British justice.

For the Anglo-Irish Agreement (or anything like it) to really change expectations, however slowly and in spite of people's very deep and usually well grounded suspicion of their internal and external opponents, it is necessary for the two governments to accept that assent may only grow slowly. At the same time they must both remain clear about their guarantor roles, because otherwise their internal groups have nothing to which they can assent. The clearer the intergovernmental understanding and the more they are committed to take the risks involved, the more Britain will have to behave towards the Republic as a joint sovereign. Instead of reassuring the unionists that nothing has really changed, and that the Agreement was mainly about improving cross-border security, the British government would then recognize that its undivided sovereignty could never undo nationalist alienation. At the same time the British input into the joint sovereignty arrangement would no longer be conditional upon a majority vote in the North. The

Ulster unionists' Britishness could be affirmed without embarrassment, because it would then be matched by, rather than in conflict with, the nationalists' Irishness. The Republic, being treated as a joint sovereign, could begin to behave like one, taking responsibility for jointly agreed decisions. Thus the claim to the territory of Northern Ireland, which has been the only internationally recognizable way of asserting the Republic's guarantor relationship to the northern nationalists, could be replaced by an institutional arrangement that is explicit about this role. Garret FitzGerald described the Anglo-Irish Agreement as the 'end of irredentism', and in this way it would actually become so.

It may be felt that this line of reasoning places too great an implied obligation upon the two governments. There is the obvious and immediate objection that the unionists are opposed to the involvement of the Irish Republic in Northern Ireland. But if that line of criticism is pursued then it is important to appreciate where it leads. When we say that such co-operation is impossible for the two governments, we are actually admitting at the same time that internal co-operation will eventually become impossible. The extent of intergovernmental cooperation that people inside Northern Ireland come to regard as normal will determine how much space there is for internal groups to accommodate each other. So the greater the cooperation at intergovernment level, the easier it would become for the nationalists to settle for devolution within Northern Ireland, using the intergovernmental cooperation as an anchor for its place as a minority party in a power-sharing administration. Under these circumstances the choice facing the unionists would also become clear; to share power or to revert to whatever joint-sovereignty arrangement evolves from the Anglo-Irish Agreement. Unionists would also be faced with clear signs that the government of the Republic and the nationalists were accepting the existence of Northern Ireland and taking responsibility for it. Following the first step from the two governments, the creation of a power-sharing administration would be the second step in realizing a symmetrical relationship between the two communities.

The absence of clearer moves towards joint sovereignty may have reduced the intensity of immediate Loyalist opposition to the Anglo-Irish process. But because the Agreement seems to be running out of new possibilities at the inter-governmental level, more and more stress is being put by different groups on the possibility of devolution. In the absence of a new intergovernmental relationship, the old problems with devolution arrangements remain. The more devolution is held up as a great goal, the more the internal parties are blamed for the failure to achieve it, and in defending themselves against this charge they end up blaming other internal parties. Thus the SDLP, having limited gains that it can attribute to the Agreement, feels obliged to magnify and use to maximum advantage what it has actually got – the puncturing of the Loyalist veto. I suppose it feels keenly the importance of fending off Sinn Féin charges that the Agreement is worthless. At the time of writing the SDLP have given very little public indication of what they expect the unionists to accept as a negotiated alternative to the Agreement. The SDLP have suggested two things that are far from any recognisable concept of communal symmetry. First, in their talks with Sinn Féin they have argued that Britain is now neutral. The suggestion seems to be that British withdrawal might be possible if it is no longer a question of capitulating to violence. Second, they are implying that the unionists must negotiate with the Dublin government. Both of these propositions tend to undermine one part of the required symmetry – the British identity of the unionist community. It seems to me as if the SDLP may simply be going through the motions of using the Anglo-Irish Agreement as a lever to draw the unionists into some kind of all-Ireland arrangement, not because they think they can succeed, but because the achievements of the Agreement at the intergovernmental level have so far been limited. It is very easy to see why they might fear that devolution now would be a false dawn.

If the capacity of the two governments to cooperate with each other turns out to be little better than it was before the Anglo-Irish Agreement, then it will be clear that while they have the capacity to break the loyalist veto symbolically they can do little else. They would then be stuck in a negative relationship with the unionists that could only be undone by making matters worse. For if the unionists were to succeed in overthrowing the Agreement, or be able to claim credibly that they have done so, then the dynamic of the old, destructive relationship between nationalists and unionists

within Northern Ireland would have been restored. It would never
again be possible to rely on British-Irish co-operation in any situation of stress.

One of the dangers now facing the Agreement is that political
leaders in Britain, the Republic, and Northern Ireland, feel that they
must keep their political cards close to their chests. If new political
possibilities are not articulated in a way that holds some promise for
the unionists, the Agreement will remain an axis of confrontation
and it will be very difficult to make it a foundation of a new co-operation. At this juncture, defending the Agreement by denouncing
unionist denunciations of it, however tempting that course may be,
simply makes the Agreement a weapon. Unionist hostility to it cannot be expected to abate until intergovernmental co-operation
brings out new possibilities of a better relationship with nationalists
within Northern Ireland. From their point of view this must mean
that their security no longer depends on the old destructive relationship with nationalists. A stable future for unionists depends on their
finding a new relationship with Britain and accepting at the same
time that the nationalist relationship with the Republic must be
symmetrical with their own relationship with Britain.

If the unionists cannot be allowed to overthrow the Agreement,
and at the same time cannot be expected to like it, it becomes clear
where the initiative has to lie. So long as the two governments cannot declare openly that they are moving towards a permanent joint
sovereignty – a move that has major consequences for both – it is
also difficult for the SDLP to say plainly what their real aspirations
are. And until at least a minority of the unionist leaders can see ad-
vantages in joint sovereignty emerging in practice, they cannot be
expected to spell out the virtues of the Republic's involvement, or
to do more than reluctantly acquiesce in it. In these circumstances,
to pretend that the achievement of devolution is a vital short term
goal is to push the internal parties into an argument about which of
them is preventing it, when in fact the two governments themselves
have not anchored the framework necessary to make devolution
worthwhile to either of the internal groups.

Note:
I would like to thank John Lampen for inspiration and encouragement in working
out my ideas in this article, and Duncan Morrow and Brian Lennon for helpful
criticism.

Repentance and Peace: A Challenge to the Churches

Joseph Liechty

As I write in February 1998, a fragile peace process, along with the many threats to it, dominates public interest in Northern Ireland. These are potentially momentous developments, but they may offer some false comfort and exaggerated hope. When the debate about peace revolves around the negotiations of politicians and governments, it is comfortably removed from the responsibility of ordinary citizens and consideration of what peace may require of us. This is a crucial moment, therefore, to remember that while the best possible outcome of the current talks, an agreed political settlement and a true end to violence, is fundamental, it is only fundamental – a foundation, not the completed structure of peace. At the social level, the perennial issues of sectarianism and reconciliation will remain as before, as will at least some justice issues. If the current talks achieve all that they aspire to, we will have a dramatically improved setting in which to work on these issues; if they fall apart, the same issues will require our attention with the same urgency.

Dealing with the legacy of sectarianism will be crucial to any full and lasting peace. If Christians and their churches have been prominent in the origin and perpetuation of sectarianism, as has been forcefully argued by the inter-church Working Party on Sectarianism,[1] then they must take the lead in repenting for sectarianism. This essay offers some reflections on what that process might look like: how repentance works, what it requires of us, and what it offers.

Repentance is both Personal and Corporate

The Christian approach to repentance is typically personal. Yet if each of us were to repent scrupulously for our own sectarian attitudes and actions, the problem of sectarianism would be diminished but not eliminated, because sectarianism is not only personal, it involves institutions and social structures.[2] Therefore our repentance must also be corporate as well as personal.

The idea of corporate repentance derives from the fact that we are social beings who find our identity in historically rooted communities. We do not feel joy, grief, hurt, and anger solely over things that have involved us directly and personally, but also over the experiences of our communities. We can feel elation at the success of the national football team, hurt at a slight to a family member, anger at a historic injustice against our church. The emotions register the strength of the bond between us and our various communities. To the extent that we identify with a particular community, we must be involved in repentance for its sins.

If corporate repentance is a necessary idea, it is also complicated. Individual repentance is already a complex operation, and as the number of individuals and groups and the span of time grow, complications increase exponentially. Who repents? For what? In what terms? The issues are too difficult to resolve here, but a few guidelines may help.

First, if a sin has been communal, as in the case of sectarianism, then ideally the community as a whole should repent, perhaps through its leaders or representative structures. But the initiative can also be taken by smaller groups of community members, even by individuals. The 1945 Stuttgart Confession of Guilt, made by the Council of the Evangelical Church in Germany for their participation in the evils perpetrated by Nazi Germany, was only possible as a result of the longstanding, steadfastly prophetic and repentant witness of the minority Confessing Church. Second, while all corporate sins need to be repented of, I am particularly interested in repentance as a way of dealing with protracted conflicts, as in the case of sectarianism. The impulse behind corporate repentance is not primarily moral scrupulousness, but the desire for a new beginning and the restoration of broken relationships. Third, authentic repentance for corporate sins requires finding terms of reference that accurately reflect our degree of complicity. Thus a group of ordinary Northern Protestants disgusted by random killings of Catholics by Protestant paramilitaries cannot say, 'We repent on behalf of the Protestant paramilitaries', but they can say, 'We are part of the community paramilitaries claim to represent, and we utterly reject their actions.' Learning of some rankling injustice committed by my ancestors, I cannot in any way repent on their behalf, but I can say, 'I stand in the tradition formed by my ancestors, and I deeply regret this action of theirs.' In general, moral maturity is likely to involve increasing awareness of our complicity in sins that we could plausibly deny or hold at a distance. In the case of the Stuttgart Confession, the people who took the lead in it were those consistent opponents of Hitler who probably had least to confess.

Repentance + Forgiveness = Reconciliation

Repentance and forgiveness can hardly be considered separately. They have a mirror-image relationship – repenting is a way of dealing with my sin, forgiving is a way of dealing with sins against me – so that what is true of one is likely to have a complementary application to the other. Each is necessary and good in its own right as a way of helping an individual or a community come to terms with past wrongdoing. They fulfil their final purpose, however, as the dynamic components of reconciliation, and then they operate not separately, but reciprocally, not for an individual or a single community, but for relationships. In this process either repentance or forgiveness can take the initiative and inspire the other, but the process is only complete when the two together have produced reconciliation. In a conflict of any duration, all parties will likely to need to repent and forgive, although there is often an imbalance, depending on which party has had more power.

Much human behaviour is reactive, marked by ascending or descending spirals, as good begets good and evil begets evil. In conflicts of any kind the spiral of descent can quickly seem all but inexorable. Repenting and forgiving, however, offer the possibility of injecting a fresh impulse that can reverse the spiral. The Jewish philosopher Hannah Arendt wrote, 'Without being forgiven, released from the consequences of what we have done, our capacity to act would, as it were, be confined to one single deed from which we could never recover; we would remain the victims of its consequences forever.'[3] The complementary action of repentance offers a similar opportunity for real change in seemingly intractable conflicts.

Repentance is a Way of Seeking Justice

Not only do repenting and forgiving work together as components of reconciliation, they are part of a larger web of virtue, in which the immediate connecting strands include at least love, humility, hope, and justice. These are equally important, but perhaps justice requires particular stress, because the language of reconciliation can too easily be used in a way that obscures justice claims, and many people disdain reconciliation for that reason. Once reconciliation is identified as the consequence of repenting and forgiving, however, the connection with justice becomes apparent. Acknowledging wrongdoing and making amends are essential to repentance, and wrongdoing will often take the form of an injustice, so that making amends will mean seeking justice.

Repenting and forgiving imply a particular kind of justice. My experience working with groups in Northern Ireland on these issues is that raising the justice theme turns many Catholics reflexively to 'what the Brits have done to us', while many Protestants turn immediately to 'how do we deal with the terrorists'. These are important issues, but the implicit definition of justice is too often backward-looking, retributive, and sometimes even vengeful. The kind of justice tied to repenting and forgiving must also look backward, of course, but its fundamental orientation is toward restored community relationships in the future. Some form of retribution may be involved (vengeance never is), but the future orientation brings flexibility about retribution – it is never mistaken for justice, it is only a possible means toward the final end of justice, which is restored relationships.

Repentance is a Form of Power

If repentance is connected to justice and holds the possibility of initiating change, then repentance can be defined as a form of power. Repentance is often associated with weakness, humiliation, surrender – anything but power – a misunderstanding derived from two sources. First, we often think of power as power-over, power-to-coerce, and these forms of power have nothing to do with authentic repentance. Alan Falconer defines forgiveness as 'integrative power', 'power with the other person',[4] power that reconciles and frees from the destructive effects of conflict. The sister virtue of repentance is also well described as integrative power, power-with rather than power-over. Second, we confuse repentance with weakness because we equate vulnerability and weakness, and repentance does operate from a stance of vulnerability. Power seems an unlikely fruit of vulnerability, and yet any change that is not coerced but freely chosen will almost certainly require vulnerability, risk-taking. The relationship of power and vulnerability inherent in repentance (and forgiveness) may be paradoxical, but it is a fundamental biblical paradox, entirely in keeping with the character of Jesus, whom God granted 'the name that is above every name' because Jesus 'humbled himself and became obedient to the point of death – even death on a cross'. (Phil 2:8, 9, NRSV) In my experience, groups reflecting on the character required of a repentant person often point to this paradox by stressing the importance of both self-esteem and humility. The vulnerable power of repentance is a practical and common demonstration that 'God's foolishness is wiser than human wisdom, and God's weakness is stronger than human strength.' (1 Cor 1:25, NRSV)

Repentance is a Process

Repentance is ordinarily not a single action, but a process. The process can be described in various ways, but these five stages are basic: acknowledging a wrong done, accepting responsibility, expressing sorrow, changing attitudes and behaviour, and making restitution. The stages as listed are like a ladder on which every rung gets harder to climb. It is one thing to acknowledge wrongdoing, but another to take responsibility, and so on up the ladder. Change is the crux and culmination of the repenting process, so that any repentance that does not reach the stage of changing attitudes and behaviour is not genuine repentance. In fact, change is so crucial that it sometimes initiates repentance, because it may be only after our attitudes have changed that we realize the need to repent – a hint of change is present already when we are able to acknowledge wrongdoing.

Of the five stages, acknowledging wrongdoing, accepting responsibility, and changing are essential, while expressing sorrow and making restitution may not always be required. If the wrongdoing has been behaviour that damaged a relationship, changed behaviour may itself function as expression of sorrow and restitution, so that formal expressions are unnecessary or even unhelpful.

However, an expression of sorrow is sometimes a necessary declaration and interpretation of changed behaviour, while restitution can be the sign and seal of sincere repentance. Certainly we would not think much of the thief who fully acknowledged wrongdoing, accepted unqualified responsibility, expressed the most abject sorrow, and vowed never to steal again – but failed to return the stolen goods.

Through studying the American Civil Rights Movement, Donald Shriver has developed the idea of public, corporate forgiveness. He identifies four dimensions which characterize this process, and these are easily transposed into terms of corporate repentance: confession of a wrong perpetrated, empathy for the humanity of the victims, willingness to pay a penalty or make restitution, and the ultimate aim of restoring the community relationship of all parties to this transaction.[5] Of the four, says Shriver, 'the single overarching theme, which binds the whole transaction together in a purpose, is the renewal of fractured social bonds.'[6] Shriver's scheme is a powerful tool for thinking about conflict situations, and its application to Northern Ireland is sobering. In the political culture of victimhood, not an inch, and no surrender, accusation is more likely than confession, empathy for the humanity of opponents is often markedly lacking, there can be no willingness to pay a penalty where no wrongdoing is acknowledged, and the ultimate aim too often seems to be victory rather than restoring the community relationship. Such a culture desperately requires the leaven of repentant, confessing churches.

Whether the repenting process is personal or corporate, it is not a mechanical process, but a grace-ful process. Certainly there are dynamics to be studied and skills to be learned, but at the heart of repenting lie mysterious impulses that Christians will recognize as the hand of God. Many people, when describing how they came to repent or forgive, point to impulses that nudged or pushed them along, moments of illumination, moments of release when what had seemed impossible became possible. Conflict invariably has a spiritual dimension. Ron Kraybill started Mennonite Conciliation Services in the U. S. in the late 1970s. Fresh from graduate school, he was eager to use his hard-earned skills. He found, however, that the intense satisfaction he felt when he had completed a successful mediation was not primarily the satisfaction of skills applied or a job well done, but of worship, of being in the presence of God. God is present in the suffering of those enduring destructive conflict, and God will be present when peace is made.

Repentance is Both Religious and Secular

On the one hand, repentance is fundamental to the biblical tradition, preached by Jesus, and essential to the church. But repentance is also fundamental to all human relationships and to a healthy, peaceful society. Any social grouping would collapse in a hurry without some functional equivalents of repenting and forgiving. In fact everyone assumes the operation of repenting and forgiving, they just want others to do it. Those who use the concepts of repenting and forgiving in relation to social conflict are sometimes accused of naïveté, but the charge is more properly made against those who think they can do without repenting and forgiving. Repentance will operate similarly in religious and secular spheres and whether Christians are involved or not. The basic difference will be between those who interpret repentance in purely social terms and those who believe that a wrong done to the neighbour is also a wrong done to God, and so repent before both neighbour and God. Beyond this, Christians will be more likely to use the explicit language of repentance, to acknowledge its roots in the Judao-Christian tradition, and to recognize the essential element of grace as God at work in the world.

Pitfalls Along the Road to Repentance

Ways of getting repentance wrong are as varied as the human capacity for ingenuity in the cause of self-deception. In a survey of the repentance theme in the bible, Mennonite biblical scholar Dennis Byler comes to the sobering conclusion that no single biblical story of repentance can stand as an unflawed model – each is marred by some element of manipulation, insincerity, incompleteness, or reversion.[7] Because we are prone to see the speck in our neighbour's eye rather than the log in our own, we may forgive when we should repent. We may settle for tinkering with peripheral matters rather than cutting to the core, although the bible links repentance to radical change, fundamental conversion. We may treat repentance as a once-off action rather than as the habit of being it

must become. We may use repentance manipulatively – I said I'm
sorry, so now you have to forgive me. The list goes on.

Again, the complications increase dramatically for corporate
repentance. German theologians Werner Krusche and Jürgen
Moltmann cite many examples of German Christians repudiating
the Stuttgart Confession: denying its implications, failing to act on
it, contradicting it. And yet for all these acknowledged failures, the
repenting impulse represented by the Confession has at times effectively called the church to account.[8]

Repentance and Renewal

The only reason to repent for sectarianism is to make right the
damage done by sectarianism – ulterior motives are a main pitfall.
The connection of repentance with conversion and change does
mean, however, that repenting holds out the possibility of a wider
renewal, and any thoughtful observer of the churches in Ireland
today cannot fail to see that the challenges facing the churches can
hardly be met without profound renewal. David Hempton and
Myrtle Hill, in their outstanding study of Evangelical Protestantism in Ulster Society, 1740-1890, illustrate the relationship between repentance and renewal in the Ulster Revival of 1859 through
the words of a young woman: 'I felt that they were my sins that had
nailed the Saviour to the cross that he was wounded for my trans-
gressions and bruised for mine iniquities, it was for this I grieved,
and not from any fear of punishment.'[9] Although the 1859 revival
has not, to say the least, been an event equally accessible to all
Christian traditions in Ireland, the basic logic of repentance and renewal should be. Perhaps one path to renewal lies along this way:
grieving that it is our sectarianism that nails the Saviour to the
cross, and repenting before our neighbour and our God.

Notes:

1. For developments of this argument, see the Working Party's report to the churches, *Sectarianism: A Discussion Document* (Belfast, 1993); Joseph Liechty, 'Sectarianism' in *Doctrine and Life,* vol. 43 (September 1993), 418-25; and idem, *Roots of Sectarianism in Ireland: Chronology and Reflections* (Belfast, 1993).
2. Liechty, 'Sectarianism', 419-20.
3. Hannah Arendt, *The Human Condition* (Chicago, 1958), 237.
4. Alan D. Falconer, 'The Reconciling Power of Forgiveness', in *Reconciling Memories* (Dublin: Columba Press, 1998).
5. Shriver identifies 'forgiveness in four dimensions: its judgement against a wrong perpetrated, its empathy for the humanity of the wrongdoers, its refusal to exact a penalty from the wrongdoers in exact proportion to the wrong, and its ultimate aim of restoring the community relationship of all parties to this transaction.' Donald Shriver, *Forgiveness and Politics: The Case of the American Black Civil Rights Movement* (London, 1987), 20.
6. Ibid.
7. Dennis Byler, 'Repentance in the Bible', a talk delivered to the European Mennonite Colloquium, Avoca Manor, Co Wicklow, August 1993.
8. Werner Krusche, *Guilt and Forgiveness: The Basis of Christian Peace Negotiations,* published with Jürgen Moltmann, *Forgiveness and Politics: Forty Years After the Stuttgart Confession* (London, 1987).
9. David Hempton and Myrtle Hill, *Evangelical Protestantism in Ulster Society, 1740-1890* (London and New York, 1992), 154.

Contributors

CAROL J. BIRKLAND is Secretary for Planning, Monitoring, and Evaluation for the Lutheran World Federation's Department for World Service. Based in Geneva, Switzerland, she has oversight of development projects in Asia, Africa, Latin America, and Europe.

MAURICE BOND is a minister of the Church of Scotland after serving ten years in the Irish Presbyterian Church. He has a Ph. D. in hermeneutics and ecumenics from Trinity College Dublin.

LIONEL CHIRCOP is Research Officer with the Future Generations Programme, University of Malta, where he is reading for an M. Phil.

GABRIEL DALY, an Augustinian priest, teaches theology in Trinity College Dublin and the Irish School of Ecumenics.

SEAMUS DEANE holds the Keogh Chair in Irish Studies at the University of Notre Dame in Indiana. He is the general editor of *The Field Day Anthology* and the author of a recent prize-winning novel, *Reading in the Dark*.

ALAN FALCONER, a Church of Scotland minister, is the Director of the Faith and Order Commission of the World Council of Churches. For over twenty years he was a staff member of the Irish School of Ecumenics, where he served as Director from 1990-1995.

JOE HARRIS taught education at the University of Ulster, Coleraine, and pioneered programmes on the theme of reconciling memories, above all in encouraging young people to understand the religious traditions in Ireland.

RICHARD KEARNEY is Professor of Philosophy at University College Dublin and visiting Professor at Boston College. He is the author of several works of philosophy and fiction, most recently *Poetics of Modernity* (1998) and *Postnationalist Ireland* (1998).

JOSEPH LIECHTY is Director of Moving Beyond Sectarianism, a research project of the Irish School of Ecumenics.

MARGARET MAC CURTAIN, recently retired as a Lecturer in the History Department of University College Dublin, is now serving as Chairperson of the National Archives Advisory Council.

GEIKO MÜLLER-FAHRENHOLZ, an ecumenical consultant and writer, lives in Bremen, Germany. He is author of *The Art of Forgiveness* (1997).

MARK SANTER is the Bishop of Birmingham. Since 1983 he has been the Anglican co-Chairman of the Anglican Roman Catholic International Commission (ARCIC).

DONALD W. SHRIVER JR is President of the Faculty and William E. Dodge Professor of Applied Christianity, emeritus, at Union Theological Seminary, New York City. His most recent book is *An Ethic for Enemies: Forgiveness in Politics* (1995).

FRANK WRIGHT taught political science at Queen's University Belfast. A member of the Corrymeela Community, he wrote two books on Northern Ireland, *Northern Ireland: A comparative analysis* (1987) and *Two Lands on One Soil: Ulster Politics before Home Rule,* published posthumously in 1996.

About the Irish School of Ecumenics

The Irish School of Ecumenics is an international academic institute, Christian in its inspiration and ethos, interdenominational in structure and personnel. It exists to promote, through research, teaching and outreach activities, the unity of Christians, dialogue between religions, and the promotion of peace and justice in Ireland and abroad.

Founded in 1970 by Rev Dr Michael Hurley SJ, the School operates in the Republic of Ireland and in Northern Ireland. In association with Trinity College Dublin, ISE offers Masters and Diploma programmes in Ecumenical Studies and in Peace Studies. Students of different denominations study together, bring to bear the insights of their particular traditions on their common research and on their exchange with one another. The international character of the student body further enriches their understanding and encounter. M Phil students undertake a dissertation as part of their studies, the range of topics chosen exhibiting a broad spectrum of interests and concerns. ISE graduates have made a significant difference in their fields of study and are active in fields of conflict mediation, development and human rights agencies, and in posts of ecumenical leadership, nationally and internationally.

The staff of the School have also conducted research and projects on a variety of themes central to reconciliation: *Inter-Church Marriage, Human Rights, Irish Neutrality, Ethics in International Affairs,* and *Reconciling Memories.* These initiatives have brought together scholars from different countries, disciplines, churches, and cultures, for conferences and seminars. Currently a major ISE research project is under way in Northern Ireland on the contextual issue of *Moving Beyond Sectarianism,* drawing upon the experience and reflection of people from almost every church tradition in Ireland and of distinguished international scholars from other contexts such as South Africa, Eastern Europe and the United States.

In Northern Ireland, the Irish School of Ecumenics offers a Certificate in Reconciliation Studies in association with the University of Ulster. Other courses are provided in co-operation with Queen's University in Belfast and Armagh, as well as in local community settings in a number of centres. Thus the ISE offers an open space where people of different religious persuasions and cultural traditions – clergy, community leaders, teachers and social workers, for example – come together and engage in a process of respectful dialogue and critical study of issues relating to peace and conflict, reconciliation and respect for diversity. Particular attention is paid to the resources and obstacles within different Christian traditions in Northern Ireland, in the context of the search for peace, mutual understanding and reconciliation.

The purpose of this series of Occasional Papers is to make available to a wider readership, public lectures and reflections on different aspects of Ecumenical Studies and Peace Studies for the furthering of justice and peace, dialogue between religions and the work of reconciliation among Christian churches.